Essays on Research Methodology

Dinesh S. Hegde
Editor

Essays on Research Methodology

Springer

Editor
Dinesh S. Hegde
National Institute of Industrial Engineering
Mumbai, India

ISBN 978-81-322-2213-2 ISBN 978-81-322-2214-9 (eBook)
DOI 10.1007/978-81-322-2214-9

Library of Congress Control Number: 2015937952

Springer New Delhi Heidelberg New York Dordrecht London

Printed on acid-free paper

Springer (India) Pvt. Ltd. is part of Springer Science+Business Media (www.springer.com)

To
Young inquisitive scholars looking forward to embarking on a research career

—Editor

Foreword

Issues of research methodology, even though of fundamental significance in the evolution of any subject, rarely receive the attention they merit. This is particularly so in the social sciences, where very often fierce controversies are contested on the grounds of irreconcilable methodological premises. This book, edited by a well-known scholar and a much respected educationist of long standing, deserves to be welcomed for putting before the academic community of teachers and research students (in the social and management sciences) a wide spectrum of methodological issues of crucial import in the social sciences.

It would not be an exaggeration to say that social science research methods have grown in the shadow of the natural science method. This is probably the legacy of the French philosopher August Comte's *Unity of Science Principle (USP)* enunciated in his book *Cours De Philosophie Positive* (1842). Loosely stated, the USP considers all sciences (natural, social, historical) as methodologically similar, but with natural sciences at a higher stage of evolution than social sciences. Thus, social sciences should aspire to attain the same stage of evolution as the natural sciences and hence follow the same (or broadly similar) methods of enquiry. The USP was methodologically challenged by a group of German philosophers (Droysen, Dilthey, and Rickert) in the latter half of the nineteenth century. These philosophers argued for a methodological autonomy of the social sciences, in which phenomena were to be *understood* rather than *explained in terms of prior causes*. In such sciences, abstract concepts like *meaning, language, intuition,* and even *rhetoric* played an important role.

An attempt at seeking middle ground between these extremes can be found in the writings of the late-nineteenth-century German philosopher Windelband (see his *A History of Philosophy* (1901)) who coined the two words *nomothetic* and *idiographic* to describe two distinct approaches to knowledge. The former is focused on finding generalities that are common to a class of phenomena and deriving theories or laws to account for these generalities. *Idiographic* knowledge, on the other hand, aims at explaining particular phenomena. Modern social science research uses both approaches in conjunction. Mathematical modeling, statistical calibration and computer simulations are resorted to routinely in economics (and increasingly now in political science, psychology, and even sociology and history) and may be said to constitute the *nomothetic* component, while the delineating of the spatiotemporal institutional context of the analysis corresponds to the *idiographic* element. The success of any specific project of social science research depends critically on the quality of the balance between these two aspects. The first two chapters (by the editor himself) elaborate on these conceptual and methodological issues further and demonstrate convincingly the limitations of interpreting statistical hypothesis testing too narrowly. Of particular interest is the discussion bearing on the Kuhn-Popperian themes of paradigm change and hypothesis *falsification*. Gupta's classic essay delves deeply into epistemological issues and should serve as a "must read" reference point for both social and natural scientific researchers.

Another issue of central methodological importance in social sciences is the relative role to be assigned to statistical methods. The history of science, right up to the previous century, was characterized by a firm belief in *determinism*, not only in the natural sciences but also in the social and historical sciences. *Determinism* essentially embraced three features: (1) a belief that all phenomena and events of the world obey unchanging causal laws; (2) a confidence in the possibility of discovering these laws, at least in principle; and (3) an unconditional belief in the method of formal logic (deduction), primarily mathematics, for understanding the external world. The phenomenal growth of biological, psychological, and social sciences occurring in the early parts of this century brought home the limitations of a purely deterministic approach to explanation (and prediction) and paved the way for probabilistic modes of explanation. However, systems in the social sciences are not adequately described by well-defined and stable statistical distributions. There is no way in which definite probabilities can be assigned to the validity of many laws in social sciences – not due to our ignorance of the systems or faulty data, but to an inherent feature of those systems attributable not only to the multiplicity of influencing factors (which cannot be averaged out by the law of large numbers) but also to the *strategic interactions* of human agents (as distinguished from the *cellular automata* of biological systems). Bandyopadhyay's three chapters expound a number of important issues in problem formulation and systems modeling while also highlighting the distinctive role of *qualitative* research. The latter aspect finds uses across a wide range of disciplines including economics, political science, management science, psychology, sociology, etc., where data is very often *categorical* and quantitative methods run into several difficulties. Recent years have witnessed in a big way the emergence of experimental methods in economics (consumer choice and social preferences), political science (voter attitudes and behavior), and management science (organizational behavior, etc.). This brings into focus the statistical subject of *design of experiments*, which unfortunately rarely figures explicitly in the standard syllabi of graduate studies in these subjects. The chapter by Kool and Agrawal attempts to capture the essence of this important subject in a few pages and should prove of immense use to those freshly engaged on any experimental research project. Similar remarks apply to the chapter by Sayeed, "Questionnaire Design for Survey-Based Research."

Another issue of paramount methodological significance is the role of *causality*. Two notions of causality seem to be dominant in the metaphysical literature, viz., (1) causality as an algebraic property of representations and (2) causality as a real-world relation. Reflecting these divergent trends, we have two distinct approaches in the social sciences, viz., *model-based* methods of causal analysis and *data-based* methods. In the former group, we may mention the causal ordering method of Simon (Simon 1953), the causal chain approach (Strotz and Wold 1960), and the informational approach (Le Roy 1995), while among data-based methods, the two most prominent are the Wiener-Granger causality (Wiener 1956; Granger 1969) and the graph-theoretic method (Glymour and Spirets 1988).

Of the above group of methods, the one method especially favored by applied economists is the Wiener-Granger method. The metaphysical basis of this method is rooted in three principles: (1) firstly, causality is being interpreted in one of its weakest senses (viz., Feigl's (1953) definition) as "predictability according to a law"; (2) secondly, it is based on the Humean concept that cause precedes effect in *time*; and (3) finally, it is not predicated on any known theoretical model and thus may be regarded as model-free. Hegde's chapter, "On the Role and Significance of Contextualization in Economic Research," touches upon the issues of causality and simultaneity, in the course of his discussion of the issue of model selection and prediction especially in the face of rapid changes in technology and tastes and preferences.

In recent years, ethical issues have increasingly come to the forefront in social sciences. The archetypical position finds expression in the by now classic statement of Myrdal (*Objectivity in Social Research*, 1969): "Social science research is always and by logical necessity based on moral and political valuations, and the researcher should be obliged to account for them explicitly."

Naturally, ethical considerations figure differently in the diverse branches of the social sciences. In the domain of psychology, some of the major issues of interest refer to (1) how human beings develop, assert, and believe in certain values; (2) how personal behavior is influenced by a specific set of values; (3) how values evolve at different stages of human development, etc. In sociology, by contrast, ethics seeks to account for the differences in the personal values held by various communities (tribal, rural, and urban) and also often concerns itself with issues of value transition and value engineering.

Whereas acceptance of the ethical dimension in several branches of social sciences presented relatively few difficulties, the situation in economic science has been much more complicated. Classical economists, steeped in the tradition of Adam Smith's *The Theory of Moral Sentiments* (1759), recognized the importance of distinguishing between the economic price of a commodity and its ethical value. In an effort to make economics *scientific*, a group of economists led by Pareto, Hicks, and Kaldor in the first three decades of the last century started the New Welfare Economics movement, which sought to rigidly delineate issues of economic efficiency from the ethical issues of distribution and equity. In recent years, however, economics has come full circle, and there is a strong movement to seek a closer rapprochement between ethics and economics. The theories of distributive justice (such as Rawls' theory of distributive justice (*A Theory of Justice*, 1971), Nozick's libertarian theory (*Anarchy, State & Utopia*, 1974), or the resources-based distributive justice theory of Dworkin (*Sovereign Virtue*, 2002)) have explored the expanding interface of economics with ethics. Bhole's chapter "Ethics in Research with Special Reference to Social Sciences" touches upon these issues apart from related issues of ethics in business organizations (e.g., moral obligations to shareholders and creditors, moral obligations to customers and clients, moral obligations to employees, etc.) as well as ethics in the conduct of social science research.

The Appendix of the volume details extremely valuable guidelines for research students embarking upon the submission of their research thesis.

The volume is a very welcome contribution to research methodology and fills an important lacuna in the reference material available to the community of research students in India.

IGIDR, Mumbai, India D.M. Nachane
University of Manipur, Imphal, India
Prime Minister's Economic Advisory Council,
India
January 2014

References

Comte A (1842) Cours de Philosophie positive, Rouen Frères, Paris (Bachelier). http://www.hup.harvard.edu/results-list.php?author=1337

Dworkin R (2002) Sovereign virtue: the theory and practice of equality. Harvard University Press, Boston

Feigl H (1953) Notes on causality. In: Herbert F, Brodbeck M (eds) Readings in the philosophy of science. Appleton-Century-Crofts, New York, pp 408–418

Glymour G, Spirets P (1988) Latent variables, causal ordering and over-identifying constraints. J Econom 39(1& 2):175–198

Granger C (1969) Investigating causal relations by econometric models and cross-spectral methods. Econometrica 37:424–438

Le Roy SF (1995) Causal ordering. In: Hover KD (ed) Macroeconometrics: developments, tensions and prospects. Kluwer, Boston

Myrdal G (1969) Objectivity in social research. Pantheon Books, New York

Nozick R (1974) Anarchy, state and Utopia. Basic Books, New York

Rawls J (1971) A theory of justice. Belknap Press of Harvard University, Cambridge, MA

Simon HA (1953) Chapter 3: Causal ordering and identifiability. In: Hood WC, Koopmans TC (eds) Studies in econometric method. Wiley, New York

Smith A (2010) The theory of moral sentiments, Hanley RP (ed), Penguin Classics (Paperback) [1759]

Strotz R, Wold HOA (1960) Recursive versus non-recursive systems: an attempt at synthesis. Econometrica 28:417–427

Wiener N (1956) The theory of prediction. In: Beckenbach E (ed) Modern mathematics for engineers. McGraw-Hill, New York

Windelband W (2001) A history of philosophy. Paper Tiger, New Jersey [1901]

Contents

Contributors

Dr. Rita Agrawal Professor and Director, Faculty of Management & Technology, Harish Chandra Post-graduate College, Varanasi, India

Dr. R. Bandyopadhyay Former Director, National Institute of Bank Management, Pune, India

Visiting Research Professor, University of Manchester, Manchester, UK

Present Affiliation: Hon. Director, CASAD, Pune, India

Dr. L.M. Bhole Former Professor of Economics, Indian Institute of Technology Bombay, Mumbai, India

Dr. Amitabha Gupta Former Professor of Logic and Philosophy, Indian Institute of Technology Bombay, Mumbai, India

Dr. Lakshmikanth Hari Assistant Professor & Chairperson, Centre for Sustainable Development, K J Somaiya Institute of Management Studies & Research, Mumbai, India

Dr. Dinesh S. Hegde Former Professor of Economics and Dean (Academic), National Institute of Industrial Engineering, Mumbai, India

Present Affiliation: Visiting Faculty, IIM Raipur, India

Dr. V.K. Kool Professor, SUNY Polytechnic Institute, New Palt, NY, USA

Dr. Omer Bin Sayeed Former Professor of Organization Behaviour and Dean (Research), National Institute of Industrial Engineering, Mumbai, India

Present Affiliation: Adjunct Professor, OB/HR, IBS Hyderabad, Hyderabad, India

Contributors

About the Editor

Dinesh S. Hegde is a former Professor of Economics and Dean (Academic) of National Institute of Industrial Engineering (NITIE), Mumbai, where he had been teaching courses such as industrial environment and policy, global economic perspectives, business analysis and econometric applications and research methodology for well over two decades. He had earlier taught at Bayero University Kano, Nigeria, and University of Dar es Salaam, Tanzania. While with the latter, he also served as a Consultant/Coordinator for a major research project on interindustrial flow matrix jointly sponsored by the University Department of Economics, Ministry of Planning and Development, Govt. of Tanzania and SIDA. Over the years, Dr. Hegde has supervised many Masters and Doctoral dissertations and numerous summer/winter projects in addition to undertaking several consulting assignments and executive training programmes for corporate across oil, gas, power, electronics, chemicals, automobiles, airports and ports on diverse techno-economic/managerial issues of concern. His areas of expertise include techno-economic studies, technology evaluation, labour and infrastructure on which he has published numerous articles in reputed journals and also contributed papers in edited volumes. Postretirement, he has been the Visiting Faculty at Indian Institutes of Management Shillong and Raipur.

Chapter 1
Introduction

Dinesh S. Hegde

1.1 Backdrop

The genesis of this work goes back to the time when I began teaching a course on Research Methodology to Fellow (doctoral) Programme students at NITIE. That was way back in 2003, a good 11 years ago. That was when the Applied Statistics forming half of the course was taken out at my insistence and began to be taught as a separate course in addition to the stream-specific courses in the first module, with the sole objective of strengthening the methodology part without neglecting the statistical tools/techniques widely used by research scholars. That my colleagues on the Board of Research concurred with my long-held view and agreed to such a change was a big step indeed, for it was only then that as the Chair I could convince the Director. Perhaps, by then it had become increasingly clear to all concerned that in most credit seminar presentations, there was confusion among students as between methodology and methods and that they took the latter for the former. Thus came the opportunity to strengthen the research methodology course with some theoretical perspectives, especially from the logical and philosophical viewpoints associated with creation, dissemination and advancement of knowledge. It felt good to experiment with new topics like knowledge claims, formal logic, dialectics, theory, empiricism, positivism, phenomenology, quantitative and qualitative paradigms and models, verification and falsification, modelling, etc. More importantly, the students seemed interested and receptive, often expressing the view that this was something totally new to which they were exposed to and that it

D.S. Hegde (✉)
Former Professor of Economics and Dean (Academic), National Institute of Industrial Engineering, Mumbai, India

Present Affiliation: Visiting Faculty, IIM Raipur, India
e-mail: dshegde108@gmail.com

D.S. Hegde (ed.), *Essays on Research Methodology*,
DOI 10.1007/978-81-322-2214-9_1

would immensely benefit them in their research work. Yet, I would increasingly feel something was amiss, and this was despite the fact a significant proportion of the batch admitted happened to come with fairly sound academic background, albeit from diverse disciplines ranging from science and technology, economics, finance, behavioural sciences to social and management sciences, IT, environment, ergonomics, etc. Admittedly, their proposed areas/topics of research were as diverse; some entailing conceptualization, modelling, testing, others involving laboratory work, others relying on primary data obtained from fieldwork/surveys and yet others taking recourse to library research using published data sources. Further, some were quantitative in their approach, others were qualitative and some others adopted a mixed type. Also, the composition of the successive batches would change.

Gradually, however, as time passed, I could see that their interest was transient, and they studied only because there was going to be an evaluation including module-end examination. It was clearly getting reflected in their course-related presentations in the class and subsequent seminar presentations on registration, literature review, credits and all the way to synopsis. While they did pay attention to issues of linearity vs. non-linearity, discrete vs. continuous or static vs. dynamic models, errors in observation, measurement and aggregation, unit of analysis, estimation/forecasting, content analysis, etc., depending on the nature of the topic chosen, they continued being myopic, constrained by their selective/narrow approaches and totally oblivious to the larger issues of theory and methodology discussed in the course. The overwhelming attention was apparently on data and tools/techniques. Eventually though, some of them would drop in to say how they benefited from the course at the stage of writing, drawing inferences, implications and the like. This was no solace, by any means. Thus, it was becoming a challenge to continue teaching the course with each passing year, especially to sensitize students to certain basic issues concerning data and theory so that such an awareness is brought to bear upon their approach to research and analyses during their research. One could, therefore, feel the need to elaborate a little more on the course. Besides, the available books on the subject, mostly dealt with data analyses with a focus on tools and techniques and the relevant software packages, only made matters worse. Given all these, one also felt that a book covering the hitherto neglected dimensions of methodology and contextualization was required, somewhat more comprehensive especially with regard to the broader issues raised and yet not dense.

By and large, data analyses tend to be taken for granted as being objective, trouble-free and safe, as they are rarely questioned except on grounds directly related to data themselves. Again, they are considered apolitical, asocial, sans-ideology and thus least controversial. It cannot be otherwise, as one's mind is conditioned that way both by years of education and the mainstream literature that research students are exposed to. There are, however, serious issues concerning data analysis. Indeed, they extend far beyond what is usually discussed by way of accuracy and adequacy of data, their being consistent availability across a cross section or time series, specification and aggregation in reporting, data cleaning and the like. For that matter, it also extends beyond the difference of opinion among scientists and social scientists as regards the distinction between primary and secondary data (scientists are treating only laboratory-generated data during the course of experiments as primary and the rest as secondary, whereas social scientists are treating data gathered directly by researchers during the course of their research through fieldwork, questionnaires and surveys as primary and those obtained from published sources, reports, etc., as secondary). Indeed, it is much more and has to do with data not being independent of theory, as claimed by many well-known scholars like Karl Popper, Tjalling Koopmans and Lionel Robbins, among others, thereby raising serious doubts as to the supposed objectivity behind data analyses since it is the researcher who decides what observations to collect; where, when and from whom to collect; etc. Inevitably, his/her subjectivity does enter into the fray. Besides, according to Popper, inferences from the particular or singular statements based on results of observation/experiments cannot be justified, as they may be falsified with single evidence to the contrary. Thus, there being such severe limitations of inductive reasoning, one cannot simply be theory-neutral or for that matter to ideology and sociocultural influences such as values and beliefs. In other words, the what, why and how aspects of an inquiry towards knowledge claim or simply put, methodology assumes great significance. So also are the related questions – when and where or contextualization.

Rarely, however, one could find discussions on methodology per se; perspectives on knowledge claims and their approaches; conceptualizing, identifying and formulating problems; drawing inferences; interpreting and drawing implications and generalizations; etc. Coming somewhat near were books by Creswell (2008), Remenyi (1998) and Krishnaswamy et al. (2006) among others, but they too were partial in their coverage and tilted more towards applied research in some particular areas such as behavioural, operations and the like. Similarly, there were others with their thrust on marketing, finance and other functional areas. Nevertheless, one tried to drive home the significance of such dimensions during lectures and students' presentations especially their tentative proposals and limited literature reviews in the class so as to orient them to some basic questions concerning research. Alongside, there was a need for a good book, more by way of a reference book rather than a textbook of the usual variety, covering a range of topics striking a common ground among students with diverse background of different subject disciplines in such a way as to be relevant and useful to them. The primary objective was to enable them to ask a few basic questions – the what, why and how of research, how else and so what (by way of inferences, interpretations and implications).

As already stated, it became evident that most available books hardly made attempts in this direction. Instead, one found that they were confined, by and large, to empirical analysis or analysis of data gathered from primary and/or secondary sources, extensive use of questionnaires, survey-based research, case studies and model applications and testing of hypotheses and subjecting them to various statistical tests, parametric or non-parametric ones, and finally interpreting the results. As expected, therefore, a large majority of students only followed such books and adopted the approaches suggested therein, rarely pausing even to question themselves as to why they did what they were doing and if there were better ways of approaching the research problem at hand and conducting inquiry in a more systematic and meaningful way. Further, the ready availability of software packages only exacerbated the problem of routine handling of data analysis. Scarcely if at all, fundamental theory-related questions were raised, leaving alone the other issues of logic and philosophy that are significant as regards knowledge claims.

1.2 Interfaces with Peers/Colleagues

Further, over the years, one had the privilege of some very senior and eminent academicians coming to address the students in this course on a few occasions, and later when I shared my views and concern with them, they seemed to concur with my view that though there were numerous books available on the subject, there was scarcely any delving into the basic methodological issues. They included Prof. R. Bandyopadhyay, Prof. D. M. Nachane, Prof. L. M. Bhole, Prof. Amitabha Gupta, Prof. O. B. Sayeed, Prof. V. K. Kool and Prof. Rita Agrawal. What is more, they encouraged me to write a book to fill this void. In this way, the project began to be conceived and gradually the contours took shape. Later, when I approached them for contributions to the volume, they readily agreed despite their many pressing commitments and tight schedules. Needless to say, no amount of formal acknowledgements would do justice to their invaluable contributions.

Also, my years of experience as a referee for several doctoral dissertations further reinforced this view, as one increasingly saw an uptrend in somewhat mechanistic interpretations of regression (being most frequently used models) coefficients, based on their sign, size and significance. Quite a few colleagues, counterparts in other institutions and friends in the profession including the peers shared my views. In fact, it came to be so common that one did not even bother to check as to their relevance or about improving model specifications by raising doubts as to the lag structure, linearity, degrees of freedom, etc. Apart from glossing over such anomalies, to one's utter surprise, it has been reported that even when explanatory power of the model, goodness of fit, etc., were weak to the extent of independent variables being able to explain only some 10–20 % of the variation in the dependent variable, research reports and dissertations continued to be produced without any blink. Thus, one is at a loss to comprehend as to what explains the remaining 80–90 % variations. Surely, the residual error term cannot be expected to capture it to such a large extent! Rarely, questions tend to be raised about the usefulness of such misguided applications and analyses based on them. Sometimes, one wonders how such works are at all allowed to proceed! As for critical reasoning, the less said, the better it is. Often, I would recall Joseph Schumpeter's warning about the latter part of the twentieth century being characterized by thoughtless empirical work as against the excessive word mindedness of the earlier part of the century. One is prompted to say, how prophetic indeed!

Hence the concern and effort to strike a common ground among research scholars from diverse backgrounds ranging from science, technology, economics, finance, IT to HR, organizational behaviour and other behavioural and social sciences with a view to equip them with knowledge about some basics of methodology and strengthen their ability to conceptualize/formulate problems in their respective areas and conduct research more meaningfully with rigour and relevance, so also their ability to reason, infer and discuss implications of the findings. It is, therefore, with this expectation and hope that the present volume is being brought out. Needless to say, conscious effort has gone into it in shaping it towards that direction. Moreover, while I continued to share the ideas with research students at NITIE as I taught several batches year after year, I found myself growing with additional reading as well as learning. Besides, there were many occasions to interact with their counterparts in other reputed institutes like IIM Shillong, IIT Bombay, Kabul University, D. J. Sanghvi College of Engineering and Mumbai University, some of them being experienced teachers themselves and others with rich industry experience. Such fruitful interactions over the years have also contributed to taking my intellectual curiosity further, and to additional preparation for the lectures year after year besides strengthening my resolve and motivation to prepare for this volume, in no small measure.

1.3 A Guided Tour of the Volume

As in any arduous work of this type, the present work has also had its fair share of trials and tribulations. While some of us took quite some time to write our chapters, some others were on the verge of retirement and preoccupied with moving places, and yet others had personal and family personal issues to resolve. It certainly goes to their credit that despite such difficulties they left no stone unturned in fulfilling their promise and professional commitment to produce some valuable contributions for this volume.

Now, it is in fitness of things that a glimpse of what is contained in the volume is given. There are three chapters by Professor R. Bandyopadhyay, namely, "Problem Formulation" (Chap. 4), "Systems Approach and Soft Modelling" (Chap. 5) and "Qualitative research and its Applications in Organizational Management and Social Research" (Chap. 6). They delve into definition, formulation and structuring, essential aspects of systems approach and significance and methods and interpretation of qualitative research, respectively. He has been an eminent academic with decades of rich and varied experience and has discussed the issues of concepts and methods with great care and attention in each of these chapters. The chapter by Professor Amitabha Gupta (Chap. 3) concerns itself with the subject of crucial significance in making knowledge claims, viz. logical and epistemological norms in scientific theory construction, cutting across sciences and social sciences. It may sound dense to begin with but very useful for research scholars in comprehending the rigour and context of building and making knowledge claims. Professors V. K. Kool and Rita Agrawal have co-authored the chapter "On Using Experimental Designs" (Chap. 8) and very ably brought out the significance of experimental method in natural and behavioural sciences in addition to showing how experimental designs act as a bridge between conceptual and statistical validity. The chapter by Professor L. M, Bhole (Chap. 10) raises some important issues of values and ethics in research, their significance and also dilemmas faced by researchers including human rights and animal welfare and positive and normative approaches. His concern with such issues needs hardly any emphasis, given his abiding interest and leanings towards Gandhian philosophy. This is then followed by Professor O. B. Sayeed's chapter, namely, "Questionnaire Design for Survey-Based Research" (Chap. 9), wherein he skilfully deals with the intricacies of designing questionnaires for survey-based research and the need for due care and attention entailed in the process of eliciting the required information and undertaking survey research, respectively, to derive maximum benefit from such research. Although it took a long time for his contribution to arrive due to some unavoidable reasons, I knew it was worth the wait, given his well-known expertise, long-standing experience and felicity with data analysis. Lastly, my own chapters, namely, "Role and Significance of Contextualization in Research" (Chap. 7) and "Knowledge Claims – Approaches and Perspectives" (Chap. 2), delve into the need and significance of contextualizing research at micro, sectoral and macro levels and into knowledge claims, types and methodologies, respectively. Some philosophy of science-related issues like paradigms, confirmationalism and falsification as may be relevant in a contemporary setting is also discussed in the latter chapter. Also, there is an Appendix titled "Writing a Doctoral Dissertation" co-authored with Dr. Lakshmikanth Hari explaining how to write a thesis on completion of the research work, with all its questions like- what, why, how and so what is being addressed, structuring it in a suitable manner, reporting the findings, drawing inferences therefrom and, finally, discussing their implications.

One may add here, in a volume of this nature with contributions from different authors with diverse backgrounds and subject specializations, and it may have been difficult to maintain a balance between depth and girth across the various chapters despite efforts in that direction. Consequently, some degree of risk of compromising on consistency with respect to level throughout the volume may, perhaps, be inescapable.

Acknowledgements First and foremost, my heartfelt thanks go to the contributors to this volume for their encouragement as well as graciously agreeing to be a part of this project and sparing some of their valuable time to write the chapters amidst their busy schedules and pressing commitments. I would like to thank Professor R. Bandyopadhyay with whom I have had the privilege of long years of fruitful interaction. In addition to sharing my concerns and appreciating the need for bringing out this volume, he also generously agreed to contribute three valuable essays to it. So also, my grateful thanks go to Professor Amitabha Gupta, Professor L. M. Bhole, Professor O. B. Sayeed, Professor V. K. Kool and Professor Rita Agrawal for their encouragement, for readily agreeing to write for the volume and for sending in their valuable contributions well in time to meet the publication schedule. Besides, I am thankful to Dr. Lakshmikanth Hari for his immense help during the process of editing and consolidation of the volume to bring it to the final shape, in addition to co-authoring the Appendix. Further, I would like to express my grateful thanks to Professor D. M. Nachane who very kindly agreed to write a foreword to the volume. His erudite scholarship, humility, kindness and unwavering dedication and commitment to academic profession have been an immense source of encouragement to many of us in our generation right from our student days onwards, who looked up to the peer group that he belonged for inspiration and guidance. Also, my sincere thanks go to the several batches of research scholars I taught and interacted with, at NITIE as well as outside, during their seminar presentations right from the stage of registration, literature review, credit seminars and all the way to synopsis stage, in various capacities, be it as an examiner, advisor, guide or dean. In fact, one learned a great deal from their trials and errors and struggles with issues of conceptualization, methodology, inference, implications and the like in addition to those of one's own, over a period of time. Also, it is an occasion to reminisce with gratitude the several interesting reading sessions on classical political economy I was privileged to have with Professor Attila Agh while I was with the University of Dar es Salaam. His erudite scholarship, deep understanding of the subject and familiarity with the original German editions of the literature were immensely helpful in appreciating a number of finer points/aspects. Besides being kind and affectionate, the Agh couple was also generous hosts. In addition, thanks are due to Ms. Sagarika Ghosh, Sr. Editor of Springer for showing keen interest in the manuscript from the beginning till the very end and helping in bringing out this publication. My thanks also go to her team especially Ms. Nupoor Singh for the attention to details, care and meticulous job done on the whole. Thanks are also due to anonymous referees. Further, I shall be failing in my duty if I do not remember my venerable teachers right from school onwards, through college and all the way to university days. As I look back in retrospect and remember them with gratitude, I consider myself fortunate to have had such a galaxy of dedicated teachers who, despite being taskmasters, were kind, large-hearted and patriotic. In particular, mention must be made of Professor VR Panchamukhi, Professor PR Brahmananda, Professor R Bharadwaj, Professor KR Ranadive, Professor VM Rao and Professor GC DeCosta. Finally, I would like to thank my loving family for their constant support and encouragement over the years.

To end, it is my sincere hope, this volume would serve as a useful reference for doctoral scholars in social and management sciences, including those from a wide variety of technology-management interface areas, and would go a long way in facilitating their research work with improved rigour, relevance and perspective.

References

Creswell JW (2008) Research design: qualitative, quantitative, and mixed methods approaches. SAGE Publications, Thousand Oaks

Krishnaswamy et al (2006) Management research methodology. Pearson

Remenyi D et al (1998) Doing research in business and management. Sage Publications, London

Chapter 2
Knowledge Claims: Approaches and Perspectives

Dinesh S. Hegde

2.1 Introduction

The present essay attempts an overview of what, why and how of knowledge claims that are usually made during research or as outcomes of research. The objective here is to familiarize aspiring research scholars with the key concepts, frameworks and essential features of knowledge claims as understood in the realm of philosophy of science so that some degree of clarity is brought about what is involved in intellectual endeavours of inquiry/search for knowledge and also its progress or advancement. In this endeavour, it is no less important to keep in view the role of theoretical rigour or elegance as also that of empirical relevance. So also is the need to recognize the methodological autonomy for different sciences, particularly social sciences, while being keenly aware of certain common threads emanating from the unity of science principle running through a wide spectrum of critical inquiry and search for knowledge. The effort here is to keep this crucial big picture in view, especially in an age of specialization leading to compartmentalization of knowledge in an almost watertight manner, and the trend, for quite some time now, has been a proliferation of unbridled empirical work with eagerness to apply the latest tools/techniques, rather than critical reasoning and content. Against this background, it would be of immense value if some deeper aspects and perspectives as already indicated are brought to bear upon a researcher's inquiry, analysis, interpretation and drawing implications and thereby results in improving and enriching the overall quality of research. Thus, the focus, largely, is to explain

D.S. Hegde (✉)
Former Professor of Economics and Dean (Academic), National Institute of Industrial Engineering, Mumbai, India

Present Affiliation: Visiting Faculty, IIM Raipur, India
e-mail: dshegde108@gmail.com

D.S. Hegde (ed.), *Essays on Research Methodology*,
DOI 10.1007/978-81-322-2214-9_2

the nature of knowledge claims, their basis, classification of types of knowledge claims and, finally, various approaches to or methodologies of knowledge claims. The sections that follow are organized in that order.

2.2 Nature of Knowledge Claims

It is well known that research is undertaken with the objective of making a knowledge claim besides satisfying intellectual curiosity; solving a problem/puzzle; answering some questions; making a thoughtful guess, hypothesis or conjecture about some ideas found in the relevant literature; extending the existing state of knowledge; using new tools of analysis; fetching a higher degree and enhancing one's academic career; and the like. It may take the form of evolving new theories/hypotheses/relationships or even new methodologies. In a more general sense, research is expected to improve our understanding of the world and people around us; universe and its planets; materials and their properties; particles, molecules, atoms and their finer aspects; theorems; certain phenomena; events; processes; organizations; societies; relationships, etc., by providing new evidence, fresh insights and arguments with logical reasoning. Clearly, some of the subject areas mentioned here belong to physical and natural sciences, whereas the others to social and management sciences. Also, there are other objectives of research such as knowledge for its own sake, satisfying intellectual curiosity, obtaining a higher degree, better explanation leading to improved accuracy in prediction and control or guide to human/policy intervention, more so in the case of applied research. It may, however, be the case that even when found useful, it gets deferred or relegated to the background for a long period of time before finding favour with the management or policy.

The question that obviously arises is, what is research and what is a knowledge claim? Broadly speaking, research has come to be understood and described as free and diligent inquiry through systematic investigation with a scientific and analytical approach; careful search for new knowledge; discovering new facts; ascertaining existing theories; extend, collect or verify knowledge; and relentless pursuit of truth taking recourse to evidence, observation, measurement, experiment, analysis, persistent thinking, logical reasoning and comparison. Now, experiment may be in a laboratory or in field; reasoning may be inductive or deductive; and comparison may be over a period of time or across space. Sometimes, a knowledge claim is also called the logical assertion of truth. It may, however, be an appearance of truth and not truth itself, as was discovered much later about the wrong assertion that the Sun moved around the Earth while in fact it was the other way around. Perhaps, over the centuries, many such optical illusions came to light, and people began to refer to such assertions as 'justified true beliefs' (JTBs). Thus, they were only true to the extent that they were believed to be true and also justified to be true. Often, it was establishments who believed and justified, and invariably it was the church, and people then followed and believed. It is likely similar confusing perceptions may have prevailed over explanations with regard to lightning, thunder, clouds, mirages, etc., and would have taken a fairly long time to clearly see the objective genuine and the subjective deception. Admittedly, until then, the latter were surely believed to be true and were also justified. This is, however, not to say that what we know and how we know are any less significant, even if tenuous, for it would have paved the way towards the very growth/progress of knowledge progress by negating the previously or hitherto justified true beliefs. Nonetheless, it is important to bear in mind that beliefs that are false and/or unwarranted such as lucky guesses, coincidences, wild unsupported claims and wishful thinking should not be confused for JTBs. Surely, such cases are to be excluded. Here one might ask, what is the extent of evidence required if the claims were to be supported? It would differ depending upon what is at stake. In court cases, the evidence often relied upon should be convincing and beyond a reasonable doubt. It seems somewhat similar criterion tends to be applied in respect of regulatory pricing/rate of return which need not necessarily be fixed on the basis of scientific analysis but on evidence of reasonable application of the mind. Clearly, in knowledge claims, much more is at stake besides the reputation of those making them, such as adverse impacts arising from flawed policies and false knowledge spreading and spilling across generations, among others. In simpler cases, however, one may rely on certificates, affidavits and the like. When faced with cases involving spurious correlations, however, the question of seeking evidence does not arise, and they are only to be ignored on grounds of coincidence, as argued earlier. However, the finer distinctions of association, conjunction and causation are deferred for the time being.

According to Thomas Kuhn (1962), a researcher's attempt is to move closer to truth, an approximation, or to be as close or similar to truth as possible. He calls it verisimilitude. This is made possible by inquires and verifications within the ruling paradigms of normal science, and the process continues until such time as the normal science tends to get replaced by revolutionary science making way for a new paradigm. By a paradigm he meant a philosophical and theoretical framework of a scientific school or discipline within which inquiries, experiments and generalizations are undertaken and solutions sought by researchers. In fact, Kuhn defines a scientific paradigm as 'universally recognized scientific achievements that, for a time, provide model problems and solutions for a community of researchers'. Broadly encompassed in this definition are what to observe, probe and question, how to experiment and interpret the results, etc. Thus, it is this thought pattern that constitutes the scientific world view or the paradigm within the realm of normal science wherein scientific progress continues until such time as large-scale changes take place which eventually bring about a displacement of the prevailing dominant paradigm, in turn making way to revolutionary science with its new paradigm. This is what he meant by a paradigm shift/change. In fact, there are no absolute truths in this mundane world of ours, but only relative ones specific to the time, space and sociocultural contexts, given that there is a broad consensus as to the interdependence between data and theory as also the advantages of using mixed methods of phenomenology and positivist approaches, rather than an either or silo kind of approach. It is increasingly being felt that the former enhances the richness of analysis and holistically attempts to answer questions like what and how, thus going beyond the reductionist approach of seeing things only partially to seek answers to the question why. Indeed, recent trend has been that one is no longer enamoured of quantitative studies for their own sake, but in favour of combining them wisely along with qualitative investigation for better understanding of the phenomena under inquiry. So also is the preference to combine hard modelling with soft modelling for this very reason. In this context, it is worth recalling Schumpeter who almost prophetically said while commenting on the proliferating quantitative studies of the 1950s that if the first half of the twentieth century was characterized by excessive word mindedness, the latter half of the century would be characterized by thoughtless empirical work! Truly, the world has witnessed such a deluge of such works that almost routine regressions or other models are fitted and run on massive data and tables and coefficients are churned out with mechanical interpretations as to the size, sign and significance of the parameters thus obtained. Scarcely does one find answers to questions such as 'what', 'why' and 'how', leave alone the question 'so what' by way of drawing implications of the results obtained. The ready availability of numerous software has only made matters worse. It is, therefore, increasingly being realized that a researcher's relative comfort with equations and coefficients needs to be balanced in combination with richness/complexity of the narrative pertaining to the subject matter under investigation.

Moreover, the powerful arguments of Karl Popper (1963) have also helped in prompting a pause, at least to a limited extent, in this rush for the so-called verification as permitted by Kuhn's paradigm framework in the realm of normal science. Popper breathed a fresh air, as it were, amidst the widely prevalent practice of accepting or rejecting hypotheses based on statistical evidence on the part of most researchers. Nevertheless, the practice still continues unabated in many empirical studies. Arguably, they continue to be guided more by statistical methods which clearly demarcate acceptance and rejection regions, and most people do not bother to go beyond them. It is only when we take the trouble of pushing the frontiers further that we begin to understand and appreciate as to what constitutes knowledge and how we know. According to Popper, verification/acceptance tantamount to confirmationism with a high inductive probability and the result is a dogma. Besides, verifiability is contingent on the distinction between observational and non-observational terms, which in turn cannot be ensured given that many a science tends to have only degrees of observability. In addition, it was posited that observation is not a neutral activity, but involves data selection and interpretation, and therefore, he viewed all observation being theory dependent. It is only when we contest a knowledge claim with critical rationalism and falsify that there is growth/progress in knowledge. In other words, the hallmark of the scientific status of a theory is its testability, refutability or falsifiability. Popper was also of the view that such a process of trials and errors should be unending so that we continue to strive for higher standards. In this way knowledge grows, in his view. He goes on to add, it may all appear like a heap of ruins to begin with, but soon, we are likely to discover the treasure buried beneath. Needless to say, the hope and promise is of a tall order, inspiring and imploring one and all towards critical inquiry. Thus, falsifiability becomes a prerequisite, as it were, for knowledge claim, and we would hardly be in a position to say we accept a hypothesis! This is because a single incidence of negation or evidence to the contrary would nullify what has hitherto been accepted no matter how many times favourable evidence has been found previously. However, falsification cannot be on the basis of empirics, but on deductive reasoning.

We can, however, reject a hypothesis when the evidence is against it, and if the evidence is in favour, we can at best say the hypothesis cannot be rejected. In this way, continuously begging questions is what leads to knowledge. In spite of all these, it is important to recognize the significant contribution of Kuhn, especially his new terms such as verisimilitude, prescience, normal science, revolutionary science, paradigms and paradigm shifts and disciplinary matrix forcefully employed to explain discontinuities in received knowledge from time to time.

Thus, from the above brief discussion, it can be seen that the larger perspectives of knowledge claims are of great significance and should inform inquiry and analysis by researchers. It goes without saying that professional organizations, journals, educators, conferences, funding agencies and governments may have to play a far more effective role in encouraging what is desirable in the long run, lest a myopic view perpetuate itself, being more often than not, overweight on numerical accuracy.

2.3 Basis of Knowledge Claims

Nevertheless, verifiability continues to dominate the scene even after Popper just as it did prior to the period of Popper as an objective operational criterion to distinguish the significance of analytic statements from others lacking in content and meaning. It is only since the postmodernists, however, that phenomenology has again been on the rise and richness of analysis rather than the verifiable specifics have begun to receive attention, bringing in attitudes, values in addition to what and how, going much beyond the why. That this has been so in social and management sciences and the trend is only on the rise does not come as a surprise. It is indeed a surprise and a pleasant one at that when a similar trend is seen in sciences too! They call it the need to moving away from the 'barren land of science' as some would call it in the debates surrounding environmental degradation, sustainable development and other related issues of equity and ethics. Of late, it is seen that some scientific journals have also been publishing papers with qualitative analysis with a view to promote a holistic understanding of phenomena rather than the specifics amenable only to measurements.

In this context, it is also relevant to distinguish formal logic, dialectics and historical materialism for a better understanding of richness of analysis and a holistic perspective. So also relevant is what Schumpeter calls 'a historical sense'. First, let us begin with formal logic with its three laws, viz. law of identity, law of mutual exclusiveness and law of contradiction. They are self-evident in that the first two must be satisfied; the latter must be negated for otherwise, anything to the contrary which violates a cogent argument made possible by the former two laws renders it untenable and hence no longer valid. While it worked well for the exact sciences like science and mathematics, there was an acute need to go beyond the formal logic in social sciences, as was realized by Karl Marx who takes recourse to dialectics. He argues contradictions are to be resolved through debate, discussion and discourse following thesis, antithesis and synthesis. This is how he combines Hegelian dialectics with Feuerbach's historical materialism to explain serfdom, feudalism, capitalism and socialism and, finally, communism and the accompanying social transformations or social formations in a dynamic sense. Further, it is in such a framework that he posits that feudalism is born in the womb of serfdom, capitalism is born in the womb of feudalism and socialism would be born in the womb of capitalism. As a consequence, one finds the coexistence of different modes of production and not one to the exclusion of others. Clearly, such a coexistence is inconceivable following the laws of only formal logic! Again, it is with such an approach that we tend to comprehend and appreciate terms like capital, labour, exploitation, length of the working day, alienation, antagonisms, commoditization, class, etc., and the complexities and contradictions involved, in a much better way. So also is the case with his various categories and social relations therein in stark contrast to the conventional economic concepts. What is more, it is such an approach which enabled Marx to pay rich tributes to capitalism, calling it the most progressive phase in human history where productive forces in the economy are unleashed on a tremendous scale. More significantly, his grandiose comprehensive inquiry gave rise to powerful alternative theories in the field of economics, sociology and political science, aimed primarily at social transformation rather than stopping at mere explanation. Hence also is the significance of the vanguard class, whose role he so fervently hoped and sought. Further, the birth of progressive institutions like the Fabian Society and far-reaching legislations like the Factory Act, Workmen's Compensation Act, Trade Unions Act, etc., would not have been possible otherwise. Needless to say, only a scholar par excellence could have achieved such a feat – and not dogmatists or ideologues! Surely, it was the flawed leadership of the latter category which advocated jumping the queue thus pre-empting several countries including some developing ones from unleashing their productive forces and pushing those decades behind. That this is so is borne by ample evidence found in the experience of the twentieth century. Worse still, it had to wait for the collapse of an eight-decade-old erstwhile Soviet system before the world realized that skipping the capitalist phase and substituting it with the euphemism socialism for what was essentially state (also known as retarded) capitalism was a monumental failure.

Next, let us try to understand Schumpeter's historical sense. According to Schumpeter, economists should not only have knowledge of history but also a sense of history. Two examples should be useful in understanding the full import of this statement. One relates to the lobbying for the Corn Law in England by the powerful landed aristocracy and later when they themselves became industrialists, also powerfully lobbied for the abolition of the very same law. Apparently, it sounds contradictory, but it is not at all so. It is just that they did not want competition from imported corn earlier when they were landed aristocrats and later they very much wanted competition from imports so that industrial workers could get cheaper food and thereby they could keep the wages low, as the landed aristocracy have now become the industrial aristocracy. Therefore, it made eminent sense for the then landed aristocracy to lobby for the Corn Law and so also for the industrial aristocracy to now lobby for its abolition! The second example relates to something the author experienced first-hand during his academic assignments in Africa. It was a common practice to arrange for faculty accommodation in star hotels while waiting for campus housing which sometimes took anywhere between a few months to a year, the waiting period depending largely on the family size both in respect of expatriates and natives returning from abroad after completing their higher studies and/or sabbatical. During those days, it was not unusual to hear some African colleagues on the dining table or the one nearby say that they were 'struggling' to get soup, dessert or water, whenever waiters are delayed in serving any of the items. The word 'struggle' came to be used so commonly even in a star hotel, and it was despite the fact that they had returned from reputed universities in the UK or USA after a sufficiently long stay abroad and that they were indeed the elite of the country. It took quite some time to realize that they were only reflecting the historical experience of the society they belonged and grew up in and that most African countries had indeed struggled for freedom for a very long time and often with blood bath, what to speak of the prolonged sufferings on account of racial discrimination and slavery of their earlier historical past. Surely, this accumulated experience has had its deep impact on their psyche for generations to come so much so that expressions like struggle had willy-nilly entered even in their ordinary daily conversations! Thus, it is not merely the legacy of the colonial past and relatively recently gained independence as may be the case in other developing countries, by way of a general comparison historically. Hence, the significance of Schumpeter's 'historical sense' makes all the difference to bring about a better understanding of the phenomena as the two illustrations amply demonstrate.

2.4 Types (Classification) of Knowledge Claims

One finds that there are different ways of classifying knowledge claims and they can all be traced to epistemology and more generally to the philosophical writings of Comte, Kant and Mill. What is more, they do tend to overlap no matter how we describe their nature, source or adoption of varying methodologies for analysis, inference and justification. Thus, for the purpose of simplicity, we have tried to capture them into a single classification – a priori or semantic, a posteriori or empirical, inferential or logical and the last being situational.

The *first* variety, viz. *a priori knowledge*, does not rely on observations about the world, but essentially it refers to knowledge 'that comes before', i.e. that which is inherent in human mind before experience, true by virtue of meanings and independent of facts. Here, one is required to follow the meanings as given in the dictionaries for the purpose of warrant or justification of true beliefs about people, relationships, events, processes or phenomena. That is to say, time, space and causation are self-explanatory by the very meaning. So, when we make a statement that unmarried persons are either bachelors or spinsters, it is a priori true and does not need any warrant or justification for the belief to be true. It is true, believed to be true and justified as such, semantically. Surely, we do not stretch its validity to absurdity to include even children in the category of persons here.

The *second* one, namely, *a posteriori* or *empirical knowledge*, does depend on observations about the world, people, phenomena, process, events, etc., experiencing or interacting with them in some manner. It is likely, knowledge is gained by acquiring certain skills such as swimming, driving or playing a musical instrument and games like tennis, cricket, etc., and then one claims such knowledge saying he/she knows swimming, driving or playing those games. Such skills acquired are also termed as procedural knowledge. Also, one may combine or extend the available or previous knowledge in various ways and come out with new or additional knowledge. It would, of course, entail familiarity with the existing state of knowledge as made available in the relevant literature on the subject matter under consideration. As Isaac Newton said, it was by standing on the shoulders of giants that he could see the future. Admittedly, a large part of research in the recent times has come to belong to this category. One may add here and no analogy is made as to quality levels here. It is, therefore, of crucial importance that a critical review of the available literature is conducted and knowledge gaps identified properly so that problem identification, its formulation, choice of an appropriate methodology along with tools and techniques and research design, deriving research findings, critically analysing them with a proper interpretation, linking the research to relevant previous works and drawing implications are greatly facilitated. Put simply, the what, why, how and finally so what of research become clearer and clearer as one proceeds with the work and continues at the same time updating the literature review till the dissertation submission. Besides, a good literature review, invariably, turns out to be a chapter in itself. Furthermore, empirical or a posteriori knowledge also encompasses narratives, in-depth case studies and critical analyses of ideas found in the relevant literature, subjects them to empirical investigation, extends the previous works in a different spatial/temporal context and data analysis based on primary or secondary data and brings in some new or *alternative* interpretations, new perspectives or grounded theories. All these are to be reflected when one communicates the research findings – what knowledge claim is being made, on what basis, relying on which sources of data and information, how the investigation/inquiry has been conducted, how it differs from or improves upon the previous works, the authorities cited wherever necessary, etc.

The *third* variety of knowledge is based on *reasoning facts, content of experience or other inferential knowledge* such as a theory. In other words, the attempt here is to construct knowledge through inductive/deductive thinking and make predictive inferences. Further, they may not necessarily be based on facts or experiences. By way of examples, we have statements like the Sun rises daily in the morning and sets in the evening, all men are mortal, all animals have tails, all birds have wings or all birds fly, etc. Here, one is speaking of validity rather than truth. That the Sun neither rises nor sets and that it is the Earth that moves are well known, and yet, statements like the one made earlier continue to be made. What matters here is not its truth, but its validity for most practical purposes of planning our working day, calendar and the like. Likewise, the truth of statements as regards all crows being black or all swans being white until after the new settlements in Australia and New Zealand also holds. They are no longer true and, yet, by and large valid with suitable riders for the Far East. Moreover, going by one's own content of experience also, one might say he/she knows that some elderly persons live happily, together as a couple or otherwise. In this category, therefore, we may include what may be called original works like novel ideas, theories, insights, experience, data generation, hypotheses, analytical frameworks and methodologies developed by researchers/authors themselves.

The *fourth* and the last type of knowledge is called *situational knowledge*. It is embedded in language, culture and tradition of a particular people/place. It may refer to art, music, dance, kinship, marriage, property rights, inheritance, medicine, tribal forms of worship and the like. For instance, there are some cancer patients visiting Dharamshala for the Tibetan cure and patients suffering from asthma, diabetes and jaundice travelling to some other places for traditional cures involving swallowing of a live fish, banana, etc., along with some concoctions. Although one does not know the truth as to their effectiveness by way of cure, patients have been continuing to visit such places for a very long time. Evidently, one is bound to recognize the sociocultural influences on the lives of individuals living in those contexts, their thoughts, reasoning, beliefs, behaviour and interaction with others. This would, in effect, impose limitations of some sort on the JTBs being asserted as logically true. One may, at best, state that their beliefs are justified, but true only accidentally (though they may not necessarily be false). If one were to ask those pursuing such traditional cures as to the truth of the claims being made, they would invariably say the proof of the pudding is in the eating!

While at it, one may begin to ponder if such responses are tantamount to words of testimony (Shabda Pramana) as espoused in the Indian philosophical system. Surely not, the latter clearly is concerned with right/sound knowledge rather than validity. Obviously, one is up against far deeper issues here such as direct perception/experience (pratyaksha pramana), analogy (upamana) and inference (anumana), all concerned essentially with the absolute knowledge on knowing which nothing else remains to be known. As noted earlier in respect of the theological interpretation, the subject matter of quest/inquiry/search is the cosmos, macrocosm (Paramatma), microcosm (Jeevatma) and the sensory world or the world of appearances (Maya) and their relationships. This it seems is the ultimate or the most fundamental to be sought/known and realized, and all others are only its derivatives, through the material world all the way to atoms and its still finer splits. The criteria indicated above have their own significance depending upon the path chosen from among those laid down, viz. Jnana yoga, Karma yoga, Raja yoga and Bhakti yoga. Thus, when it comes to the word of testimony that we raised a little while ago, it is really the word of testimony from a self-realized master. We may, however, put such matters to rest, as our interest and focus are confined to the world of sensory perceptions and validity of knowledge claims within it. Nevertheless, reference is made here only to bring in the Indian perspective in a somewhat similar manner as made earlier in respect of theological and metaphysical explanations from the Western perspective and left at that for similar reasons such as spirituality, power, force and the like.

Now to return to validity from the brief digression, the basis, surely, must be on logical reasoning or evidence. As for the logic, one may rely on inductive logic or deductive logic, and in either case, generalization is to be attempted while making knowledge claims. It is worth noting that while inference is drawn from the particular or singular to the general or universal (from microcosm to the macrocosm based on data/evidence) in the former, it is the other way around in the latter (from macrocosm to the microcosm based on deduction or premises based on well-established theories or laws). Also, it is precisely because of this reason that empirical studies of the positivist stream involving data analysis entail randomness and representativeness of samples and, in effect, large samples, the exceptions being in-depth case studies involving close/intense interaction with subjects as in ethnographic and other studies of the phenomenological stream where sample size can only be small, given the very nature of interactive, experience-based interpretivist inquiry/analysis. Hence their appeal and large scale following in many an application, as compared to the deductive approach with tightly knit arguments, though academically elegant.

Evidently, we have refrained from discussing the details of weak and strong induction here and other nitty-gritties of inductive and deductive logic to avoid digression. It is, however, important to bear in mind such a distinction so that one may not fall into the trap of wishing it away with a few riders here and there, as weak inductive arguments are rarely made good by riders that are mostly meant to soft-pedal the categorical nature of statements if and when made based on comparisons and analogies by highlighting the context-specific situations and bring in a degree of modesty. Thus, the overall purpose is not to generate watertight compartments in the name of classification by hair splitting, but an understanding of what constitutes knowledge in all its variety, complexity, evidence, arguments, thesis, antithesis and finally synthesis. Needless to say, one is better off refraining from the stringent conditions of infallibility and reliability. Perhaps, it would be wise to follow David Hume's well-known advice that one should adopt practical scepticism instead of severe scepticism for otherwise, we run the risk of starving not being certain to infer as to whether bread is sure to nourish us in the future as well (on the basis of it being so in the past)! After all, our day-to-day reasoning is more guided by experience than deductive arguments. It may be worth recalling here philosophers have gone as far as to suggest that knowledge should bring peace to the intellect, which, perhaps, would also include relevance and benefit to the larger good of society.

In practice, however, we find a mix of different types of research works, more so in doctoral dissertations, with differences being seen across chapters depending on the aspects covered. For instance, two or three chapters may be the main ones by way of empirical analysis, and the remaining one or two may deal with some other aspects of the topic like tracing the recent trends in descriptive terms, discussing some relevant theoretical aspects, attempting a comparative analysis as between different industries, countries, historical and periods, etc. By adopting mixed types, however, care should be taken to avoid a mix-up within a chapter lest it leads to confusion. So, it is important to bear in mind that the purpose is to bring in fresh insight and new perspective and contextualize better, and so long as such clarity prevails, it really does not matter what mix is followed.

Finally, it is not uncommon to find yet another classification with studies being categorized into *theoretical*, *empirical* and *grounded theories*. While the first variety involves conceptual and modelling, the second type covers studies involving data analysis and interpretation, and the last category refers to some regularity in the patterns observed or grounded theories emerging out of the empirical work and repeated interaction of data and analysis. Needless to say, the first two types do not call for an explanation, as one is all too familiar with what is commonly being practised. It is the third variety which needs to be explained. I have often seen research scholars coming up with their literature reviews for progress seminar presentations and getting confused as to where to position some studies not neatly into their chosen taxonomy of theoretical and empirical studies. In such cases, one may as well introduce a third category called grounded theories, if the studies can rightly be treated as such. To elaborate, one may recall Adam Smith's theory of specialization based on the *division of labour* observed in a pin factory. Again, the high repayment ratios (in the range of 93–98 %) seen in the case of women borrowers in many countries including even poor ones like Bangladesh, Nepal and Niger (Timbuctoo, especially) have been attributed to what is now famously known as *economy of affection* referring to larger commitment and responsibilities on the part of women to their families than on the part of men. The latter were seen to be more prone to drinking and gambling and failing to repay the loans they borrowed in turn resulting in poor repayment ratios; women are performing far better in terms of credit worthiness owing to economy of affection. This has been amply demonstrated by the relative success of a number of microfinance schemes/institutions in several parts of the world, inspired largely by the now famous Grameen Bank in Bangladesh, started with the initiative and dedicated efforts of Dr. Mohamed Yunus. It is noteworthy, similar initiatives have been seen in the health sector as well, in some developed and developing countries. It becomes clear, therefore, that such cases of the economy of affection exemplify the phenomenon and also justify the classification. As pointed out earlier, the classification often tends to blur, especially when we take cognizance of the fact that the word paradigm also connotes exemplar and pattern, among others.

2.5 Approaches (Methodologies) to Knowledge Claims

Often, there exists some confusion among research scholars, as between methodology and methods and the two are used interchangeably. We had earlier described research as a systematic search for knowledge with scientific methods of investigation. Now, methodology is nothing but a procedure of going about research, the overall approach to its what, why and how, which in turn leads to certain tools, methods and techniques of inquiry/analysis. It may be said different methodologies tend to be used to address different types of research issues/questions and each of them seems to have their own advantages. What is more, researchers may have their own preferences depending upon their ontologies and epistemologies (whether implicit or made explicit), the former referring to their views of the world and the latter to their views about how knowledge is created. It becomes difficult, therefore, to regard one methodology better than another. Moreover, scientists themselves do not agree as to what is strictly scientific and regard science as a socially embedded activity. This would imply we have to reckon with a researcher's beliefs, his/her subject discipline and past experiences having a bearing on his/her philosophical approach and, in effect, the paradigm choice. Thus, analytical frameworks differ as between researchers belonging to radical left, centrist and rightist or market fundamentalism. This is particularly true of research in social sciences. Elsewhere, it may be somewhat subtle, with interest groups often hidden behind smokescreens of objectivity, as in respect of research related to defence, environment, energy security, strategic regional alliances, etc., ostensibly in the larger national interests while being ideological in essence, and yet, in others like some medical and pharmaceutical research, it may be commercial interests at play. It is in such contexts that *ethics in research* assumes significance. We may recall here it was only after four decades of denial by the establishment that the US President Bill Clinton finally apologized to the nation for the unethical use of prisoners and mentally ill patients as guinea pigs in clinical trials without their or their parents/guardians' consent. Until then, there were only denials even as the uproars continued.

Nonetheless, a researcher should be able to adopt a sound conceptual framework as also justify the same, as being relevant for the *purpose of the study* under consideration. Often, it is found that such attempts tend to be made with much reliance on the available literature comprising previous studies on the problem area or closely related to it. There may, of course, be exceptions where higher level of rigour is attempted with new frameworks, research designs and strategies put forth as original contributions of the researchers themselves. Most certainly, such contributions would stand on their own as knowledge claims in themselves. As we may recall from the earlier sections, a knowledge claim may take several forms including new insights, evidence, relationships, patterns, theories and methodologies. In any case, it is important that such details are elaborated under the methodology chapter/section while communicating research findings in a dissertation/paper, including the objective of research, paradigms and models adopted, design and clarity as regards the study being, exploratory, descriptive, explanatory, causal, experimental, ethnographic (study of families, tribes and organizations) historical or evaluatory. Also required is information concerning the unit of analysis, degree of control, sampling, nature of data, sources, kind of relationships hypothesized, tools/techniques, measures and locus of location.

Against this backdrop, the different approaches or methodologies are broadly grouped under two categories – phenomenological and positivist. In so doing, we have been guided more by the philosophy of science, the paradigms put forth by it, their continuity and/or sudden shifts and, finally, the possibility of bringing about synthesis of thesis and antithesis. This is what prevailed over the choice of classifying the different approaches into quantitative and qualitative types. Again, as mentioned earlier, either the confusion between methodology and methods or for reasons of area-specific needs, ease of convenience, etc., it is often observed different classifications such as evolutionary methodology, phonetics and cladistics in biological sciences and expert systems, logistic regressions and neural networks in computer and telecom network researches tend to be adopted. For our purpose, however, there is no need to get into the nitty-gritty of such variety of classifications as they are mostly not considered relevant in the context of social and management sciences, not to mention the overlapping in many a case. Also, it is seen that sometimes, pragmatism becomes the deciding factor and simplicity, practicality and elegance seem to matter and not merely truth or falsity in itself, as eloquently argued by some authors. In what follows, their essential features, differences, contexts and advantages and disadvantages are dealt with. This is then followed by a discussion on mixed methods, wherein the synthesis part is brought in.

2.5.1 Positivism

It was Auguste Comte, one of the founders of sociology, who propounded positivism to begin with, in the second quarter of the nineteenth century, followed by others subsequently. He posited that the human mind goes through three historical stages – (1) *the theological* wherein natural and social phenomena, including famines, earthquakes and wars, are explained by making reference to divine will or spiritual forces (no wonder, the church ruled and was so powerful as not to forgive Galileo for three centuries), (2) *the metaphysical* which is characterized by search for the ultimate causes like power and force taking the place of divine will and (3) *the scientific* or *positive* seeking correlations and conjunctions among the phenomena rather than explaining them. The third stage, then regarded as an evolved stage science, eventually led to a convergence of views by Comte, Kant and JS Mill making way to what came to be termed as unity of science principle according to which all sciences tend to have similar methodologies. However, despite this broad consensus, debates and discourses continued for long as to how far one can stretch association to imply causation if at all and whether scientific endeavour is to discover truths or construct models/hypotheses confronting data for an improved understanding of phenomena, events, processes, etc., and also whether theory or empiricism is capable of solving problems. Perhaps, such debates beg more questions than they answer, as the world has witnessed many path-breaking contributions purely on the basis of studying huge mass of data, as discussed elegantly by Nachane (2003) who goes on to cite the great works of Charles Darwin and other famous studies of Mitchell, Tinbergen, Kuznets, etc., based solely on huge mass of data, but continuing to stand tall even in the face of severe criticisms and reservations on empiricism by Robbins, Koopmans and Keynes. Nevertheless, it is a fact that mainstream economists were greatly influenced by logical positivism leaning heavily towards analytic statements with definitions or testable (synthetic) statements of fact and on the unity of science and the principle of verifiability, saying only they were meaningful or made cognitive sense. The rest, according to them, were metaphysical and unscientific. Later, towards the mid-twentieth century or so, it culminated into logical empiricism with its hypothetico-deductive approach and statistical tests relying heavily on observation, measurement and confirmationalism. It was then followed by Thomas Kuhn's *Structure of Scientific Revolutions* with his concepts of prescience, normal science, revolutionary science and paradigm shifts. In fact, this approach too came to be challenged by Popper with his powerful principle of falsification and the argument that observation itself was not a neutral activity but entailed data selection and interpretation implying, in effect, all observations being theory dependent. Given such deeply involved issues of logic and philosophy, suffice it to say, we have only made an effort to provide a link among the loose threads in a historical perspective. Hence, for the purpose at hand here, we would prefer to continue referring, in the pages to follow, to the broad category called positivism. Nevertheless, it may not be out of place to mention here that positivism does not hold sway since the last few decades or so, with the rise of postmodernism.

In a positivist framework, the whole is reduced to its parts or components, and they are studied in part(s) and then generalization attempted. Further, the observer/researcher is considered independent of the observed, and hence, the analysis becomes objective and value-free. Also, the concern is with the observations that are amenable to measurement/quantification and other details get ignored. Moreover, the reasoning and inferences tend to be deductive, by and large, based on well-founded theories, principles and laws, as the results are often tested against the criteria established therein. Lastly, there is an attempt to study possible relationships, be they associative or causal. Hence, the why aspect assumes significance here. In so doing, however, the day-to-day experiences of people and their beliefs, obstacles, attitudes and values do not get captured, despite the fact that an understanding of these aspects of life may have potential for enriching the analysis. That is to say, the 'what' and 'how' aspects tend to receive scarce attention. Again, a large number of samples become a prerequisite for the generalizations attempted.

Meanwhile, during the intervening period of the 1950s, positivists seemed to receive a booster with Milton Friedman's (1953) advocacy of judging competing theories and empirical hypotheses (formulated about the real world whose entities may be amenable to quantification and being made to face the test of data) on the accuracy of their predictions rather than the realism of the assumptions. They, however, came to be challenged by Samuelson (1963), Wong (1973), Boland (1979) and proponents of social choice theory like Arrow and Sen on grounds of violating canons of logic and wishing away methodological and value judgments which are not empirical but important nonetheless for purposes of policy advice.

2.5.2 *Phenomenology*

In the later part of the nineteenth century and early part of the twentieth century, however, some severe limitations of positivist analysis began to be recognized. As elaborated by Remenyi et al. (1998), this movement was mainly led by Franz Brentano and Edmund Husserl arguing that reductionism and determinism imposed stringent constraints in the understanding of the world in which we live and many human affairs and related issues, relationships, interactions, etc., go a long way in shaping the world. Thus, abstracting the analysis from such factors deprives us from a holistic understanding of systems and its elements and can only provide us with partial and limited view as the world is widely believed to be socially constructed with all its beliefs, attitudes and values at play. An observer/researcher, therefore, is necessarily required to be sensitive to capture such softer aspects in order to develop an understanding of the subject matter under study in all its complexities, with alternative perspectives and interpretations. At times it may so happen that tradition, authority, orientation and stance about what is directly experienced or perceived by people are regarded more reliable than the appearances, though hard to understand outside those contexts. Therefore, interpretation holds the key in such situations rather than verification/validity based on large samples. That is the reason why researchers choose a small sample or even a case study for in-depth analysis in phenomenological studies. This is quite unlike the case with positivist studies which require large samples ensuring representativeness and enabling deductive generalizations. This, in effect, makes the analysis subjective and value laden, but also throws light on what is going on and how so. Besides, the description and discussion become richer and more valuable with fresh insights/new perspectives. In this way, the analysis becomes inductive, qualitative and interpretivist, rendering measures, quantification and clear-cut procedures superfluous if not redundant. What is more, new hypotheses, theories and methods may evolve in the process of such an inquiry/research often conducted with the help of fieldwork. Needless to say, certain normative issues do tend to crop up here. A word of caution here is in place, however. The language of research and the researcher's felicity with it would also matter a great deal such that the results of the analysis and their implications are adequately communicated with clarity, fairness and modesty, lest rhetoric or erudition takes the better of the situation to claim more than warranted.

2.5.3 *Mixed Approach*

Notwithstanding the taxonomy of methodologies discussed above, a researcher should take due care so as not to be carried away and fall into the trap of watertight compartmentalization. It should be possible to combine the two approaches (also called triangulation in the literature when methodologies or data are mixed) depending upon the situation at hand, especially on the part of scholars pursuing their doctoral dissertations or large research projects wherein some aspects of the phenomenon under study may yield to quantitative analysis and the others only to descriptive or narrative variety. In such cases, while some chapters may adopt a positivist methodology, the others may go in for a phenomenological methodology. After all, the purpose is to improve one's understanding of events, processes, organizations and people and thereby make a contribution to the society's fund of knowledge and not to be bogged down with a tunnel vision. As said a little while ago about model selection criteria, here also, simplicity, parsimony, rigour, relevance, comprehensiveness besides elegance matter. To put simply, one should be able to explain much with a little. As the saying goes, try feeding a mouse to get an elephant, but not the other way around!

References

Boland LA (1979) A critique of Friedman's critics. J Econ Lit 17:503–522

Friedman M (1953) Essays in positive economics. Chicago University Press, Chicago

Kuhn TS (1962) The structure of scientific revolutions. Chicago University Press, Chicago

Nachane DM (2003) Causal inference and scientific explanation in economics. Presidential address to the 39th Indian econometric conference, Baroda

Popper KR (1963) Conjectures and refutations: the growth of scientific knowledge. Routledge, London

Remenyi D et al (1998) Doing research in business and management: an introduction to process and method. Sage Publishers, London/Thousand Oaks

Samuelson PA (1963) Problems of methodology – discussion. Am Econ Rev 53:231–236

Wong S (1973) The F- twist and the methodology of Paul Samuelson. Am Econ Rev 63:312–325

Chapter 3
Logical and Epistemological Norms in Scientific Theory Construction

Amitabha Gupta

The article is concerned with theory construction in both natural and social sciences and the issues relating to such efforts. It provides a historical perspective and debates relating to the nature of theories – "concrete," "middle range," and "abstract" or "grand" – and the logical (deductive and inductive) and epistemological norms (empirical and rationalistic) involved with them. The article highlights an alternative mode of theory construction in the social sciences in contrast with the formal, abstract, grand theories so common in the natural sciences. It argues that this alternative is characterized by *grounded contextualist epistemology*, *causal generalizations*, and *local realism*. Finally, the article provides two good illustrations of what counts as *local contextualist epistemology* and *causal generalizations* in theory construction in the social sciences from the works of Amartya Sen and M.N. Srinivas.

3.1 Introduction

Since the formative period of science in the antiquity, the logic of induction and deduction and the role they play in formulating scientific theories have been the concern for both the practicing scientists and the philosophers of science. It is commonly believed that science (and specifically a scientific theory) does not consist of discrete and random collection of factual statements, but comprises a network of both empirical and theoretical, particular and general, and observational and law statements in a coherent structure and framework. The role of logic in science, especially the job of the construction of scientific theories, essentially relates to spelling out the nature of these connections andrelationships among the

A. Gupta (✉)
Former Professor of Logic and Philosophy, Indian Institute of Technology Bombay, Mumbai, India
e-mail: agcg503@gmail.com

D.S. Hegde (ed.), *Essays on Research Methodology*,
DOI 10.1007/978-81-322-2214-9_3

various types of statements in this network, explaining what entitles the scientists to move from one type of statement to another or justifying on what basis they do so.

The two logics of induction and deduction have bearing also on the relationship between science and experience and foundation of scientific knowledge (the epistemology of science). For traditional epistemology or theory of knowledge, the question of finding *the method(s)* of arriving at acceptable scientific knowledge (or for that matter any knowledge) is interwoven with the issues relating to the basis of *generation or genesis* and *justification* of scientific knowledge, i.e., the issues of genesis and justification are not thought to be independent. History of science reveals that logic, epistemology, and science, especially at the time of the scientific breakthroughs in the form of production and defense of new scientific knowledge, have a close and intimate relationship.

3.1.1 Science: Scientific Method(s) and Logical and Epistemic Norms

In all ages science was considered as one of the paradigm examples of a successful logical and epistemic enterprise; hence, the method(s) science followed in achieving knowledge was thought to be indicative of the very nature of knowledge.[1]

Sciences in the antiquity (such as astronomy, cosmology, mathematics, medicine, biology) developed in tandem with the concern for explicating the nature of "scientific method(s),"[2] i.e., the contention that by using these method(s), science is interested in accurately describing (with the help of mathematics) what we observe or claiming to know how things really are.[3]

During the formative period of classical physics, epistemologists, such as Locke, Herschel, Whewell, and Kant, took scientific knowledge as a paradigm of epistemic enterprise and looked upon themselves as crusaders (or according to Locke, assumed the role of "under laborer") for vindicating the cause of the new knowledge and epistemic claims that were being made by the scientists of their time, especially Newton. Their job as epistemologists consisted in describing the processes and the logic through which this paradigmatic knowledge is acquired and spelling out the norms appropriate for this knowledge.[4]

---

[1]Suppe (1977).

[2]Losee (1972), p. 6, Jones (1952), Arnold(1974).

[3]The detailed study of the Babylonian mathematical astronomy can be found in (1) Neugebauer (1957, pp. 105–113). For Egyptian mathematics and astronomy, see Chap. IV, pp. 77–96; for Babylonian mathematics, see Chap. II, pp. 25–70; for astronomy, see Chap. V, pp. 97–144. (2) Neugebauer (1975). For Babylonian astronomy, see Pt. I, Bk. II, pp. 347–555; for Egyptian astronomy, see Pt. II, Bk. III, pp. 559–70.

[4]Locke (1968).

At the turn of this century, when the modern physics was being shaped, logical positivists too felt the necessity of articulating a new paradigm of scientific knowledge and accepted the goal of providing and justifying an account of the nature of scientific enterprise. In this endeavor, the logical positivists pursued with messianic fervor the search for the epistemic norms that would avoid the pitfalls of metaphysical traps in which science, according to them, could be enmeshed, particularly while asserting regularities of nature by invoking entities, which are not directly observable, such as "atom," "electrical field," "molecule," etc. The logical positivists fashioned their account of science on logic and epistemic norms that were solely empirical, exact, quantitative, logical, universal, and objective and found that the social sciences did not measure up to such standards of scientific adequacy.

3.1.2 Logical and Epistemic Norms in the Social Sciences

This alleged difference between natural and social sciences did raise a new set of epistemological and methodological questions concerning the character and possibility of knowledge of social phenomena. The comparison led to a close examination of the main epistemological themes, viz., the foundational and axiomatic systemic models, logic of confirmation and explanation, epistemological status of scientific laws and accidental generalizations, and nature and structure of scientific theory. By focusing directly on these logical and epistemological themes, one gets at the heart of the many different but related issues and questions in the social sciences: the issue of objectivity and causality; the issue of social ontology and realism, naturalism, reductionism, and pluralism; the foundational questions concerning the nature of rationality, self-interest, and preference; and the moral questions concerning welfare, justice, equality, and freedom, which are of abiding significance to social scientists in general and economists in particular. Thus, logic and epistemology indeed play a pivotal role in any scientific endeavor.

3.2 Logics of Induction and Deduction, Epistemology, and Goals of Science

The logics of induction and deduction evolved alongside the two dominant epistemological views of empiricism and rationalism. Both the logics and the associated epistemological views are directly linked with the *nature* and *goal of science.*

Kant in *Metaphysical Foundations of Modern Science* and *Critique of Pure Reason* claimed that his main concern was to explain how *synthetic a priori* judgments are possible in science and mathematics.

3.2.1 Two Logics Defined: Aristotle's Definitions

Till the advent of mathematical logic, there was a widespread view espoused by Kant that Aristotle had discovered all there was to know about logic. Indeed, Aristotle was first to systematically develop logic and define the inductive and deductive arguments.

3.2.2 Inductive Logic

For Aristotle, induction (*epagôgê*) is a cognitive process that moves from particulars to their generalizations, which is the basis of knowledge of the indemonstrable *first principles of sciences* (*Posterior Analytics*).

An *inductive argument* is an argument in which it is thought that the premises provide reasons supporting the *probable* truth of the conclusion. In an inductive argument, the premises are intended only to be so strong that if they are true, then it is *unlikely* that the conclusion is false.

The great intuition Aristotle had was that deduction in natural sciences rests upon prior induction. The universal general premise of a deductive argument is obtained not only through our contacts with the physical world, but because of our ability to grasp the *essential property* the particulars share in common. For Aristotle, essential properties are those without which an object would not be what it is and enable us to categorize an individual object as belonging to a class. So, according to Aristotle, our knowledge of generalization (*noûs*) depends on apprehending or grasping the essences (*archai*).

Aristotle made a distinction between enumerative induction and (intuitive) induction based on *essences*. Enumerative induction amounts to establishing a universal proposition or making a generalization by an exhaustive or complete enumeration of all the instances and ensuring that each satisfies a given property, e.g.,

All observed A's are B's
Therefore, all A's are B's

The more significant generalizations are based on (*intuitive*) *induction* arrived at on the basis of *essences*. Aristotle believed that human beings alone have the ability to acquire *noûs* by apprehending or grasping *archai* through their contacts with individual objects of the physical world.

3.2.3 Deductive Logic

According to Aristotle "a deduction is speech (*logos*) in which, certain things having been supposed, something different from those supposed results of necessity because of their being so."[5] Each of the "things supposed" is a *premise* (*protasis*) of the argument, and what "results of necessity" is the *conclusion* (*sumperasma*).

The most important claim made by this definition relates to the notion of "resulting of necessity" (*ex anankês sumbainein*). This corresponds to the notion of "logical consequence." In a deductive argument, the premises are intended to provide support for the conclusion that is so strong that if the premises are true, it would be *impossible* for the conclusion to be false.

Aristotle's *theory of syllogism* is the first and most comprehensive study of a class of *valid* deductive arguments based entirely on their *structure* or *form* (represented in terms of their "figure" and "mood") and not on their *content* or what these arguments are about.

3.3 Concrete Science: Pure Empiricism, (Phenomenal) Generalizations, and Prediction

The evolution of science in the antiquity – particularly generalization based on accurate observation in sciences, such as astronomy, cosmology, science of motion, and biology – may provide us with insights leading to the contrast between the "concrete" and the "abstract" science.[6] The contributions in astronomy by the Egyptian (c. 2000–500 B.C.) and the Babylonians (c. 1800–150 B.C.) characterize what may be called "concrete science," which is mainly observational and computational in nature and was driven by practical problems.

Generalizations made in these sciences are founded on systematization of data by specifying the relationship between "directly observable" and "explaining" observable phenomena in terms of other observable phenomena but never stepping out of the domain of concrete or observables. The generalizations thus arrived at in concrete science may be called *phenomenal generalizations*,[7] which are derived from the features of the phenomena being observed and investigated. The generalizations never assume any underlying (causal) structure.

The development of the "mathematical" astronomy[8] in these civilizations was dependent on the contrivance of many early astronomical instruments facilitating naked-eye observation (e.g., gnomons, sundials, etc.) and computational techniques by developing relevant mathematics (e.g., number system, spherical geometry, etc.). These aids enabled the early astronomers to make meticulous observation and record them motivated by the desire to solve practical concrete problems they were faced with.

[5] *Prior Analytics* I.2, 24b18-20.

[6] Gupta (1989), Freund (1968), Caneva (1978).

[7] Cartwright (1983, 1989), Little (1993).

[8] Neugebauer (1957, pp. 105–113; 1975), *op. cit.*

3.3.1 *A Case Study: The Babylonian Observational Astronomy and (Phenomenal) Generalizations*

The practical problem the Babylonian astronomers set out to solve exhibited their remarkable command over arithmetical techniques leading to *(phenomenal) generalizations*, which enabled them to develop calendar and *forecast* many natural events (e.g., the first visibility of the new moon, lunar eclipses, floods, tides, etc.) with remarkable accuracy. However, they achieved all these without having or never formulating any idea about the physical nature of the system of the heavenly bodies.

Babylonian civilization is often known as "calendar civilization." The demands of trade and commerce, religious rites, and astronomical prediction led the Babylonian to develop calendar. The Babylonians devised a lunar calendar which defined a month as the interval between the successive sightings of the first crescent of the moon. Hence, the basic problem underlying the Babylonian astronomy was to predict the visibility of the first crescent each month in order to mark the beginning of the month on the basis of this astronomical phenomenon.

3.3.2 *The Problems Faced by the Babylonian Observational Astronomers*

O. Neugebauer[9] shows how the Babylonians came to look upon the "first visibility of the crescent" as a complicated periodic phenomenon. The *observational astronomy* of the Babylonians recognized this problem as highly complicated because it was dependent on several other phenomena: the *conjunction* of the sun and the moon just preceding the first visibility, the so-called elongation between the sun and the moon (which increases about 12°per day. In fact, the daily elongation might vary between 10°and 14°, bringing to light the problem involved in detailed knowledge of the variation of both solar and lunar velocities), the *seasonal variation of the angles between the ecliptic* and *horizon* also effecting the visibility of the new moon (the number of days from one new moon to the next is not always the same – sometimes it is 29 days and other times it is 30 days; hence, it is difficult to work out beforehand the point of the first visibility since it is hard to foretell whether any given month would be 29 or 30 days in duration), and *the problem of keeping the lunar calendar in step with the annual cycle of seasons*, i.e., the apparent movement of the sun.

[9]Neugebauer (1957, pp. 105–113).

3.3.3 Solution: An Example of (Phenomenal) Generalizations

The Babylonians devised an arithmetical procedure for making astronomical prediction and computation. The table (given in the Appendix 1) shows the monthly conjunction of the sun and the moon (this table is a direct transcription of a cuneiform tablet referring to the year 133–132 B.C.).

According to Neugebauer, the arithmetical technique of the Babylonians consisted of obtaining over-all averages for the main periods of astronomical phenomena. These averages then were improved by occasional individual observations. At the same time, short-range predictions of phenomena could be made on the basis of a series of observations immediately preceding the event. Once the Babylonians had at their disposal extensive and accurate data, they analyzed them (as men who prepare tide table or economists working on "time series" at present times would do) to look for recurring cycles. Having detected a cycle, they observed deviations from the average and saw whether there was any cycle to be found there. Finding an average cycle in these deviations, they next examined the departures from the fresh average and so on. By taking the process far enough, it was possible for the Babylonians to solve the practical problems they set out with and to predict not only when the new moon would be visible but also whether a particular opposition between the sun and moon would result in a lunar eclipse or when the retrogression of planets would take place.

3.4 Abstract Science: Rationalism and Deductivism – The Platonic-Pythagorean-Euclidean Tradition

The shift from the pure "empirical" or concrete science to the anti-empirical, idealistic, and rationalistic character of science and mathematics was advocated by Eleatic, Platonic-Pythagorean-Euclidean tradition, which spearheaded the use of reductio ad absurdum arguments[10] introduced earlier by Parmenides (fl. 540 B.C.), the most famous of the Eleatic thinkers. Plato (428–348 B.C.) turned away from the study of the world as revealed in sense experience in favor of the abstract world of "ideas" and rational methods.

The distrust of sense experience led to the introduction of the "methods of proofs" thought to be more reliable. Pythagoras (c. 570–c. 540 B.C.) and Euclid (fl. 300 B.C.) developed the logically valid deductive patterns of reasoning by constructing "proofs" for such claims as the irrationality of "$\sqrt{2}$" and the existence

[10]The reductio ad absurdum argument essentially involves a technique of proving a claim or theorem Γ by assuming that "not Γ" is true and then deducing from "not Γ" and the axioms of the system both a statement and its negation. It is clear that if the assumption of "not Γ" entails contradiction where the axioms of the system are taken to be true, then "not Γ" must be given up, and "Γ" must be admitted as true.

of an infinity of prime numbers.[11] Euclid in his *Elements*[12] developed geometry, especially in his first two books, out of an earlier hodgepodge of practical methods of measurement and calculation recipes. These were finally brought together under a single set of axioms by Euclid in his *Elements*, when he built a "deductive structure"[13] in his axiomatic system.

Euclid did not rely on experience and observation and used exclusively rational arguments, such as reductio ad absurdum and the *method of exhaustion*[14] (mainly used the latter in Books XI and XII to develop solid geometry), in order to justify and establish his theorems, conclusions, or claims. Euclid's 13 books, constituting the *Elements*, not only cover geometry (plane rectilineal geometry, circle and regular polygons) but also theory of proportions and magnitudes, arithmetic, irrational lines, solid geometry, and regular polyhedral, all in a deductive structure in the axiomatic form.

3.4.1 Norm of Science as an Axiomatic System with Deductive Structure

Following Euclid, Archimedes (287–212 B.C.) was the first to cast an empirical science in the axiomatic mold. Since Euclid and Archimedes, it was expected that empirical science must be an axiomatic deductive system of statements comprising axioms, definitions, and theorems organized in such a manner so that the truth of the theorems follows from the assumed truth of the axioms. Archimedes went on to prove from his axioms on the lever that two unequal weights balance at distances from the fulcrum that are inversely proportional to their weights.

Even during the Renaissance, the "new" science of Galileo (1564–1642) and his treatment of "local motions" (freely falling bodies and projectile motions) in his *Dialogues Concerning Two New Sciences Pertaining to Mechanics and Local Motion*[15] and mechanics of Newton (1642–1727) in his *Philosophiae Naturalis Principia Mathematica* (*Mathematical Principles of Natural Philosophy*)[16] followed the axiomatic method (although in his *Optics* Newton used the inductive method of analysis, but gave it up in his *Principia*).

---

[11]Szabó (1978), Hardy (1940).

[12]Heath (1861–1940, 1956).

[13]Mueller (1981/2006).

[14]The *method of exhaustion* consists of showing that each possible contrary of a theorem Γ has consequences that are inconsistent with the axioms of the system.

[15]Galileo (1638).

[16]Newton (1729).

3.4.2 Plato's Thesis of "Saving the Appearance"

"Abstract science" consists of speculative, theoretical activity yielding ideas, concepts, axioms of theories and models, and explanatory structures, where knowledge claims and explanations are evaluated in terms of deducing consequences, which corresponds to finding answers to such questions as: "How or why do things happen?" "What are the grounds that determine their occurrence?"

Stephen Toulmin, in his *Foresight and Understanding*,[17] has criticized the predictivist thesis (espoused by concrete science). Prediction or forecasting, according to Toulmin, "is a craft or technology, an application of science rather than the kernel of science itself." On the other hand, Toulmin claims that the function of science is to build up systems of ideas about nature which has some legitimate claim to "reality." For Toulmin, these systems of ideas provide explanatory techniques which not only must be consistent with data but also must be acceptable, for the time being at any rate, as "absolute" and "pleasing to the mind." Moreover, Toulmin says that although scientific theories inter alia are used to predict, their main function, however, is to provide explanations of recognized regularities and explain away anomalies and irregularities in observation.

Some of the anomalies and irregularities in *apparent* motion that were discerned by the ancient *observational* astronomers had to do with the *retrograde* motion, i.e., the motion in a loop of the planets, nonuniform motion of the sun, and irregularities in the motion of the moon, as opposed to the strictly uniform and circular motion expected of all celestial bodies. Plato, who is searching questions that dominated the subsequent astronomical inquiry, is said to have asked:

> What are the uniform and orderly movements by the *assumption* of which the apparent movements of the planets can be accounted for?

The Greek (theoretical) astronomers used three geometrical figures to "model" the observed motions of celestial bodies. The models accounted for the anomalies and irregularities at the same time claiming that the "real" motion described in terms of the these geometrical figures remains strictly uniform and circular. The three geometrical figures that were used for modeling are the deferent and epicycle system (by Claudius Ptolemy to explain the *retrograde* motion of the planets) and the eccentric and the equant circles.

"Abstract science" construes scientific models and theories, such as astronomical theories, as devices for "*saving the appearance*." This view, having a lineage from Geminus (first century B.C.), Plato, Pythagoras, and Ptolemy (c. 100–c. 178 A.D.) and attributed to Copernicus (1473–1543), maintains that scientific theories are mere hypotheses, without any claim to truth, superimposing mathematical relations on phenomena in order to "save the appearance," i.e., to remove the discrepancies and anomalies in observation and making them coherent. It is opposed by *realism*,

[17] Toulmin (1961).

upheld vociferously by Galileo (1564–1642), who maintained that scientific theories must not be viewed as mere computational devices to "save the appearance," since they make claims to *physical truth*.

3.5 Marriage of Concrete and Abstract Science

History of science does not support the conception of theory that differentiates abstract science from the science of the concrete to the exclusion of each other. The abstract science invariably reaches beyond empirical co-occurrence to postulate a representation or structure for the phenomena under investigation, one which *accounts for* the co-occurrence and potentially for other aspects of the phenomena not yet observed. Further, scientific theory, according to abstract science, is not an economic presentation of accumulated propositions claimed as "known." Rather, it goes beyond mere logical organization of given facts in *reinterpreting our experience* in terms of fresh concepts, methods of representation, explanatory procedures, paradigms or ideals of natural order. A theory is intended not as a description of what one already knows but as a hypothesis: something that goes beyond the evidence by introducing a *postulated physical structure* that could provide an inferential or causal account of the data to be explained.

3.5.1 Alleged Incongruence Between Deduction and Induction: A Critical Examination

There is a widespread view that the notion of "deduction" founded on rationalistic epistemology is fundamentally and essentially disparate or incongruent to induction. Moreover, it is argued that unlike deduction, induction cannot be justified as a legitimate form of inference[18] nor could induction be regarded as the characteristic method for scientific investigation.[19]

3.5.2 "Mixed Method" in Geometry

The view stated in 5.1 is countered by those who maintain that deduction and induction are more intimately related than is presently common,[20] and in spite of the overwhelming emphasis on deductive structure of science, induction, "probability theory, and statistical inference" now emerge as better foundations for scientific

[18]Hume (1739/1888).

[19]Popper (1963a, b, 1968).

[20]Beth (1967).

models.[21] Hence, it is necessary to reconceptualize induction in a different way and in a more "favorable light."[22] Euclidean geometry can give us a clue.

3.5.3 Close Relationship Between Deduction and Induction: Geometrical Generalization

An analysis of the deductive structure of proofs in the axiomatic framework of Euclidean geometry will show that *induction is inbuilt* in the Euclidean deductive proofs. In other words, the passage from a particular to a generalization is inherent in all deductive proofs in the Euclidean system.

Consider the structure of the proof of Proposition 1, Book I, of the *Elements* consisting of the following parts:

Enunciation
(*protasis*) On a given finite straight line to construct an equilateral triangle.

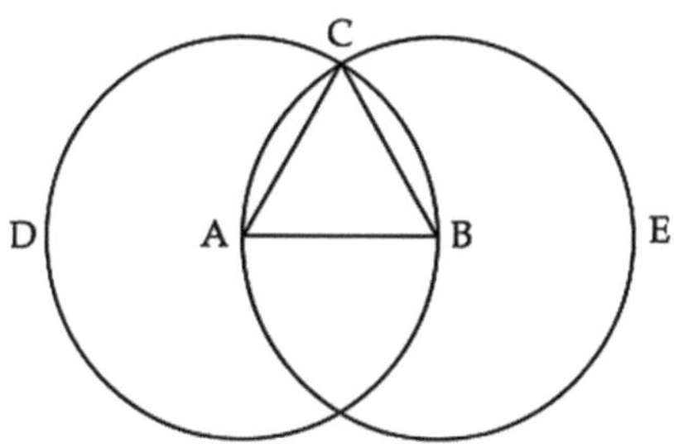

Setting-out
(*ekthesis*) Let AB be the given finite straight line.

Specification
(*diorismos*) Thus, it is required to construct an equilateral triangle on the straight line AB.

Construction
(*kataskeuē*) With center A and distance AB, let the circle BCD be drawn; again, with center B and distance BA, let the circle ACE be drawn; and from the point C, at which the circles cut one another, to the points A and B, let the straight lines CA and CB be joined.

[21]Mumford (1999).

[22]Macnamara (1991, pp. 21–48).

Proof (in modern sense)	
(Apodeixis)	1. Since the point A is the center of the circle CDB, AC is equal to AB [by Def. 15]
	2. Again, since the point B is the center of the circle CAE, BC is equal to BA [by Def. 15]
	3. But it was shown that CA is equal to AB (restatement of 1)
	4. Therefore, each of the straight lines CA and CB is equal to AB [from lines 2 and 3]
	5. And things which are equal to the same thing are also equal to one another; therefore, CA is also equal to CB [by CN 1]
	6. Therefore, the three straight lines CA, AB, BC are equal to one another [by CN 1]

Conclusion
(sumperasma) Therefore, the triangle ABC is equilateral; and it has been constructed on the given finite straight line AB, which was required to be done (Q.E.F.).

The six parts of the Euclidean proof of Proposition 1, Book I, show that geometrical proof, according to Euclid, does not rest merely on part 5, i.e., apodeixis (proof) [which essentially is similar to our familiar concept of "proof," viz., a sequence of steps each justified by an appeal to either Euclidean definitions or common notions (or other initially given assumptions of Euclid) or a step following from the previous line(s) already justified].

If the apodeixis (proof) exists, then why does Euclid need the other components of his demonstration, especially enunciation (*protasis*), setting-out (*ekthesis*), specification (*diorismos*), and then a summary in conclusion (sumperasma)? This is because, as Beth points out, although the entire demonstration – from *protasis* to *sumperasma* – is about a *specific* geometrical figure, in this case it is about a *specific* line AB; the conclusion being arrived at, however, applies to *all* lines. If the *apodeixis* concerns only to a specific line chosen, then the entire exercise of doing geometry is pointless.

3.5.4 The Condition Legitimizing Euclid's Passage from Particular to the Universal Generalization

The important issue, which needs to be brought out here, is: what is the condition that legitimizes Euclid's passage from particular to the universal generalization? The answer has to do with the fact that universal generalization is permitted only when *no special assumptions* are made about the particulars in terms of which the proof was carried out. The axiomatic system of geometry must ensure that *no properties* of the geometrical figure under consideration are being used in the entire geometrical proof.

The violation of this condition did take place owing to the common practice, since Euclid, of the use of figures as part of proofs in geometry and resultant smuggling in unstated assumptions relating to their properties (as documented by Lakatos[23] in the case of Descartes-Euler conjecture on polyhedra). This was the main justification given for *formalizing* mathematics (geometry and arithmetic), as was done by Hilbert (1862–1943) in formalizing Euclidean geometry in 1903, completely banning the use of geometrical figures and permitting symbols to represent them only under interpretation.[24] The rule of universal generalization in logic essentially performs induction by using variables and allowing them to range over *arbitrary* objects or individuals without invoking any of their properties. (However, there is debate whether generalizations in geometry and the rule of inference, called UG, are similar.[25])

3.6 "Mixed Method" in the Natural Sciences

It is believed that generalizations engendered by geometry in its axiomatic form are no different from those in the empirical sciences. The articulation of the view combining inductive and deductive approaches to scientific knowledge can be traced back to Aristotle. In his study of local motion exhibited by, for example, freely falling bodies, Aristotle combines the inductive-deductive method.

3.6.1 Aristotle's Notion of Science: Demonstrative Science

For Aristotle, scientific knowledge (*epistêmonikon*) involves the processes of both induction and deduction. Deduction in the sciences rests on induction. Unlike many thinkers even in contemporary times (some denouncing and censuring induction), Aristotle maintained that induction and deduction in science form a single system.

With this distinction between empirical and rational abstract, speculation was forced. Scientists relate the visible changes in nature to the permanent principles underlying them ("*logos*"). There is a prevailing conviction that nature functions, not willfully but "rationally," i.e., according to some principle. The scientists' essential task is to get an intellectual grasp of the character of natural order, showing in this way why the events had to happen as they did. The "method of hypothesis" or postulational method is regarded as one of the main ways the (scientific) knowledge of this natural order can be articulated.

---

[23]Lakatos (1976).

[24]Hilbert (1902).

[25]Fine (1985), Stoll (1961), Macnamara (1991, pp. 26–27).

Aristotle claimed that *science is demonstrative* (*apodeixis*), i.e., deducing "what is unknown" from "what is better known." According to Aristotle, providing (epistemic) explanation and justification of what is unknown amounts to deducing the unknown from its cause, i.e., giving some sort of causal explanation based on generalizations attained through the process of "intuitive" induction. Aristotle's inductive-deductive method looks like this[26]:

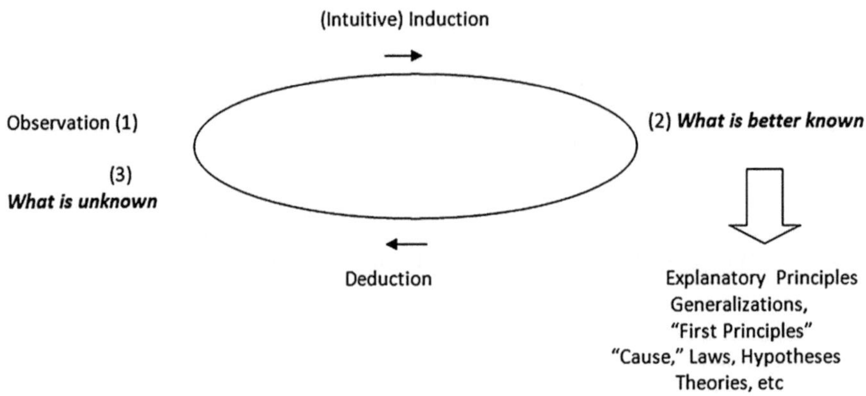

3.6.2 *Congruence Between Deduction and Induction in Aristotle's Science*

Using the *inductive-deductive method*, Aristotle developed his *science of motion*, starting with four *doctrines*, four *first principles*, and the *laws of motion* (based on his claim to establish generalizations founded on (intuitive) *induction* arrived at on the basis of his notion of *essences*), and then derived *deductively* empirical consequences from them (see Appendix 3.2).

In the history of epistemology, one observes a tension between access to reality through empirical facts (empiricism) and through predictive mathematical laws (rationalism). Aristotle saw this tension while justifying any particular conceptual framework or theoretical paradigm. For him the tension was between (1) the abstract ideal character of mathematics appropriate to describe the underlying ideal structure that forms the basis of our understanding of the observed world and (2) the possibility of its (i.e., mathematical modeling or idealization) grasping the complex real world because of the alleged inappropriateness and possible lack of "fit" between the ideal and the real. However, he resolved it by introducing the concept of *mixed science*.

[26] Adapted from Losee (1972, p. 6).

For example, according to Aristotle, arithmetic is useful since it signifies the quantitative characteristics embodied in matter or the real world, the *numerical* dimension of sensible object. Similarly, Aristotle believed that geometry is necessary for a proper understanding of such natural phenomena as an eclipse or a rainbow.

The reason for this is that the explanation of the occurrence of such natural phenomena would be given in terms of certain physico-mathematical properties (e.g., a certain spatial configuration between the sun, the moon, the spherical raindrops, and the observer, the rectilinear path of the light ray, etc.) that exhibit the closeness or fit between nature and geometrical idealization. Such closeness or fit was thought to be the basis for the so-called mixed sciences, such as astronomy, optics, mechanics, and harmonics, in which Aristotle took the use of mathematics for granted. In the Middle Ages and the Renaissance, the followers of Aristotle, e.g., Robert Grosseteste, Albert the Great, and Thomas Aquinas, endorsed the "mixed sciences."

3.6.3 The Method of Hypothesis

In due course, the task of science consisted of relating the "phenomena" (or even departure from the regular order of things) to paradigms (i.e., an "exemplar" or "ideals of natural order"). A community of scientist proposes or assumes that certain behavior patterns are natural and expected; the expected does not require explanation – only the unexpected does. The job of a scientific theory, then, is to specify these expected patterns of behavior and to explain deviations from them. All behavior within a given domain, then, is to be accounted for either by its conformity to expectations or by explaining its deviations from expectations. However, this presupposes that a community of scientist agrees upon certain natural course of events, paradigms, or "ideals of natural order," e.g., the law of inertia, the principle of rectilinear propagation of light, etc.

It is this conception, a scientific theory that does not differentiate abstract science from the science of the concrete to the exclusion of each other. Moreover, a scientific theory reaches beyond empirical co-occurrence to postulate a representation or structure for the phenomena under investigation, one which accounts for the co-occurrence as well as the potential explanation for other aspects of the phenomena not yet observed. Further, scientific theory is not an economic presentation of accumulated propositions claimed as "known." Rather, it goes beyond mere logical organization of given facts in reinterpreting our experience in terms of fresh concepts, methods of representation, explanatory procedures, paradigms, or ideals of natural order. A theory is intended not as a description of what one already knows but as a *hypothesis*, something that goes beyond the evidence by introducing a *postulated physical structure* that could provide an inferential or causal account of the data to be explained.

Thus, it became a norm that a completed science will have two components:

(a) Observational laws, e.g., in Newton's mechanics, Galileo's laws of freely falling bodies and projectile motion, as well as Kepler's three laws of planetary motion
(b) The axioms or hypotheses from which the observational laws could be derived and thereby explaining them, e.g., the three laws of motion as axioms of Newton's theory of mechanics

Another example of this postulational hypothetical structure of science accounting for and explaining the observational laws can be found in kinetic theory of gases (see Appendix 3).

3.7 Axiomatic Systemic Notion of Theory

The other epistemological view, known as the received view of theory, maintains that the basic principles are materially true a priori and constitute the starting point of the axiomatic structure of a scientific theory, often called "the *axiomatic systemic* notion of theory." An outline of this has been given in Sects. 3.5 and 3.6.

3.7.1 Axiomatic Systemic Model in the Social Science

The received view on modern mathematical exact sciences supports a lofty vision of a world completely ordered by a single elegant theory. One of the most cherished goals of the logical positivists was a unified science bound by a common rationale. It was claimed to have the structure of a pyramid with a system of few simple, elegant, abstract, all-embracing, general, universal axioms on the top and a vast array of relatively less abstract but specific domains with their observational laws below it.

Mill in his essay *On the Definition and Method of Political Economy*[27] draws an analogy between *economics and geometry*.

The rationality assumption in social sciences turns some part of social life into an abstract a priori game of skills. Hobbes in Leviathan also endorses a similar comparison by comparing the rules of social life with the rules that enable us to do arithmetic or geometry.[28]

Lionel Robbins in his *An Essay on the Nature and Significance of Economic Science* (1932)[29] draws an analogy between *economics and mechanics.* There are reasons for preferring mechanics, if we have to seek analogies, since it allows phenomena as countervailing causes, whereas it is hard to envisage the presence of

[27]Mill et al. (1963).

[28]Hobbes, Leviathan (1651).

[29]Robbins (1932).

causes in geometry. Thus, Robbins claims that economics is a species of mechanics and that laws in economics are "necessities to which human action is subject."

The usual textbook introduction tends to create an impression that the basis of economics lies in approximate truths about consumer and producer behavior together with some acknowledgement that different assumptions would produce different theories.

Generally, theory-governed explanations are a priori. Many of these theories amount to the blueprint of the underlying mechanism we want to study, manifested in the behavior of the phenomena. The underlying mechanism, say in classical mechanics or kinetic theory of gases, is often formulated in terms of certain assumptions or axioms.

Milton Friedman in his *The Methodology of Positive Economics* (1953)[30] fashions any sound economic theory into a "logical language" and "a body of substantive hypotheses." The former, according to him, is a "set of tautologies" and "its function is to act as a filling system." The latter is "designed to abstract essential features of a complex reality."

Friedman raises the question: "Can a hypothesis be tested by the realism of its assumptions?" His answer is that the "realism of assumptions" is irrelevant to the assessment of a theory. For him the only test of the theory is its success with prediction; realism is not the criterion. However, he does not support the standard instrumentalist position.

Ludwig von Mises (1960, 1962)[31] attempted to construct one unique great axiomatic economic theory with complete and deductively closed set of precise statements into which all our knowledge relating to diverse intelligible phenomena can be fitted. For example, Ludwig von Mises argued that all statements of economic theory followed deductively from an axiom that he held to be materially true a priori, the so-called basic concept of action and its categorical conditions. He claimed that all the theorems of economics can be derived from these axioms. Thus, according to von Mises, the empirical testing of economic theory becomes totally superfluous. At best we can check the deductive reasoning to make sure that the conclusions do in fact follow necessarily from the axioms.

The recent example of the use of *axiomatic systemic model* in social sciences can be seen in "social choice theory," mainly authored by economists and political scientists. The theory aims at modeling the mechanism of collective decision making.[32] Logic has also been found to be useful in formally specifying and verifying the properties of procedures of social choice by developing *social software*.[33] (For a comprehensive coverage of this important development, refer to *Logic and Social Choice Theory*.)[34]

---

[30]Friedman (1953).

[31]von Mises (1960, 1962).

[32]Arrow (1951, 1963), Sen (1986, 1970, n.d.).

[33]Parikh (2002).

[34]Endris (2011).

3.7.2 *Construction of "Scientific" Sociological Theories: "Grand" and "Middle-Range" Theories*

Talcott Parsons tried to develop a general theory of society in his *The Social System* (1951).[35] Parsons attempted to present a general theory of society or "social system theory," influenced by "systems theory" and "cybernetics" and adopting their basic ideas and concepts to the realm of sociology and social sciences, such as "feedback," "latent function," "pattern maintenance function," "equilibrium," etc. The Parsonian paradigm was meant to generate a "grand" inclusive theory and the scientific laws of society similar to the natural sciences.

In contrast with "grand" theories, the idea of "middle-range" theories in sociology was mooted by a group of sociologists in the 1950s, such as Robert Merton (1949/1957/1968),[36] Hans Zetterberg (1954/1963/1965),[37] Llewellyn Gross (1959),[38] and others. Zetterberg said: "In physics, the theory of relativity and the quantum theory are inclusive theories in terms of which most laws of physics can be explained. The goal of the scientific enterprise is to know such a theory." However, Merton acknowledging the present limitations of the "theoretical paucity" in sociology asserted that "between twentieth century physics and twentieth century sociology stand billions of man-hours of sustained, disciplined and cumulative research. Perhaps sociology is not yet ready for its Einstein because it has not yet found its Kepler – to say nothing of its Newton, Laplace, Gibbs, Maxwell or Plank."

3.7.3 *"Dust-Bowl Empiricism" or "Barefoot Empiricism" in the Social Sciences*

Naïve or simple empiricism and positivistic tradition or what has been characterized as "dust-bowl empiricism" or "barefoot empiricism" derives its character from the insistence on the *epistemic primacy of observation* and the rejection of a priori theorizing as an epistemic source of explanation.

The methods codified by the advocates of this approach in social scientific theorizing, more commonly known as verificational approach, emphasize on data collection, statistical analysis, hypothesis formulation, and testing them against empirical facts. This approach raised the hope (expressed by, e.g., Lipset[39]) of a truly "scientific" social science.[40]

---

[35]Parsons (1951).

[36]Merton (1949/1957/1968).

[37]Zetterberg (1954/1963/1965).

[38]Gross (1959).

[39]Lipset (1994).

[40]Gibbs (1972), Cohen (1980).

3.7.4 Objections to the Empiricist Positivistic Approach

Some of the objections to the epistemic primacy of "dust-bowl" or "barefoot empiricism" are:

(1) Scientific *observation is theory laden*: granting that the objects that are observed and the properties possessed by them are independent of the observer, but what kind of objects they are observed to be and the properties that are observed are ***relative*** to and determined by the observer's theory, belief, prior knowledge, i.e., observer's *conceptual perspective*. Hence, the adherents of two different theories will view the same phenomenon in two different ways. Hanson maintains that Tycho and Kepler would see different things while watching the same dawn.

(2) *Underdetermination of theory by facts*: the *same set of facts may be explained by more than one theory*. What counts as a fact is determined by the *conceptual perspective* associated with a theory.

(3) *The meanings of a term* in a given theory cannot be considered in isolation. Its meaning is derived from being part of a theoretical system. The meaning of any term, say *mass*, common in two different theories, for example, in classical mechanics and special theory of relativity, will not be the same in the two theories as different and incompatible equations about mass hold in the two theories. Hence, the condition of *invariance of meaning* across the theories does not hold, and different theories are noncomparable or *incommensurable*.

(4) *Conceptual relativism*: the incommensurability thesis stated in (iii) implies conceptual *relativism* – the acceptance of one theory over another is relative to a prior commitment to a paradigm or a *conceptual perspective*, rather than to a neutral, objective criteria of evaluation. The *conceptual perspective* analysis not only reduced scientific knowledge to a subjective enterprise, but made it ***relative*** to a sociocultural group.

(5) Since the 1960s, the static positivistic model of scientific knowledge was replaced by the *dynamic model*. This led to a historical approach and an analysis of the actual scientific practices in order to develop an understanding of the principles that govern rational transitions or justifiable change of belief in the growth of scientific knowledge.

(6) Based on detailed historical studies, the view that has emerged is: *there is no uniquely correct methodology of science as* there exists *plurality of methodologies* which are employed for all sorts of reasons.

3.8 The Character of Knowledge of Social Phenomena

Otto Neurath (1935)[41] exhorted us to give up our belief in the "system," one great scientific theory, i.e., a unique, complete, and deductively closed set of precise statements, into which all intelligible phenomena of nature can be fitted. Recently, Nancy Cartwright supported these ideas in her *The Dappled World*,[42] in which she argues that the idea of unified theory that models all situations is a myth since "we live in a dappled world, a world rich in different things, with different natures, behaving in different ways." These differences can be accounted for in terms of the approaches toward understanding of nature typified by their own theoretical concepts, models, experimental and observational techniques, the objects of investigation, which are *characteristic of each domain.*

This prompted a local realistic view of scientific explanation. According to this view, we posit natural mechanisms whose working is responsible for the way the phenomena appear and "laws of nature" get their depth not from the fact that they express something about the essences of things or are based on statistical generalizations but from the fact that similar mechanisms are seen to underpin very different seeming phenomena.

3.8.1 Karl Popper's "Situational Logic"

Popperian pluralism is a form of rationalism or a halfway position in the struggle between rationalism and empiricism. In opposition to psychologism of Freud and interpretative (*verstehen*) methodology of Max Weber, Popper claims that there exists a *purely objective method* in the social sciences, which may well be called *situational logic*. It consists in realizing that an action is *objectively appropriate to a situation*. Popper says:

> The man with certain wishes therefore becomes a man whose situation may be characterized by the fact that he pursues certain objective aims; and a man with certain memories or associations becomes a man whose situation can be characterized by the fact that he is equipped objectively with certain theories or with certain information.[43]

Popper's *Models, instruments, and truth*: *The Rationality Principle in the Social Sciences* is a significant contribution on *practical inference* in which the situation and the actor's decision scheme jointly imply "the thing to do."[44]

[41]Neurath (1983).

[42]Cartwright (1999).

[43]Popper (1963a, b).

[44]Popper (1963a, b, 1970).

3.8.2 Grounded Contextualist Epistemology and Local Realism

The works of Nancy Cartwright (1983, 1989),[45] Arthur Fine (1986, 1996),[46] and Ian Hacking (1983)[47] have shown the futility and sterility of a generic, global epistemic debate on the realism-antirealism and its replacement by a local contextualist epistemology grounded in doing science, getting involved in actual specific issues faced by a given science and taking a natural ontological attitude. Hacking calls this change from global to local epistemology a shift from representing to intervening.

Harold Kincaid (1996)[48] and Nicholas Huggett (2001)[49] claim that this attitude of epistemology in philosophy of science is reflected in downplaying global concerns of representation, correspondence, or truth and explaining the possibility of knowledge in terms of specific models of entities with causal powers under particular circumstances. This is called "localism" or "local realism."

3.8.3 Local Realism and Causal Generalizations: W. Salmon and N. Cartwright

Wesley Salmon (1971)[50] rejects the Humean conception of causation as linked chains of events by attempting to articulate an epistemologically sound theory of continuous causal processes and causal interactions. It reads not so much as an analysis of the term "causality" as a set of instructions for producing a causal explanation of a particular phenomenon or event.

One begins by compiling a list of statistically relevant factors and analyzing the list by a variety of methods. This procedure terminates in the creation of causal models of these statistical relationships and empirical testing to determine which of these models is best supported by the evidence. Salmon insists that an adequate explanation has not been achieved until the fundamental causal mechanisms of a phenomenon have been articulated.

Nancy Cartwright (1983, 1989) also forcefully endorses the idea that regularity or, for that matter, causal explanation of a phenomenon involves identifying the causal processes, *capacities*, and relations that underlie the phenomenon.

---

[45]Cartwright (1983, 1999).

[46]Fine (1986, 1996).

[47]Hacking (1983).

[48]Kincaid (1996).

[49]Huggett (2001).

[50]Salmon (1971).

3.8.4 Generalization in Social Sciences: H. Kincaid

It has been argued that social sciences cannot have laws and generalizations (John Searle (1984),[51] P. Churchland (1979)[52]) because it is built around folk psychology that invokes mental states like beliefs, desires, etc., and there can be no laws relating mental states and behavior.

N. Cartwright (1989) and Harold Kincaid (1996) reject these largely a priori arguments against the constraints put on lawlike explanations in the social sciences. They argue that if the constraints of complexity, redescription, and ceteris paribus conditions were cogent, they would succeed in preventing laws in most of natural sciences as well. They defend the possibility and reality of generalizations and well-confirmed laws in the social sciences based on the discovery of causal mechanisms underlying various social processes.

With the help of substantive arguments, Kincaid goes on to demonstrate that in terms of a local contextualist epistemology, it is possible to produce well-confirmed laws according to standard scientific procedures *in certain sections* of social sciences. The laws of market behavior, which are fundamental and common to divergent economic theories – neoclassical, Austrian, and Marxist – are confirmed if the relevant ceteris paribus clauses hold. The laws are *a rise in the price of a good will result in a decrease in quantity demanded*, and *a decline in the supply of a good will result in a rise in price*. Empirical evidences have shown that the relevant ceteris paribus clauses for these laws do hold. Studies by A. Weinstein show that *the preferences are* frequently *transitive*. Based on the empirical work by G. Becker, it is reasonable to believe that even when preferences are not orderly, little deviation from the above laws will result. Claiming that these two laws are not rare jewels in the morass of otherwise *soft* social sciences, Kincaid goes on to extend the same conclusion to the best empirical work on cultural evolution and ecological adaptation in small-scale societies carried out by anthropologists and economists. These works are similar to the scientific work in evolutionary biology and ecology producing lawlike claims, such as *the law of succession*.

3.8.5 Phenomenal Regularities and Causal Realism: D. Little

The reason for caveats and avoiding sweeping claims about well-confirmed laws in social sciences in general prompts Daniel Little (1991, 2003)[53] to assert that the regularities that can be found within social sciences are *phenomenal*, produced by the specifics of the social- and individual-level causal mechanisms and processes.

[51]Searle (1984).

[52]Churchland (1979).

[53]Little (1991, 2003).

The objective of social science is to discover such causal mechanisms, processes, and powers or capacities that derive from agents and institutions and the regularities they produce, instead of looking for lawlike generalizations or providing interpretation of behavior. This view on social explanation aims to give "... a true description of underlying causal factors sufficient to bring about the phenomenon in question." Little calls this view *causal realism*. He says: "... against current anti-positivistic criticisms among social scientists, I will argue for causal realism in social explanation: causal explanation is at the core of much social research, and causal hypotheses depend on appropriate standards of empirical confirmation for their acceptability."

Claiming that the justifications for causal realism are not a priori but based on empirically informed analysis, Little suggests that the philosophy of science and the metaphysics of social causation must be in close proximity to the scientific discipline that is its subject. With reference to the ontology of social causation, Little subscribes to a naturalistic view maintaining that the causal influence that social entities have is through their effects on individual action. Thus, social phenomenon supervenes but is natural since it is the result of the actions and states of human beings, who themselves are natural organisms. However, Little denies that strong lawlike regularities exist at the social level.

Following Nancy Cartwright's distinction, made in her *How the Laws of Physics Lie*, between fundamental and phenomenal laws, Little differentiates between "governing" and "phenomenal" regularities. A law of nature is a paradigm example of governing regularity as the law describes the behavior of a given natural kind (See Appendix 3.4). He denies that social concepts, such as "state," "class," "market economy," "share-cropping land-tenure system," etc., serve to identify social kinds, analogous to natural kinds. They function rather as ideal types or cluster concepts, permitting us to classify a range of diverse phenomena under a single concept.

The phenomenal regularities comprising social concepts are *emergent* inductively discernable patterns that derive from the underlying causal properties of things and mechanisms. Such regularities, however, are not accidental generalizations as they support counterfactuals and qualify as lawlike. Little gives examples of a variety of regularities concerning the state suggested by social scientists: states create entrenched bureaucracies, states maximize revenues, state crises cause revolutions, etc. Although these regularities hold across a number of cases and support counterfactuals, they derive their strength on the basis of the underlying institutional and individual-level circumstances that give rise to the regularities of state behavior mentioned above.

In his *Varieties of Social Explanation* (1991), Little explains the idea of causal ascription in terms of attributing causal mechanism and causal power: to assert that A causes B is to assert that A in the context of *typical causal fields* brings about B (or increases the probability of the occurrence of B). This concept is further elaborated in terms of the idea of a causal chain: A causes B just in case there are structured circumstances of agency of the individuals at the microlevel making up social institution and representing the causal mechanisms that link the occurrence of A to the occurrences of B.

The causal power of a social institution operates through incentives, opportunities, empowerments, information preference formation, etc., that are embodied in a social structure affecting the actions of the individuals. A "social institution," unlike "brute facts," has a logic and is the result of a set of constitutional rules, which defines it. This idea of a "logic of institution" attempts to capture the notion that a social entity has an entrenched set of incentives and constraints on individual actions that follow from these defining constitutional rules. By altering incentives, preferences, and beliefs, the logic of social institutions has effects on the intentionality of individual behavior, which in turn produce aggregate social outcome. The concern of the social scientist is to provide explanations of social phenomena by laying bare this logic and the causal mechanism on which it is grounded.

Little illustrates how social entities have causal influence on agents in terms of the structuring of incentives and opportunities for them. For example, it is not a brute fact that transport system and patterns of settlement are highly correlated. The logic of the transport systems as a social institution dictates that it has the causal capacity to influence patterns of settlement: settlements arise and grow at the hubs of the transport system because proximity of the transport system is economically desirable for agents. The regularity that increasing the tariff on imported running shoes leads to an increase in consumption of domestic running shoes can be explained in terms of price sensitivity of the consumers resulting in a shift in consumer behavior.

In the same way, the observation that centralized bureaucratic states have greater capacity to collect revenue from the periphery than decentralized feudal states would require explanations in terms of an account of the causal capacities of these states. Similar accounts need to be given for generalizations such as "low GNP is correlated with high infant mortality" or "political development produces political instability."

Since we cannot expect to find a strong underlying order in the social system (may be because it is a "dappled world"), the regularities in social world, according to Little, are not deterministic and "governing" as they are conditioned by ceteris paribus clauses, incomplete knowledge of causal fields, and other similar problems. Hence, the *predictive capacity* of the social sciences is very *limited*.

Yet for Little, such "phenomenal" regularities pertaining to social domain are lawlike, support counterfactuals, and are grounded on complex causal influences conveyed by microlevel individual agency. This means that macro-level theories, such as rational choice theory, game theory, theory of institutions, collective action theory, systems theory, etc., require microlevel foundations in terms of microeconomics or micro-sociology. The job of such theories is to unravel underlying causal mechanisms that produce phenomenal regularities.

In order to illustrate the work on this genre, I wish to select two substantive examples of social scientists: the works of Amartya Sen and M.N. Srinivas.

3.9 Two Case Studies

3.9.1 Amartya Sen

The work of Amartya Sen and his prolific research contributions in welfare and development economics touch on several key foundational issues in philosophy of social science: (A) methodological issues in philosophy of social science, (B) methodological and ethical issues in social sciences, and (C) issues relating to applied sciences, such as poverty, famine, and gender. I shall try to spell out briefly what I consider to be the main contributions in each one of these areas. This is not an exposition of his technical contributions in economics, but a brief summary of some of Sen's contributions on methodology and philosophical issues in social science.

In (A) methodological issues in social sciences, especially in welfare and development economics, Amartya Sen is mainly concerned with two important problems: (1) the search for an overarching unified theory and (2) the problem of objectivity in the social sciences.

Let me state a few salient points relating to Sen's contributions in methodology of economics and general philosophy of science.

First, the received view on modern mathematical exact sciences supports a lofty vision of a world completely ordered by a single elegant theory. One of the most cherished goals of the logical positivists was a unified science bound by a common rationale. It was claimed to have the structure of a pyramid with a system of few simple, elegant, abstract, all-embracing, general, universal axioms on the top and a vast array of relatively less abstract but specific domains with their observational laws below it.

Serious questions have been raised about this approach and its attempt at unification. A careful analysis of the actual scientific practices at the ground level reveals that there is very little in common in terms of both methodology and content between any two given domains of science. Moreover, as Nancy Cartwright has pointed out, our world is rich in different things, with different natures, behaving in different ways.

Sen arrives at the same conclusion by maintaining that the grand theories or very abstract theoretical assumptions, such as the self-interest assumption (i.e., we act to maximize our own utilities) or the assumption of rational conduct (i.e., certain behavior can be proved to be rational by rational choice theory or game theory) or the concept of "economic man" or the assumption of "perfect foresight" or "perfect competition" or "general equilibrium," are false.[54] For Sen, this amounts to claiming that (a) distinct scientific domains and even within a given domain distinct theories model different situations in the world and are severely restricted in scope and (b) each theory at best can model highly simplified situation and cannot model every situation within its purported domain. Although some of Sen's earliest work dealt

[54] Sen (1977).

with the technical details of some of the macro-level theories, such as rational choice theory, collective choice and game theory, and the critical assessment of their basic assumptions, his main concern was with their microlevel foundations in terms of human agency.

Rather than treating the abstract models as vehicles of truth, he construed the macro-level theories as merely expository devices for understanding the specific socioeconomic structures and causal mechanisms true in a society given in terms of different probability measures appropriate for the quantities appearing in the causal relations. In the work of Sudhir Anand and Ravi Kanbur on Sri Lanka's welfare program, Sen was criticized for not adopting a causal relation that holds among designated quantities across all developing countries. Some of these causal variables are per capita income, technological advance, social welfare expenditure, living standard, and the like. Instead, Sen adopted a hypothesis representing different causal mechanisms for different countries. Cartwright has shown that Sen is right in his approach.

Sen is concerned with the issue that if abstract models contain empirical falsity, how much falsity should be allowed within an empirical theory? In his *Standard of Living*,[55] Sen compares two concepts that are often used as indicators of development: one abstract amenable to accurate measure and mathematical treatment and the other that does not readily admit of such treatment. Sen demonstrates that the two relevant concepts, viz., the concept of gross national income or what he calls the opulence measure and the concept of standard of living defined in terms of a set of functioning and capabilities, are indeed different and therefore cannot be identified. While evaluating the standard of living, one should look at those situations in which one must function, such as health, life expectancy, infant mortality, primary education, shelter, etc. They, however, cannot be aggregated. But its traditional alternative, viz., "national income aggregate," would admit of mathematical treatment but be useless and a false description, say, for devising planning strategies. It would be useless because such data would hide information vital for planning, such as distribution of resources. Moreover, it would be harmful if planning strategies are formulated based entirely on such measures since strategies based exclusively on this information would be quite misleading for the planners.

Second, absence of grand global theories might appear to lead to relativism and lack of objectivity in the social sciences. Sen avoids relativism and lack of objectivity in the social sciences by upholding what he calls "positional objectivity"[56] and the role it plays in selecting scientific data and acquiring scientific knowledge. While addressing issues such as "gender bias" or "cultural relativism," Sen maintains that although observation is unavoidably position based, scientific reasoning need not be based on observation from one specific position only. If under appropriate conditions one fails to see a mirage, it would only demonstrate that there is something wrong with one's vision. However, the explanation of mirage in terms of

[55] Sen (1985).

[56] Sen (1993).

a theory in optics based on refraction of light passing through an atmosphere having an unusual distribution of air density indicates the possibility of a *transpositional perspective*, which takes into account distinct observational positions.

Hence, the issue here is whether economics can produce *transpositional perspective* in its explanation, yet at the same time invoking its local categories. Sen highlights the importance of "internal criticism" in social sciences in order to arrive at the transpositional perspective. For example, a transpositional assessment may necessitate a revision of the received view in gender studies, viz., inferiority of women. In spite of applying diverse categories to the social world, there exists the possibility of discovering an order and the same criteria of credibility and cogent argument. This underlying notion of what is valid or credible *transpositionally* in social science is thought to be the essence of objectivity of social scientific knowledge. This notion of valid scientific knowledge constitutes the hard core, the common ideology in all branches of social science.

(B) On the question of the disjunction between facts and values (or ethical considerations) in the social sciences, one is naturally reminded of Hume's injunction that the normative can never be derived from the descriptive premises, i.e., *ought* not to be deduced from *is.* This led to a serious distancing between economics and ethics. Efforts to keep values out of economics motivated some to endorse what Milton Friedman calls positive economics claiming that it is a purely observational science and consequent states of affairs. However, not all consequences are either of equal importance or desirable. Desirability and the evaluation or prioritizing consequences is dependent upon the values we uphold. Hence, fact-value dichotomy cannot be maintained, and in the last analysis, positive economics is subsumed under normative economics. Moreover, a forceful denial of the rigid distinction between fact and value has come from several philosophers in the recent past, such as Max Black, John Searle, Hilary Putnam, and Sen. Keeping their contributions in mind, it is important to make a distinction between universal naturalism (i.e., the view that all value judgments can be derived from factual premises) and existential naturalism (i.e., values can be derived from factual premises only in certain contexts). It appears that Sen endorses only the latter view. This position, however, requires some analysis.

It is well known that the dominant form of naturalism in ethics is self-interest or utility, and through utilitarian ethics, economics has come to embrace self-interest maximization as the definition of rationality as is evident from the work of Edgeworth, Arrow, Hahn, and Samuelson. Utilitarianism, however, is supported by following theses: welfarism (i.e., the judgment of relative goodness of alternative states of affairs must be exclusively based on, and taken as an increasing function of, the respective collection of individual utilities in these states), sum-ranking (i.e., one collection of individual utilities is at least as good as another if and only if it has at least as large a sum total), and consequentialism (i.e., goodness of a state of affairs has to be judged on the basis of goodness of the consequent state of affairs). There are aspects of utilitarianism, viz., act utilitarianism, which evaluate actions in terms of the consequences.

Sen argues that this consequentialist view, i.e., taking self-interest maximization as the only possibility, could not be an essential part of man's rationality. Hence, Sen considers non-gains maximization as a viable alternative to self-interest maximization. Moreover, preferences in revealed preference theory are quite different from what is actually chosen in a given situation. Finally, the first two theses, viz., welfarism and sum-ranking, cannot deal adequately the issue of *well-being* of a person. Sen shows that since an economic theory requires other relevant concepts, such as justice and liberty, naturalism and utilitarianism have to be jettisoned.

From the ruins of utilitarianism, is it possible to reconstruct a viable form of naturalism and utilitarianism? Sen suggests a viable alternative. Sen's alternative is based on his views on "existential naturalism" (i.e., values can be derived from factual premises only if they are contextualized) and "plural utility" (i.e., a vector view of utility that accepts nonutility considerations also in moral discourse and the possibility of their co-existence).

Sen develops an alternative by falling back on the concept of *well-being* and other associated ethical concepts, such as justice, equality, liberty, freedom, etc. Sen's approach emerges not only out of his pure theory of social choice and critique of the works of many leading moral philosophers and political thinkers, such as Rawls, Nozick, Berlin, etc., but also the constructive possibilities that the new literature in these areas produced based on informational basis of judgments and available statistics for a variety of economic and social appraisals: measuring economic inequality, judging poverty, evaluating projects, analyzing unemployment, famine, assessing gender inequality, investigating the principles and implications of liberty and rights, and so on. On this informational and factual basis, Sen shows how individual well-being can be defined more satisfactorily in terms of "basic capabilities" and not in terms of "primary goods," which Sen dubs as commodity fetishism.

Sen carries out a systematic analysis not only in interdisciplinary research involving epistemological and ethical issues, but implicit in his monumental work are explorations and implications of the conditions of developing countries and characterization of the nature of human agency in terms of a new vocabulary in welfare and development economics, such as well-being, basic capabilities, empowerment, etc., which takes us away from Western utilitarian self-centered concept of welfare and toward democratic and pluralistic norms in organizing society. Sen himself admitted that many of his ideas on human development and human rights were inspired by the teachings of Buddha and Ashoka.

In (C) issues relating to applied sciences, such as poverty, famine, and gender, Sen has been concerned with more practical problems that were totally ignored by the practitioners of mainstream economics. This is an interdisciplinary area in which Sen collaborated with development economists and field scientists.

3.9.2 M.N. Srinivas

M.N. Srinivas was one of the most distinguished Indian sociologists and social anthropologist. He was deeply concerned with methodological issues in these disciplines and wrote on issues relating to the significance of fieldwork, participant observation in social science research, the observer and the observed, and the insider and the outsider in cultural studies. Many of these methodological writings can be construed as good illustrations of the principles of *local contextualist epistemology* (though he never explicitly articulated this position) rather than flights of global theory, such as structural functionalism or systems theory. Srinivas' work covered a vast terrain: village studies, caste and social structure, social change, religion and cultural studies, gender studies.

Srinivas' most fundamental methodological contribution consisted of his breaking out of the confines of the textual authority of Sanskrit studies that defined the scope of his discipline. During the colonial period, the Indian society and its social structure were viewed as static and unchanging. The approach to the study of Indian society was through the mediation of a combined approach of Indology and sociology and heavily relied on the classical texts. Srinivas' first book entitled *Religion and Society among the Coorgs of South India* (1952)[57] based on an ethnographical study of the then little known Coorg community marked a complete departure from, what he himself called, the "book view" to "field view" of the study of Indian society.

From then onward, his social laboratory became the village, factory, and home: the places where people lived, worked, and in general played out a multiplicity of social and cultural roles. This prime importance given to close and insightful observation of men and their changing roles in the society could be the foundation for innovative theory construction. Srinivas had the rare gift of converting insightful observations into major innovative sociological *concepts* and *theories* that have changed the theoretical landscape of Indian sociology.

The best example of Srinivas' fieldwork is his socio-anthropological studies of the village of Rampura near Mysore carried out in 1948 and published in 1976 in the form of a book entitled *The Remembered Village*.[58] This won him international recognition and firmly established his unique scholarly position.

However, he is more well known for his ideas on social change and modernization anchored in another study, which could be regarded as the finest example of "local realism" and "contextualist epistemology."

Based on the painstaking ethnographical study of the Coorg community in 1952, Srinivas introduced certain seminal ideas in the theory of social change in India. In opposition to the colonial notion of a static and unchanging Indian society, Srinivas sought to capture the fluid and dynamic nature of Indian social structure and caste as a social institution in terms of some of the most innovative concepts that have now become an integral part of Indian sociological theory, such as "sanskritization," "dominant caste," and "vertical intercaste and horizontal intracaste solidarities." The concept of "sanskritization" seeks to describe the process by which castes placed lower in the caste hierarchy seek upward mobility by emulating the rituals

[57]Srinivas (1952).

[58]Srinivas (1976).

and practices of the upper or "dominant castes." This analysis of change in the social structure had several methodological lessons for social scientists: (1) it validated the importance of fieldwork as an essential methodology for Indian sociologists and social anthropologists, and (2) it replaced the widely held idea of a rigid pan-Indian caste system by the regional dimensions of caste system conveyed in terms of another innovative idea introduced by Srinivas, viz., the "little tradition" of Hinduism. The more recent theories of modernizations had to take note of the fact established by Srinivas that with certain adaptations, the caste system in some form is here to stay.

3.10 Conclusion

The problem of generalization and the assumptions about unobservable entities and mechanisms plagued the logical positivistic account of scientific knowledge. A viable alternative to this account appears to be a *local contextualist epistemology* grounded in doing science, getting involved in actual issues faced by a given science, and taking a natural ontological attitude. Two good illustrations of this approach were given from the works of Amartya Sen and M.N. Srinivas.

Appendices

Appendix 3.1: The Transcription of a Babylonian Ephemeris

(a) The Transcription

Year	Successive months of the year	Monthly progress of the sun across the zodiac	Anticipated position in the zodiac of the conjunction	Sign of the zodiac
2, 59 {Seleucid era, i.e., 2 X 60 + 59 = 179 after 312 B.C. or 312–179 = 133–2 B.C.}	I	28, 37, 57, 58	20, 46, 16, 14	Taurus
	II	28, 19, 57, 58	19, 6, 14, 12	Gemini
	III	28, 19, 21, 22	17, 25, 35, 34	Cancer
	IV	28, 37, 21, 22	16, 2, 56, 56	Leo
	V	28, 55, 21, 22	14, 58, 18, 18	Virgo
	VI	29, 13, 21, 22	14, 11, 39, 40	Libra
	VII	29, 31, 21, 22	13, 43, 1, 2	Scorpio
	VIII	29, 49, 21, 22	13, 32, 22, 24	Sagittarius
	IX	29, 56, 36, 38	13, 28, 59, 2	Capricorn
	X	29, 38, 36, 38	13, 7, 35, 40	Aquarius
	XI	29, 20, 36, 38	12, 28, 12, 18	Pisces
	XII	29, 2, 36, 38	11, 30, 48, 56	Aries

(b) The rule for computing the position, taking the example of month II to month III and the transition from Gemini to Cancer

From the given position in Gemini	19, 6, 14, 12
Add the monthly progress of the sun	+ 28, 19, 21, 22
	47°, 25, 35, 34
Subtracting 30°	−30°
The position of conjunction at cancer	17, 25, 35, 34

(c) The table indicates a cycle based on arithmetical progression, i.e., increase and decrease with constant fixed difference between two limits (between 28 and 30)

Months	Decrease	Increase
I–II	18′	
III–VIII		18′
IX–XII	18′	

Appendix 3.2: Aristotle's Science of Motion Based on Inductive-Deductive Method

In his treatises, *Physics* and *De Caelo (On the Heavens)* upheld *four doctrines.* They are:

- Doctrine of essentialism: discovering the *essential* of an individual/object ("*phusis*" = nature) and demonstrating why, in order to fulfill its *function*, it has to have the essential property.
- Doctrine of four elements: that all naturally occurring substances are made out of four fundamental elements – earth, water, air, and fire.
- Doctrine of natural place: each of the fundamental elements has a *natural* level of existence, i.e., when displaced, they seek/have a tendency or desire to revert back to their natural level of existence.
- Doctrine that presented a *worldview* that the universe is an organism, anthropomorphic or human centric, and teleological.

Aristotle's anthropomorphic or human centric and teleological imply that any attempt to explain the behavior of an inanimate/material body:

- Must be made in the analogy with a living organism
- Must be given in terms of its own nature (essence), tendency, desire, motive, goal (teleos), or final cause

For example:

- *The nature (essence) of a heavy element*, such a lump of earth, is to go down.
- *The nature (essence) of a light element*, such as air/fire, is to go up.

These are *natural motion* of these objects.

From this doctrine of essentialism, attributing *essential property*, *Aristotle's* four first principles (*archai*) follow:

Aristotle's four first principles (*archai*)

- All motions are either *natural* or *violent.*
- All *natural motion* is a motion toward a natural place.
- All *violent motion* is caused by the continuing action of an agent.
- Vacuum is impossible (because in that case all bodies will move with equal velocity, which is impossible).

Based on the three doctrines and four first principles, Aristotle and his followers go on to formulate certain "laws of motion":

Aristotelian laws of motion
Further assumption of Aristotelian laws of motion:
For Aristotle, in all motion (natural or violent), two major factors play a role:

- The motive force, denoted by F
- The resistance of the medium, denoted by R

The statement of Aristotle's laws of motion:

From observation, Aristotle concluded that for motion to occur, it is necessary that:

- The motive force must be greater than resistance, i.e.,

$$F > R \tag{3.1}$$

In other words, when motive force overpowers/overcomes resistance, motion takes place.

- The greater the resistance, the smaller the speed, or speed is inversely proportional to the resistance of the medium through which the body moves, i.e.,

$$V \propto 1/R \tag{3.2}$$

[Note: this should not be read quantitatively, i.e., as double the speed 1/2 the resistance.]

- Consequently, the greater the force to overcome the resistance, the greater the speed:

$$V \propto F \tag{3.3}$$

- Combining Eqs. (3.2) and (3.3), we get a single equation, viz.,

$$V \propto F/R \tag{3.4}$$

That is (*in modern language*), speed is proportional to the motive force and inversely proportional to the resistance of the medium. Or speed is proportional to the force divided by the resistance.

Consequence of Aristotle's Law

Consider dropping two objects in the same medium, say air, where the weight of one is exactly twice the weight of the other.

- For Aristotle, the speed of the heavier object, which has twice the motive force (since it has twice the weight of the other), should be exactly twice that of the lighter one.

Based on such reasons, Aristotle concludes that the speed of a falling body is proportional to its weight.

- For a constant distance of fall, the speed would be inversely proportional to the time such that the heavier the object, the less time will it take to descend, i.e.,

$$V \propto 1/T$$

That is, the speed is inversely proportional to the time of descent:

- $V1/V2 = T2/T1$

That is, the time of descent of the heavier object would be just half the time of descent of the lighter one.

- Hence, for Aristotle, the time of free fall in a given medium is inversely proportional to the weight of the object.

Appendix 3.3: Kinetic Theory of Gases

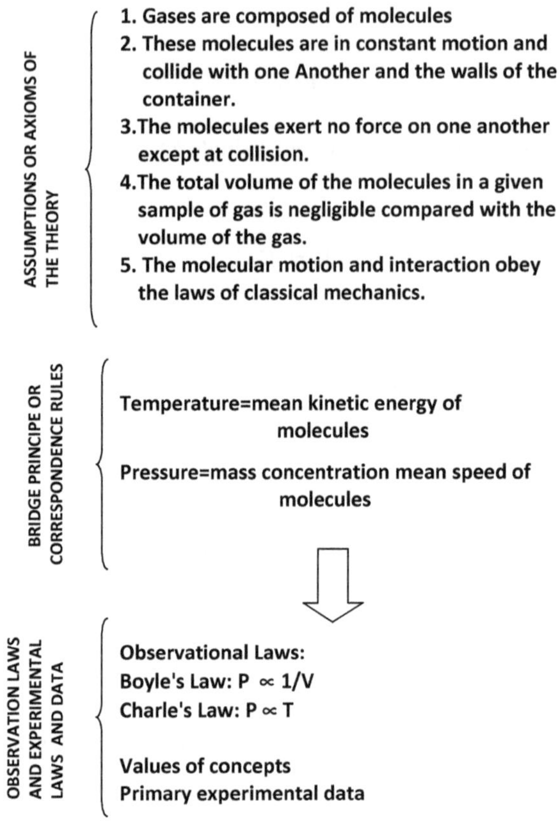

Appendix 3.4: A Note on Reconceptualizing Induction, Induction and Natural Kinds

Problem with Induction: "Hume's Problem"

Hume (1711–1776) in his *Treatise* (1739/1888) raised a serious problem relating to universal general statement or scientific hypothesis arrived at as an inductive conclusion from evidence statements. The universal general statements in science are the hypotheses and laws that make up theories; the particular statements are observations or reports on experiments. Specifically, Hume targeted induction as not being a logically sound form of inference. The problem of induction is the problem of justifying the formation of universal statements from particular ones – with incomplete data at hand.

Induction by virtue of going beyond the evidence – from particular to the general – is *ampliative* (meaning "to enlarge" or "to extend": adding to that which is already known). Hume maintained that there are no objective necessary connections among the attributes of phenomena given in ordinary experience. It follows from this that the only grounds that we have for inferring from a sample to a population or from the past to the future are given by present experience or memory. Hence, induction lacks *soundness* [59] and is *nondemonstrative* (i.e., an inductive argument is not necessarily valid, and it is not the case that whenever the initial statements, i.e., premises or axioms, of an inductive argument are true, the conclusion is also true). Unlike deductive argument, inductive inferences can never achieve apodictic certainty.

Reconceptualization of Induction: The Notion of "Natural Kinds"

Hume's problem does not lead, as some have suggested, to skepticism about all events beyond present experience; nor does it imply that all such judgments are somehow unreasonable or unjustified.[60] Particular observations are treated by many logicians as "good reasons for belief" in a universal generalization.[61] One of the implications of this is that our notion of rational justification ought to be adapted to this fact.

New Way of Looking as Inductive Generalization: An Essentialist Response to Hume

Essential properties typically involve reference to the microstructure of things. Having atomic number 79 is said to be the essential property of gold,[62] being H_2O the essential property of water.[63] Genetic makeup similarly enables us to identify essential properties for animals and plants, and the mean molecular kinetic energy is taken to be the defining property of temperature. These essential properties characterize *natural kinds* and are furnished by the natural sciences:

> In general, science attempts, by investigating basic structural traits, to find the nature, and thus the essence (in the philosophical sense), of the kind. (S. Kripke [1972], p. 330)

---

[59] Proofs given by Broad (1918, 1920) and Salmon (1967).

[60] Strawson (1952/1962).

[61] Black (1967).

[62] Kripke (1972, p. 327, 1971).

[63] Putnam Hilary (1975).

Natural Kind and Generalization

Natural kinds, therefore, are characterized by the possession of an essence, that is, a set of intrinsic, causally explanatory properties that are necessary and jointly sufficient to belong to the kind.

The causal notion of natural kind has been developed by Boyd[64] and Griffiths[65]: a class C of entities is a natural kind if and only if there is a large set of scientifically relevant properties such that C is the maximal class whose members tend to share these properties because of some causal mechanism.

Moreover, the causal notion of natural kinds in these cases is not vacuous. It implies that *nominal kinds*, for instance, the class of physical objects that weigh more than 30 kg, are not natural kinds, for their members don't share (scientifically relevant) properties. For example, many *subsets* of natural kinds, e.g., white dogs, are not natural kinds, for such properties are accidental and true of the subset. Hence, the natural kind assumption says that it possesses three characteristics:

- There is a set of properties that a specific natural kind tends to possess.
- These properties of natural kind help in making generalizations about its members.
- A given natural kind possesses these properties because of some causal mechanism.
- Natural kind terms feature in laws, i.e., in generalizations that are temporally and spatially unrestricted and that support counterfactuals.[66]
- Natural kind expressions feature or could feature in the laws in natural sciences or scientific laws and theories.

Natural Kind and Induction

The notion of natural kind is essentially tied up with induction as claimed by Mill, Quine, Boyd, and Hacking.[67] For the notion of natural kind supports nonaccidental, scientifically relevant inductive inferences. Kornblith in his *Inductive Inference and Its Natural Ground*[68] says:

> Natural kinds make inductive knowledge of the world possible, because the clustering of properties characteristic of natural kinds makes inferences from the presence of some of these properties to the presence of others reliable.

[64] Boyd (1990), And (1991).

[65] Griffiths (1997).

[66] Collier (1996).

[67] Mill ([1843] 1905), Quine (1969), Boyd (1990), And (1991), Hacking (1991).

[68] Kornblith (1993).

References

And (1991) Realism, antifoundationalism, and the enthusiasm for natural kinds. Philos Stud 61:127–148

Arnold (1974) Knowledge and society. Pegasus, Indianapolis

Arrow KJ (1951, 1963) Social choice and individual values. Wiley, New York

Beth EW (1967) Aspects of modern logic. Reidel, Dordrecht

Black M (1967) The article on induction. In: Edwards P (ed) Encyclopedia of philosophy. Macmillan, New York

Boyd R (1990) What realism implies and what it does not. Dialectica 43:5–29

Broad CD (1918) The relation between induction and probability I. Mind 27:389–404

Broad CD (1920) The relation between induction and probability II. Mind 29:11–45

Caneva KL (1978) From galvanism to electrodynamics: the transformation of German physics and its social context. In: McCormmach P, Pyanson L (eds) Historical studies in the physical sciences, vol 9. The Johns Hopkins University Press, Baltimore, pp 60–160

Cartwright N (1983) How the laws of physics lie. Oxford University Press, Oxford

Cartwright N (1989) Nature's capacities and their measurement. Oxford University Press, Oxford

Cartwright N (1999) The dappled world: a study of the boundaries of science. Cambridge University Press, Cambridge/New York

Churchland P (1979) Scientific realism and the plasticity of mind. Cambridge University Press, Cambridge/New York

Cohen BP (1980) Developing sociological knowledge: theory and method. Prentice-Hall, Englewood Cliffs

Collier J (1996) On the necessity of natural kinds. In: Riggs P (ed) Natural kinds, laws of nature, and scientific reasoning. Kluwer, Dordrecht, pp 1–10

Endris U (2011) Logic and social choice theory. In: Gupta A, van Benthem J (eds) Logic and philosophy, vol 30. College Publications, King's College, London, pp 333–377

Fine K (1985) Reasoning with arbitrary objects. Basil and Blackwell, Oxford

Fine A (1986) The shaky game: Einstein, realism and the quantum theory. University of Chicago Press, Chicago

Fine A (1996) Bohmian mechanics and quantum theory: an appraisal. Kluwer, Dordrecht. (Co-edited with J. Cushing and S. Goldstein)

Freund I (1968) The study of chemical composition: an account of its method and historical development. Dover, New York, pp 2–30

Friedman M (1953) The methodology of positive economics. In: Essays in positive economics. University of Chicago Press, Chicago

Galileo (1638) Dialogues concerning two new sciences pertaining to mechanics and local motion (trans: Crew H, Salvio de A). Dover, New York

Gibbs J (1972) Sociological theory construction. Dryden, Hinsdale

Griffiths PE (1997) What emotions really are. University of Chicago Press, Chicago

Gross L (ed) (1959) Symposium on sociological theory. Harper and Row, New York

Gupta A (1989) The concrete and the abstract science: description versus explanation. J Indian Counc Philos Res VI(3):67–88

Hacking I (1983) Representing and intervening: introductory topics in the philosophy of natural science. Cambridge University Press, Cambridge

Hacking I (1991) A tradition of natural kinds. Philos Stud 61:109–126

Hardy GH (1940) Mathematician's apology. University Press, Cambridge

Heath TL (1861–1940) The thirteen books of Euclid's elements translated from the text of Heiberg with introduction and commentary. Three volumes. University Press, Cambridge, 1908. Second edition: University Press, Cambridge, 1925. Reprint: Dover Publication, New York, 1956

Heath TL (1956) The thirteen books of Euclid's *elements*, 3 vols. Dover, New York

Hilary P (1975) The meaning of 'meaning'. In: Hilary P (ed) Mind, language and reality. Cambridge University Press, Cambridge, pp 215–271, 233

Hilbert D (1902) Grundlagen der Geometrie (The foundations of geometry, trans. E.J. Townsend, Chicago)
Hobbes T (1651) Leviathan, Revised Edition. Martinich AP, Battiste B (ed) Broadview Press, Peterborough, 2010
Huggett N (2001) Physics meets philosophy at the Planck scale, (with Callender, C). Cambridge University Press, Cambridge
Hume D (1739/1888) Treatise of human nature (Selby-Bigge LA, ed). Clarendon, Oxford
Jones WT (1952) History of modern philosophy. Harcourt, Brace and World Levison, New York
Kincaid H (1996) Philosophical foundations of the social sciences. Cambridge University Press, Cambridge
Kornblith H (1993) Inductive inference and its natural ground. MIT Press, Cambridge, p 7
Kripke S (1971) Identity and necessity. In: Munitz MK (ed) Identity and individuation. New York University Press, New York, pp I35–I64
Kripke S (1972) Naming and necessity. In: Davidson D, Harman G (eds) Semantics of natural language. Reidel, Dordrecht, pp 253–355, 763–769, 327
Lakatos I (1976) Proofs and refutation. University Press, Cambridge
Lipset SM (1994) Search of "scientific sociology". In: "The state of American sociology," Sociological Forum, vol 9. pp 199–220, 201
Little D (1991) Varieties of social explanation. Westview Press, Boulder
Little D (1993) On the scope and limits of generalizations in the social sciences. Synthese 97(2):183–207, Empiricism in the Philosophy of Social Science
Little D (2003) The paradox of wealth and poverty. Westview Press, Boulder
Locke J (1968) An essay concerning human understanding. Meridian Books, New York
Losee J (1972) A historical introduction to the philosophy of science. Oxford University Press, New York
Macnamara J (1991) Understanding induction. Br J Philos Sci 42(1):21–48
Merton R (1949/1957/1968) Social *theory and social structure*. The Free Press, New York
Mill JS ([1843] 1905) A system of logic. Reprint. Routledge, London
Mill JS et al (1963) Collected works of John Stuart Mill. University of Toronto Press, Toronto
Mueller I (1981/2006) Philosophy of mathematics and deductive structure in Euclid's elements. Dover, New York
Mumford D (1999) A paper based on a lecture delivered at the conference "Mathematics towards the Third Millennium", held at the Accademia Nazionale dei Lincei, May 27–29, 1999
Neugebauer O (1957) The exact sciences in antiquity, 2nd edn. Brown University Press, Providence
Neugebauer O (1975) A history of ancient mathematical astronomy. Springer, New York
Neurath O (1983) The unity of science. In: Philosophical papers 1913–46 (ed and trans: Cohen RS, Neurath M). Reidel, Dordrecht
Newton I (1729) Philosophiae naturalis principia mathematica (mathematical principles of natural philosophy) (trans: Motte A (1729) revised by Cajori F (1962)), 2 vols. University of California Press, Berkeley
Parikh R (2002) Social software. Synthese 132(3):187–211
Parsons T (1951) The social system. The Free Press, New York
Popper KR (1963a) Conjectures and refutations: the growth of scientific knowledge. Harper and Row, New York
Popper K (1963b) Models, instruments and truth: the rationality principle in the social sciences. Karl Popper Collection, Hoover Institution Archives at Stanford University, Stanford
Popper KR (1968) The logic of scientific discovery, 2nd edn. Harper and Row, New York
Popper K (1970) Logic of the situation. In: Watkins JWN, Borger R, Cioffi F (eds) Explanation in the behavioural sciences. Cambridge University Press, Cambridge, pp 206–208
Quine WVO (1969) Natural kinds. In: Quine WVO (ed) Ontological relativity and other essays. Columbia University Press, New York, pp 114–138
Robbins L (1932) Essay on the nature and significance of economic science, 2nd edn. London, 1936, pp 152–158

Salmon (1967) The foundations of scientific inference. The University of Pittsburgh Press, Pittsburgh
Salmon W (1971) Statistical explanation. In: Salmon W (ed) Statistical explanation and statistical relevance. University of Pittsburgh Press, Pittsburgh, pp 29–87
Searle J (1984) Minds, brains and science. Harvard University Press, Cambridge
Sen A (1970) Collective choice and social welfare. Holden-Day, San Francisco
Sen A (1977) Rational fools: a critique of the behavioral foundations of economic theory. Philos Pub Aff 6(4):317–344
Sen A (1985) *The standard of living*: the tanner lecture on human values delivered at Cambridge University. http://www.tannerlectures.utah.edu/lectures/documents/sen86.pdf
Sen A (1986) Ethics and economics – Royer lecture at University of California Berkeley, Blackwell Publishing, First Published in 1987
Sen A (1993) Positional objectivity. Philos Pub Aff 22(2):126–145
Sen A (n.d.) Impossibility of paretian liberal. J Polit Econ 70(1):150–157
Srinivas MN (1952) Religion and society among the coorgs of south India. Clarendon, Oxford
Srinivas MN (1976) The remembered village. Oxford University Press, Delhi
Stoll RR (1961) Set theory and logic. Dover, New York
Strawson PF (1952/1962) Introduction to logical theory. Methuen, London
Suppe F (1977) The structure of scientific theories, 2nd edn. The University of Illinois Press, Urbana, p 716
Szabó Á (1978) The beginning of Greek mathematics. Reidel, Dordrecht
Toulmin S (1961) Foresight and understanding. Hutchinson, London
von Mises L (1960) Epistemological problems of economics. Princeton, van Nostrand
von Mises L (1962) The ultimate foundation of economic science. Princeton, van Nostrand
Zetterberg HL (1954/1963/1965) On theory and verification in sociology. The Bedminster Press, Totowa

Chapter 4
Problem Formulation

R. Bandyopadhyay

4.1 Objectives

In any problem-solving exercise, whether it is an academic research problem or a sponsored research or a problem-solving exercise to solve certain real-world problems, it is essential to know the exact nature of the problem to be solved or researched. Today, there has been a significant development in terms of novel solution methods and solution theory; the corresponding development has not taken place in terms of problem identification, problem formulation and problem structuring. To advance the science of problem-solving, we must be able to solve relevant and right problems in the efficient way. It is of no use to solve an irrelevant and wrong problem in the most efficient and elegant manner. It is therefore necessary to give adequate attention in defining and specifying the problem to be investigated in a proper scientific manner (Ackoff 1962). The present chapter is devoted to this. Thus, the objectives of the present chapter will be as follows:

- To understand the manner of classification of problems for different types of problem-solving exercises (academic research for advancement of knowledge, academic research for solving real-life problems, sponsored research, etc.)
- To appreciate various aspects of problem formulation
- To clearly understand the difference between primary and secondary problems
- To develop skills in specifying secondary problem components
- To develop capabilities for identification of various factors affecting and influencing a problem

R. Bandyopadhyay (✉)
Former Director, National Institute of Bank Management, Pune, India

Visiting Research Professor, University of Manchester, Manchester, UK

Present Affiliation: Hon. Director, CASAD, Pune, India
e-mail: rangband@gmail.com

D.S. Hegde (ed.), *Essays on Research Methodology*,
DOI 10.1007/978-81-322-2214-9_4

- To appreciate the basic logic of modelling
- To appreciate the basic importance of good problem formulation in overall success of problem solution

4.2 Taxonomy of Problems

Any problem to be investigated may fall in any of the following classes:

(a) The research study of a problem is basically meant to explore a new area for developing concept theories or for understanding in greater depth and clarifying some existing phenomena. Many PhD, MPhil and academic studies fall under this category.
(b) Sponsored studies on some real-life problems or on some conceptual, theoretical or exploratory issues.
    In all such cases, understanding the objectives which the sponsors want to achieve is very important in formulating the profile of the problem to be investigated.
(c) Solution of an existing problem within a system, society, country, organisation or environment.
    Here, again understanding what exactly are causing concerns is very important before exploring solution methods.

For all the above three types of studies, understanding and specifying the problem to be studied and issues to be explored are very important, these are generally covered under the general label of '*problem formulation*'.

Thus, problem formulation consists of having a clear idea about (White 1969):

1. Who – The main person and group interested in getting the problem explored or solved.
2. What – We must be clear what the group wants to achieve through such exploration or solution.
3. How – It is also necessary in this connection to know exactly what are the alternative methods available to carry out exploration or to solve the problem.

The implications of these three things are quite different in the three classes of study that we discussed earlier. We may like to discuss each of these in respect of each class of problems.

4.3 Secondary and Primary Problems

The problem or study that we want to explore or solve is the primary problem. We also want to explore data to be collected, techniques to be applied and expertise to be employed. These are parts of the secondary problem. Good problem formulations specify both primary and secondary problems (White 1975).

In case of each type of problem class (a), (b) and (c), we shall discuss these aspects in detail.

Examples:

1. Let us assume that a candidate is doing a PhD level research and he/she wants to design an incentive scheme for the production workers. Here, he/she has the primary problem of designing an incentive scheme for the production workers. For solving the primary problems, he/she has to decide the nature of standard measures, what techniques and statistical tools to be used and what data have to be collected in these respects.
2. A chief executive of a large manufacturing organisation wanted to improve the overall effectiveness of the organisation. This is the primary problem to solve. Here, we have to define measures of organisational efficiency, find ways of measuring performance and relate such measures to resource use and with the volume and quality of output. Decisions regarding data to be collected for purposes of analysis, analytical and synthesising tools and techniques (both qualitative and quantitative) that can be used are also secondary problems.
3. In a rural development study, the idea was to design a framework of employment generation in the rural sector. This was the primary problem. The secondary problems were assessment of skills and capabilities, assessment of potential for productive economic activities, tools and techniques (both qualitative and quantitative) to be used, experts to be consulted and nature of environmental and natural resource data to be collected. These details were all components of the secondary problem.

Thus, problem formulation becomes complete when primary and secondary problems are fully and adequately specified. In doing so for primary problem, we are concerned with whom and what are specified earlier. For secondary problems, the answer to the question 'how' will be useful.

We shall now discuss each of these in the case of three classes of problems.

4.4 Problem Formulation in Academic Study

In academic study, the first issue relevant to problem formulation is the selection of the area of research that is of interest and importance and then comes the selection of a specific topic within the selected research areas/fields.

For any academic research study, the following determine the contours of selection:

(i) What areas of study are of interest to the candidate – is it also approved by the guide or selected research advisors?
(ii) Candidate's background and knowledge about the area and his/her enthusiasm and determination to explore the selected topic even when the background is not adequate initially.

(iii) Based on preliminary assessments, the candidate should be able to decide with the help of the guides and supervisors how difficult it would be to undertake the study in the proposed area. He/she should then decide (in case of background knowledge and skill gap) whether bridging the gap will be feasible without much difficulty. Thus, if a candidate's interest is in optimisation of production in steelmaking, relevant knowledge, technical and managerial, in respect of steelmaking in modern era must be adequately grasped before the study can be cracked. Candidate's existing knowledge may/may not be adequate for the purpose. In case of inadequacy, it has to be assessed how difficult it will be for the candidate to bridge the gap of managerial and technological knowledge needed for conducting the study successfully. These are also secondary decision problems. These aspects need to be resolved before selecting the right primary problem in terms of selecting an area of study and a specific area within the selected area.

(iv) In case the required expertise is not available within the institution, expertise can be made available during the period of study or it is possible to acquire the expertise in collaboration.

Thus, a candidate has selected a study area in biomedical engineering in respect of surfactant and their local production for premature born babies. The study area and topic selected required expertise and research equipment which were not available where the candidate was registered for his/her PhD work.

However, collaborative institutes were identified where required expertise and instruments were available and the candidate felt confident to use these effectively for the purpose of his/her research. He/she completed his/her experimental work in the collaborative institute.

(v) Whether data required for the research to be undertaken can be obtained easily? In certain research on say defence-related studies or organisation studies, many data may not be shared or made available. Any topic selected where such data are needed will therefore run into difficulty and therefore should not be attempted in the first place.

For selection of study area and a specific topic within, we must prejudge reasonably easy access to relevant data particularly when we are attempting time bound research studies.

(vi) Lastly, any research area and a specific topic to be taken in the area must be subject to the constraint of time available. This we have already mentioned in (v) above.

Basic criteria for selecting an academic cum research project are therefore the candidate's interest, his/her state of prior knowledge about the subject and difficulties of the subject matter in question in terms of access to new skills, new knowledge, new equipments and new sources of data.

So here again, basic ideas of the problem to be studied should not be left vague and should be adequately detailed and formulated to fix the various contours of the problem to be studied.

4.4.1 *For this It Is Necessary to Classify a Research Idea/Ideas into Three Types*

1. *Area*
2. *Field*
3. *Aspects*

Area is a broad field of scholarly endeavour, say economics, production engineering, system science, etc. These are all areas of research.

Field This is a component of the area representing a subdiscipline. For example, process control is a field of control engineering, macroeconomics is a field of economics, and recruitment policies are a field of human resource management.

Aspect These describe the detailed facts of a field. The use of continuous casting of steel and its effects on the level of output is an aspect of production problem study; an effect of financial incentives on the worker's productivity is also an aspect of a study of an employee's productivity. If the researcher can fix these three parameters, he/she will be able to narrow down the choice, and the task of selection of the research topic will be relatively easy. Thus, a research candidate for PhD research on incentives can specify the topic as incentive problems of manufacturing workers with special reference to financial incentive and productivity. In this case, the selected area is manufacturing; the field selected is productivity, and its relationship with incentive aspects is confined to financial incentives. Thus selected, the topic provides adequate focus.

For academic research, it is necessary to appreciate that the selection of the title of the topic should not be kept vague; it should be precise and as specific as possible.

Thus, the research topic selection should go through the following steps:

(i) Listing of possible topics and ideas
(ii) Identification of a few key attributes of the topic
(iii) Listing several topics for each of the attributes selected
(iv) Consideration of different combinations in (iii) above

In deciding the topic finally, the candidates should broadly consider for various topics selected the secondary problem areas regarding techniques and tools and methods to be used, persons to be contacted and consulted and data to be collected. All these should be within the prima facie realm of feasibility.

Comparing our framework of who, what and how with what we have discussed so far, we find in academic research, the guide and the candidate are the relevant persons who decide the problem selection, and in doing so, we have discussed the steps that should be followed.

The next question of importance would be what does the candidate intend to do and how does he/she intend to do it?

Any good academic research must display originality and generalisability having relevance beyond the situation and setting, in which the data were gathered.

Research projects identify the issues to be investigated by referring to a theory, concept or group of ideas. A research project makes its contribution by extending or adding to the existing theories, concepts and ideas in some way. Findings of good research project in applied areas like economics, sociology, management and organisation should be applicable to real-world problems. Someone somewhere should be able in principle to put the recommendation into good effect.

It may be pertinent to say that all good research projects (for PhD, MPhil, etc.) should be efficient and effective. Efficiency of a project has to do with technical possibility and feasibility.

Effectiveness on the other hand is concerned with constraints on the applicability of technically acceptable recommendations. A solution is effective if it is feasible given the various constraints.

4.5 Problem Formulation for Types (b) and (c)

We have discussed the special nature of consideration in the case of type (a) or academic research studies. We shall now discuss about the framework for sponsored, in company or consultancy, studies of real-world problems. What we discuss now on will be applicable generally for all types of problems. Wherever considered appropriate, we shall refer the methods discussed and their relevance to type (a) academic problems.

4.5.1 Who Owns the Problem?

In understanding the basic nature of a problem, it is necessary to know the decision-maker(s) who will act on the basis of recommendation after the problem/issue is resolved.

In sponsored research or in the case of consultancy problems, consultant/consultants and researchers are expected by the sponsoring agencies (of decision-maker(s)) to examine certain issues and recommend solutions for implementation. In the case of policy issues, policymakers are the owners of the problem. In organisational decision-making, the decision-maker is often known. In a sponsored project, the head of the sponsoring organisations decides the fate of the project. These are easily identifiable and do not create much difficulties, but for implementable solutions, recommendations must appreciate the viewpoints of all stakeholders. Thus, in a manufacturing organisation though the head of the organisation is the ultimate decision-maker, any recommendation that affects employees or workers adversely may be resisted, and it may become very difficult to implement the resolution.

Thus, the Industrial Development Corporation and its chief may decide a policy of industrialisation and sponsor a research study for appropriate location. In this case, the relevant 'who' as decision-maker is the head of the state government, but if location involves dislocation of status quo at the local level like the diversion of local land from agricultural use to industrial use, the people affected must be included as part of 'who' to be considered because their opinion can affect the implementation of the ultimate optimal solution. In river valley projects, certain groups will be benefited, and certain groups will be disturbed. Both groups need to be taken as relevant section of decision-makers, and their views and interest must be given appropriate considerations while arriving at final solution to a problem.

Even in the case of academic research problems involving real-world issues, this aspect is relevant. Firstly, all groups who can influence solution and implementation must be included as relevant for seeking opinion and conducting discussion. Thus, in the case of PhD and MPhil research, the guide and the candidate can influence the research, and therefore both these groups should be in the loop. The researcher will benefit immensely by knowing what the guide wants in the ultimate analysis.

The next step in the process of problem formulation is the identification of what. What is/are being intended to be achieved through the solution of the problem? Often, the objectives are not being clearly specified. There is also confusion between constraints and objectives. In a PhD level research, the intention was to design an optimal strategy of land distribution. Here, the objectives are not clearly specified because we do not what are the criteria of optimality.

In case of a sponsored study, the sponsoring agency may suggest that the criterion of optimality is the maximisation of production, subject to the prescribed limit of unequal distribution or alternatively the policymakers may suggest that the criterion of optimality is the minimisation of skewness of the ownership of land-based assets of different sections of the farm household subject to a certain level of production being achieved from the total amount of land-based resources.

In the third place, the decision-makers may define objectives by a statement that the country wants the most egalitarian distribution of landed assets with the maximisation of production. The first two propositions are workable, but the third specification is vague because neither the statement most egalitarian nor maximisation of productions is free of ambiguity.

Similarly, the head of a railway organisation wanted minimisation of cost per passenger kilometre between station A (Glasgow) and station B (London). Of course, the least cost solution (if feasible) starts the train at Glasgow and let it stop at London without any intermediate stop. Quite clearly, this was not acceptable. The chief of the railways then specified the minimum number of stations where the train must stop and the maximum speed that may be permissible.

These examples suggest that the often concerned decision-makers are not clear about their objectives and the researcher must find out what the decision-makers want by asking relevant and appropriate questions. For example, when the policy-makers suggest that they want a land distribution which is most egalitarian, it may be pertinent to point out that such egalitarian distribution may make landholding nonviable and thereby the production may suffer; similarly, where we want to maximise production, the land distribution may become very skewed.

In actual practice, telling the top-level policymakers/lawmakers regarding infeasibilities of their statements and pronouncements may not be very much favoured. Similarly, if such statements are made by guides and advisor, the researcher faces similar dilemma. No one likes to be told that his/her statements are infeasible or illogical.

To solve this issue it is necessary to proceed in two stages. Stage one consists of defining boundaries of problem to be investigated. The problem boundary in land distribution may be the agricultural cultivable land of a specific state, district or a block. Once the boundary of the land problem is drawn, various factors outside the boundary may influence distribution. So, after drawing a problem boundary, relevant environment for the problem needs to be selected. Thus, socio-economic condition, political environment and distribution of other assets will all affect land distribution. We should identify all relevant factors that affect the strategy of land distribution and agricultural production. Similarly, all factors that affect costs of passenger per kilometre must be identified (French and Papamichail 2009).

In this connection all environmental factors that affect the internal factors identified must also be specified. In theory everything depends on everything else, and no problem-solving exercise can deal with all factors exhaustively. We will only consider those factors which have an influence on the ultimate outcome variable; the rest of the factors may be ignored.

The questions that need to be answered are what factors and variables are to be studied for the purpose of our study, how to identify them and how do we relate these variables in terms of their effects on ultimate result.

The first step in this is the identification of variables.

4.5.2 *Variable Identification Method*

We have to understand that in any problem, we have three types of variables: (1) uncontrolled environmental variables, (2) control variables and (3) output/input variables. Thus, in the case of land distribution, equitable distribution is an outcome variable. The amount of land allocated to a household is a control variable. These are also decision variables. Socio-economic conditions and political environment are uncontrolled variables (Bandyopadhyay 1975).

In a costing exercise of safe-deposit lockers, the idea was to decide remunerative price for lockers. Here, the ultimate price was the outcome variable, and the demand of safe locker service will determine the volume provided and will affect the cost. These are uncontrolled variables. Various inputs needed for producing safe locker service are input variable and partly controlled variables. Environmental socio-economic conditions influence demand; they are environmental variables and are not controllable.

So, for any problem to be studied, we have to identify these three types of variables.

$$c \longrightarrow d \longrightarrow p$$

Fig. 4.1 Forward formulation (Safe deposit locker study)

These are three methods for identification of variables:

1. Forward formulation
2. Backward formulation
3. Combined backward/forward formulation

We explain and illustrate these in the next subsection.

4.5.2.1 Forward Formulation

In this type of formulation, we take our known or given concept and ask the question what other variables or factors it will influence. For example, cost of inputs will affect cost of locker service. We can ask the questions what factors of the cost of locker service will have an influence; obviously, it will influence demand – demand will influence chargeable price. This is called forward formulation.

Thus, forward formulation is obtained by starting with a variable and by repeatedly asking the question 'what will it affect?' till we reach the ultimate outcome variable or variables.

Thus, in the safe-deposit locker service case, we have the cost of input (ci) influencing the demand for locker service (d), and this will affect the chargeable price (p) – Fig. 4.1 depicts this.

Case (ii): In a maintenance study, it was necessary to determine optimal frequency of maintenance for a machine part, so that the cost of maintenance is optimal. In this case we may start with the variable frequency (f) of maintenance. Frequency will influence cost of maintenance (c); it will also influence downtime for production (dp). It will also influence the breakdown maintenance (bm) need. Breakdown maintenance need will influence production downtime and also the cost of maintenance.

Thus, Fig. 4.2 depicts this.

Both these formulations are forward formulation.

4.5.2.2 Backward Formulation

In identifying variables instead of starting with a given or known variable, we may start with the desired outcome variable and then ask the question 'what factors will influence this?' Thus, in the study of safe-deposit locker service, we are concerned with the outcome variable of chargeable price.

If we start with the variable chargeable price (pc) and ask the question which other variable will affect this, we can get the idea, socio-economic condition (SE)

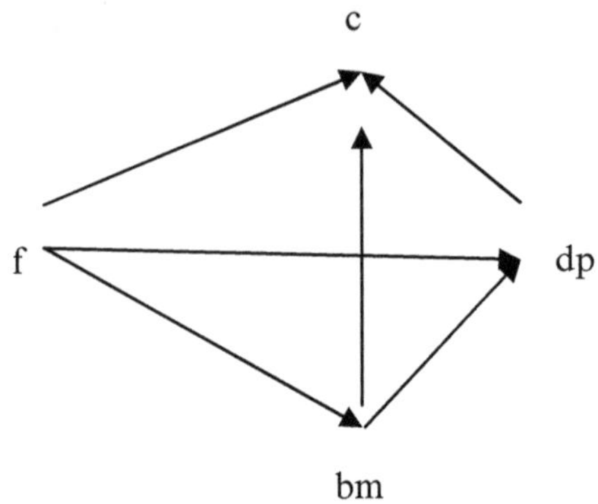

Fig. 4.2 Forward formulation (Maintenance study)

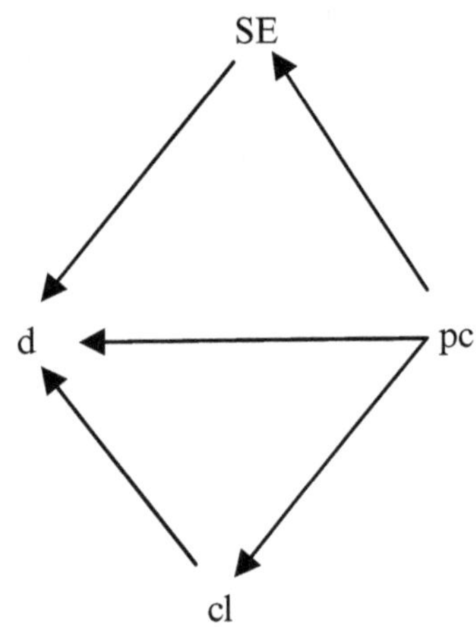

Fig. 4.3 Backward formulation (Safe deposit locker study)

of the community will affect the chargeable price, because that will affect demand (d); further chargeable price will be influenced by the cost of providing safe-deposit locker service (cl). We have the diagram of Fig. 4.3.

Here, starting from the outcome variable, we proceed backwards to identify variables by asking the question 'what influenced these factors?' The arrows show the direction from the outcome variable to the influencing variable.

4.5.2.3 Combined Backward/Forward Formulations

Here we may start with the identified variable and proceed forward and again start with the outcome variable and proceed backward. These forward/backward movements provide a network of variables.

Take the example of the inventory control problem as an illustration. In an inventory control problem, if stocks are not available to meet the demand, then we have lost sales, and there is a penalty for not having a stock. There is a cost for

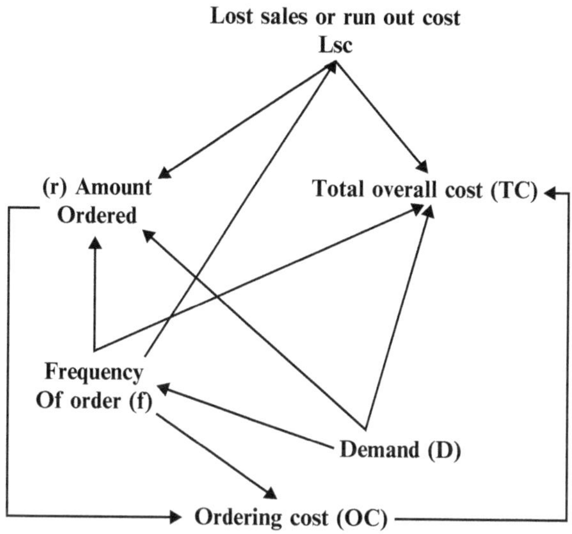

Fig. 4.4 Present the network of variables obtained through backward and forward formulation (combined) processes

ordering or for having a stock. Demand will decide the amount of order and also the frequency of order. These will determine the cost of ordering; in addition, if there is more stock than demand, there is always a stockholding cost. Thus, the overall cost is composed of runout penalty cost, stockholding cost and ordering cost. These can be identified as a network by adopting combined backward and forward formulation as shown in Fig. 4.4

In a study of energy balance in an area, the following variables were identified:

Air pollution
Biomass available
Price of kerosene
Price of diesel
Price of petrol
Price of coal
Price of wood
Industrial activities
Agricultural activities
No. of GW wells with pumps
Domestic cooking
Lightings
Transportation energy

All these can be identified as combined backward and forward formulation. Energy balance will depend on demand and supply equilibrium of energy and proceeding systematically by identifying factors affecting demand and supply and also starting from energy price and then proceeding to identify factors affected by energy price.

4.6 Clarification of 'What'

We started our discussion on determination of 'what' is intended to be achieved by the study and before completing that discussion digressed to the identification of variables. When objectives and constraints of a research study are not adequately specified, it may be pertinent first to identify relevant variables conceptually and then ask concerned people to specify which variables they want to optimise. Say in an energy balance problem related to rural developments, we identify variables like:

- Lifestyle
- Increased agricultural activities
- New industries
- Employment generation
- Migration
- Air pollution

The concerned decision-makers then identify employment generation as the main concern subject to non-deterioration of lifestyle, nonmigration and adoption of new industry subject to acceptable level of air pollution. Thus, pollution levels become constraints, employment generation becomes objective and agriculture and industry become the 'means' variable. Thus, problem is properly defined as maximisation of employment through improvement of agricultural and industrial activities so as to ensure that there is no deterioration of lifestyle and no migration takes place. Pollution is at an acceptable level, and energy balance is maintained.

Once the research problem is defined this way, we proceed to the next stage of further elaborating on available alternatives in elaborating on 'how'.

4.7 Alternatives Available and Feasible

Any problem can be resolved by following different options. The idea is to select the best option. Each option adopted will have consequences; some of them are positive and some of them will be negative. For example, the option of creating new industrial activities for generating employment by enhancing production will be increasing wealth (positive consequence). It will have negative effect in terms of creating pollution, diversion of land from agricultural use to industrial use, etc. Different options may affect different sections of the society differently. Thus, a river valley project may give irrigation facilities to certain areas, whereas it will submerge certain villages and create displacement in some other areas.

Further effects at different time periods for different options may also differ. Then, some options may give immediate beneficial and favourable results but can lead to disaster and bad long-term results. Thus, drawing of water for irrigation from groundwater by means of electric/diesel pumps may result in a better irrigation and increase agricultural production in the short term. But where the withdrawal is much more than recharge, the process can create serious problems of groundwater quality and may force the groundwater level downward, increasing the cost of pumping up water significantly.

Any research study be it academic or sponsored if it has to have any relevance must consider all available options for solving the problem holistically considering the effects on the total system and also overtime. Only after that, we can proceed to determine the optimal.

4.8 Relations

Once variables and options are identified, it is necessary to establish relationship among variables. Unless, at least conceptually, we are able to visualise these relationships, we shall not be clear what data have to be collected. Supposing we are studying migration, we conceptually identify various factors affecting migration and also identify options available for affecting migration. We must identify how various options affect migration and in what manner. Once these things are known, we are clear what data should be collected and how these data should be analysed. Thus, for solving any problem, real-life issues have to be depicted in our research proposal either through description or through some modelling. Thus for every research study, modelling is essential.

4.9 Representation of the Problem Reality

Modelling is nothing but representation of reality. It is not reality but it gives a picture of reality. We have an esoteric view of a model. 'All models must be mathematical'; thus, the statement is not at all true; on the other hand, no good research is possible without a picture or description of what is to be done, how it is to be done and for whose benefit it is to be done. This is what modelling is for.

Thus in any research study, we must know the present state; we must specify the desired state to be obtained through study, options available to us and various factors that will influence the result. Some of these variables or factors are under our control for which we will take the appropriate actions. Some variables and factors are not within our control; these are called uncontrolled and free environmental variables. These variables can be anticipated and projected. So, forecasting of free environmental variables is needed.

Thus, following 'White' (White 1975), we can draw a simplified diagram for research problem modelling (Fig. 4.5).

Any research is based on certain basic assumptions and measures adopted for the particular study; by varying the assumptions, relations and measures, we can generate different solutions. Of course, any research has limitations regarding time and resources. Within those limits various solutions can be generated, and effects can be assessed.

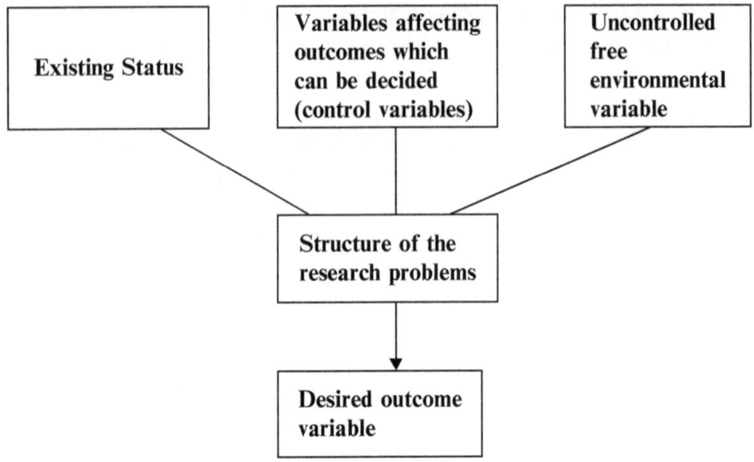

Fig. 4.5 Model of research problems

4.10 Benefits of Problem Formulation

Thus, problem formulation consists of (Ackoff 1981):

1. Identification of decision-makers
2. Identification of objectives and constraints
3. Identification of alternatives
4. Establishing of relationships outcome
5. Formulation of total framework for representing reality

Once problems are structured this way (Rosenhead 1996), the data requirements for the study become clear. Quite often data demands are excessive, and access to data is difficult. Problem to be studied may be modified both in nature and scope to suit data availability. Even for academic research, these steps are very essential. It relieves much trouble later on. It is advisable that for every problem researched, the problem should be properly specified by following logical scientific processes and methods. We have demonstrated these methods. We shall explain the methods in details by means of a few case studies.

4.11 A Few Case Examples

4.11.1 Case A

A PhD level, the thesis title was 'Evolving Sustainable Urban Transportation for India'. The topic as a presentation is not very explicit about the range of analysis, factors to be dealt with and other related aspects. To write a comprehensive proposal based on scientific problem formulation, we may precede as follows. As for our earlier discussed framework of academic research, at present, research area is multidisciplinary – it encompasses the disciplines of economics, civil engineering, energy engineering and environmental science. Field within these disciplines is transportation and urbanisation and other related technologies. Aspects to be dealt with are pollution levels and satisfactory urban transport system in India (for intercity and intracity transportation).

The next question to be satisfactorily answered is to identify the ownership of this problem. Obviously, PhD guide and PhD advisory committees expect some results out of the research study which will extend the frontiers of knowledge, but to be relevant, the study should produce outcomes that can influence policy related to urban transport planning and sustainability. Thus, policymakers and community as a whole are interested in the project outcome. What exactly is expected is difficult to decide, but quite clearly broadly speaking, most of the groups identified above would like to have a clear idea of a profile urban transportation that will be efficient, effective and sustainable. If these are the objectives we have in mind, how should we proceed to structure the problem further. As it is to sketch, the urban transportation profile for the country as a whole is a gigantic problem, so we need to specify the exact boundaries of the problem. The overall transport framework, intercity and intracity, transportation and intermodal character (road, railways, air and water) are to be tackled. Both goods and passenger traffic have to be handled. However, apart from the broad framework, no detailed statewise or districtwise or areawise framework development may be feasible.

Thus, the problem boundary can be defined as India and its broad transport system for urban areas. The next stage will be the identification of various factors and variables relevant to the resolution of the research study.

Here, we must specify alternatives and their effects. We are to identify consequence variables for alternative transport profiles. These consequence variables can be identified by the forward or backward formulation or by combined backward/forward formulation. Thus, we can take ultimate consequence of speedy urban travel and then ask the question, 'which will affect the speed?' Another ultimate consequence may be congestion and also the degree of pollution, and we then ask the question 'what factors will affect congestion and pollution?' So, we can identify factors like volume of traffic, technology, technology of travel, mode of travel energy use pattern, energy use efficiency, width of road, frequency of public transport, number of vehicles in use and their polluting effects. Demand of transportation will be influenced by the location of economic activities and centralisation and decentralisation of such activities. Sustainability as a consequence variable will depend on available sources of energy, efficiency of energy conversion, capacity utilisation of vehicles and efforts for demand management.

We can also start with existing alternatives in urban transportation, how these will be influenced in the future and identify various factors till we reach the ultimate consequence variables. Thus, continuing with these processes, we may be able to identify the following variables (neither illustrative nor exhaustive):

Consequence variables: Congestion, speed, accident, cost, energy consumption and pollution infrastructure profile for various transportation modes

Intermediate variable: Public-private partnership for urban transport infrastructure, administrative system, capacity utilisation, traffic control, pollution control arrangement, location of economic activities, etc.

Decision variable: Intermodal mix,
selection of technologies and energy use levels,
methods of demand management and capacity utilisation,
selection of mode of public transport,
relocation of activities and
creation of infrastructure

Once most critical variables are identified, we can then identify the data requirement. Here in this case, we should get data regarding technological modernisation and options available in different transportation modes and their relative costs and advantages. Energy source, data affecting demand for transportation, growth of economy (GDP), scale of urbanisation and trend of migration from rural hinterland to rural areas. Polluting effects of each type of vehicles and transport modes, total effects on demand on available energy sources and data of various energy resources available.

In addition, we may like to have data regarding global trends in urbanisation and urban transportation. Special stress may be given to data regarding evolution of urban transportation of developing economies like Brazil and China. For sustainability assessment, we must obtain data on polluting effects of various alternatives and data regarding means available for reducing congestion, pollution and causing better capacity utilisation (so we should have data about urban infrastructure for present and projected future needs and present level of capacity utilisation). Effects of public transport and creating vehicle free zones – not encouraging private transportation in certain areas – may be studied. We should then have data in respect of these aspects.

Broadly speaking Indian urban transport will be partly influenced by global trends of urban transport. Thus we can draw a broad conceptual model of the problem (Fig. 4.6).

Once this broad conceptual framework is developed, w can then see that there are various aspects that we are ignoring, for example, with the growth of demand, more volume of traffic will emerge; with the dominance of private transport, the demand on transport infrastructure will grow; the requirement of land for broadening of road network may create diversion of agricultural land and create non-sustainability. Sustainability has to be therefore assessed in respect of all non-renewable resources. We may deliberately avoid certain factors to tackle a problem that is manageable. Thus we may assume that social tension arising out of diversion of land will not be a part of our study.

When the problem is formulated this way, we can write a proposal defining the primary problem of urban transportation and second problem of understanding transport technology and choice between private and public transport. Secondary problem will also be the determination of effects on sustainability of different transport options – secondary problem will also be the location of economic activities, strategies of rural development and their effects on rural-urban migration, degree of urbanisation and demand for urban transportation. We should try to

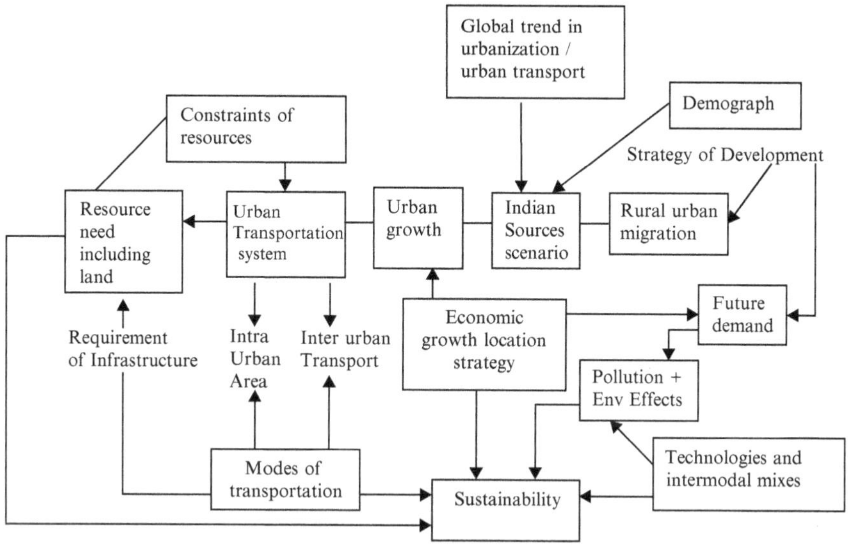

Fig. 4.6 Models of urban transportation. Major components to be studied

specify all important secondary problems to understand clearly the range of expertise, skill and data required to successfully tackle the primary problem. If necessary we can suitably modify the specification of the primary problem based on our details of problems of formulation, identification of variables, constraints and various secondary problems.

4.11.2 *Case B*

There was a sponsored problem to be resolved. Sponsoring agency was the Department of Science and Technology/Government of India. The sponsoring agency was working on behalf of the 'Pulse Mission'. The project was entitled as pulse production strategy for making the country self-sufficient in pulse within the next 10 years, so that dependency on export is brought down to nil.

The primary problem was to increase production of pulse to meet the total demand of pulses in the economy. Here, the owner of the problem was early identified – it was the Pulse Production Mission set up by the Government of India. 'What' are the objectives of the owners are also very clear. The objectives are improving the total production of pulse within the next 10 years so that the total pulse produced in the economy is sufficient to meet the total demand for pulses. However, such specification of objectives is not complete. We must know the constraints involved in the solution of the problem. The amount of land that can be allocated to pulse production was limited. People's preferences of different types of pulses and effects of such choices on production decision of farmers have to be considered. Thus after properly specifying constraints and objectives, we wanted to identify various factors affecting pulse production. Here, we can use combined forward and backward formulation described earlier in this section. On the basis of such method, we identified the following variables.

Different type of pulses
Demand of different pulses
Costs of production
Productivity
Land allocated for pulse production
Land needed for self sufficiency
Technology of pulse production

These basic concepts can be used to generate further important variables for solving the problem. Thus the cost of production will depend on technology, seeds, water requirement, labour and farm management practices. Existing land for cereal production cannot possibly be diverted to pulse production, because that will affect cereal production. So there is a constraint of pulse production in terms of land available that are dedicated only for pulse products. Intercropping may release the constraint to some extents. Thus 'intercropping' becomes another important concept.

For each of the above concepts, there are constraints and boundaries.

These constraints are being adhered to. Secondary problem identification consisted of the identification of technologies available for production, estimation of demand for pulses and estimation of productivity. Having identified the basic objectives, constraints and available options for improvement of productivity and related cost, we can formulate a conceptual model of the problem (Fig. 4.7).

Here, free environmental variables were population growth and their pattern of pulse consumption. These are uncertain environmental variables and have to be projected on the basis of past data and trends.

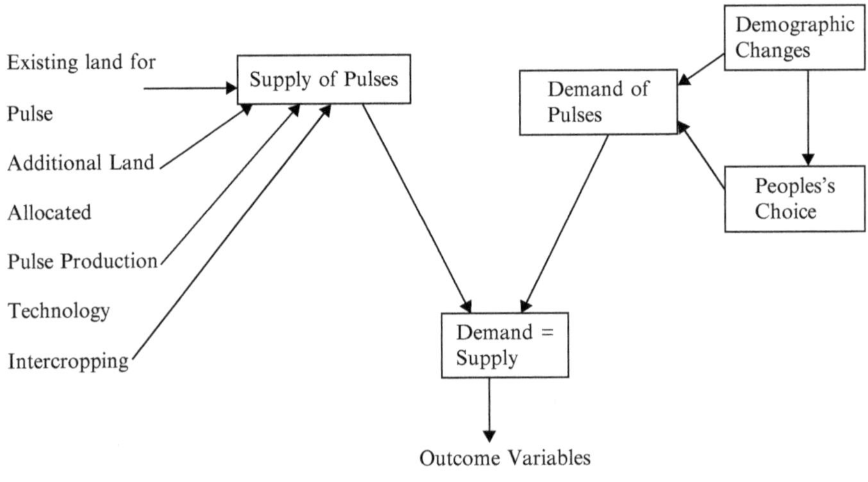

Fig. 4.7 Model for optimising pulse production

Existing situation of land devoted to pulse production and available technologies are state variables.

Once these aspects are identified, data requirements for the project can be easily specified.

4.11.3 Case C

In this case, it was needed to assess the impact on pollution of chemical industry with special reference to chemical industry in Gujarat. This problem is a better specified problem. It deals with areas of chemical engineering and environmental science. It specifically deals with chemical industries in Gujarat. The owners of the problem (which was a PhD level problem) were of course the guide and research advisors, but the results will be used for policy formulation at state and national levels, so their views should be taken, in considering ownership of problem.

The objective of the research is to assess the impact of various chemical production technologies in creating pollution in the environment – thus the objective is to objectively assess environmental impact of various chemical manufacturing

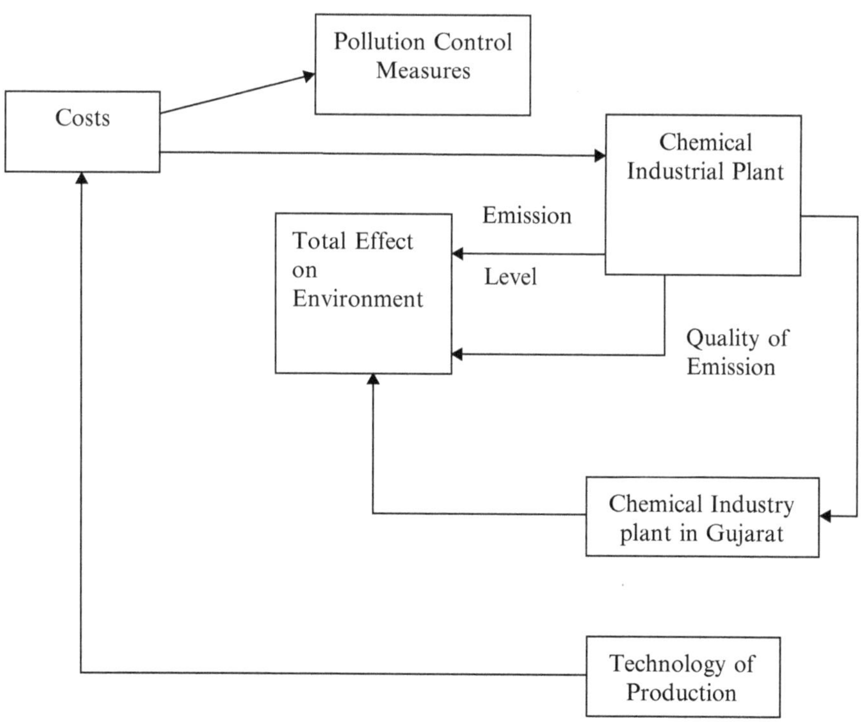

Fig. 4.8 Model of polluting chemical industry

plants and also specifically to asses such impact in the case of industry in Gujarat. Relevant variable can be identified by following forward and backward formulation. The pollution levels are affected by emitted gases and their compositions. The pollution levels also depend on pollution control measures taken by various chemical manufacturing units in Gujarat (Fig. 4.8).

The above figure defines the various components of the proposed research study. It provides guidance regarding data requirements for the study of pollution of chemical industry in general and in Gujarat in particular.

We have discussed three cases of which we have discussed two cases in detail.

It may be stressed that whatever may be the nature of the research problem, some attention initially in formulating the problem scientifically always helps. It helps in working the research proposal, planning the study and also in data collection.

References

Ackoff R (1962) Scientific method – optimising applied research decisions. Wiley, New York

Ackoff R (1981) The art and science of mess management. Interface 11(1):20–26

Bandyopadhyay R (1975) On approaches to O, R modelling. Omega 3(1):59–69

French S, Moule J, Papamichail N (2009) Decision behaviour analysis and support. Cambridge University Press, Cambridge

Rosenhead J (1996) What's the problem? An introduction to problem structuring methods. Interface 26(6):117–131

White DJ (1969) Decision theory. Allen Unwin, London

White DJ (1975) Decision methodology. Wiley, Chichester

Chapter 5
Systems Approach and Soft Systems Methodology of Organization and Management Studies

R. Bandyopadhyay

5.1 Need and Importance of Systems Approach in Management and Social Research – Concepts, Theories and Ideas

5.1.1 Objectives

The present chapter deals with the essential aspects of systems approach and explains the concepts and ideas on the basis of systems thinking. The objectives of this chapter are given as follows:

- To give an idea of systems approach and its need in the modern world of complex problems
- To explain the various concepts underlying systems approach and systems thinking
- To appreciate the application of systems approach in solving complex real-world problems
- To explain the difference between soft systems and hard systems methodologies and in this connection to appreciate the beneficial effects of soft systems methodology in tackling complex, social, economic, management, and policy problems in the complex real world
- To expose the readers particularly with major tools, techniques, and diagrammatic methods of problem solving and problem structuring by adopting soft systems method

R. Bandyopadhyay (✉)
Former Director, National Institute of Bank Management, Pune, India

Visiting Research Professor, University of Manchester, Manchester, UK

Present Affiliation: Hon. Director, CASAD, Pune, India
e-mail: rangband@gmail.com

D.S. Hegde (ed.), *Essays on Research Methodology*,
DOI 10.1007/978-81-322-2214-9_5

- To illustrate the applications of systems approach and soft systems methodologies by means of various real-life case studies

5.1.2 Needs and Benefits of Systems Approach

The present chapter details the essential aspects of systems approach for conducting management, organizational, and socioeconomic studies. The term "systems" is derived from the original Greek word "synistanai." Synistanai basically means "to bring together and combine." "Systems approach" as a field of enquiry emerged as the real-life problems in the modern technological world started becoming too complex. It appeared as an affective approach to tackle complex problems of the real world. The approach basically has four ways or concepts (Checkland 1981):

- The larger system is divided into smaller components and subsystems are studied in a concentrated manner with adequate depth. This would require *specialization* to study individual components.
- In order to avoid greater complexity with greater level of specialization, various components and subsystems are grouped in the form of a discipline or subdiscipline. This is called the process of *grouping*.
- While generating groups and combining subsystems and components, it will be pertinent to coordinate interactions among various groups. Thus, systems approach requires *coordination*.
- In describing systems into subsystems, one must not forget to recognize that the system as a whole is greater than the sum of the parts and the system has a property which is not the property of the elements of the subsystem. This is called the *emergent property* of the system. We have further explained the property emergence later in this chapter.

Thus, specialization, grouping, coordination, and emergence are the four basic concepts constituting systems approach.

The group and interface between groups can be elements or processes. Thus, some elements or processes are grouped. There can be a variation within each group. Understanding these variations is critical to application of systems approach to problem solving.

Most research studies generally tend to apply the analytical reductionist approach, thereby only achieving partial solutions. Every problem depends on a large number of variables, and these are interdependent variables; often by taking only a few elements and subsystems into considerations, we tend to ignore affects by and on other subsystems and therefore the solution obtained are not wholly satisfactory. We can give a few illustrative examples of how partial consideration affects solution. In a transport study, we want to remove the congestion of a road. Widening of roads and building of overbridges and flyovers are suggested. However, it is often found that such solutions only remove congestion for a limited period. More vehicles get attracted with wider roads and often congestion reappears. This happens because of a narrow approach to the problem. It tends to ignore the effect of the widening of roads and creation of flyovers on volume of traffic and their resultant effects on congestion. Quite often, while trying to solve a problem in certain parts of the social system, we create a more intractable problem in some other parts of the social system.

As already pointed out, the present chapter details out the essential aspects of systems approach for conducting management and organizational studies. Most research studies generally tend to apply analytical reductionist approaches, thereby only attempting partial solutions. It is therefore necessary that for all real-life social, organizational, and management problems, we should complement analytical and reductionist methods through systems approach where aspects of bringing changes in any part of a system is considered on other relevant parts. Systems approach considered the total effects on all elements of a system and is not confined to a narrow partial solution. In this chapter we shall illustrate the approach along with soft systems methodologies of solution. Hard systems methodologies are already dealt with in other chapters of this treatise. For undertaking systems approach and soft systems methodology, understanding few basic concepts, ideas, and laws will be necessary. The chapter is therefore divided into three parts. The first part deals with some of the important concepts and their definitions. The second part outlines the basics, concepts, methods and available techniques which are normally used in a systems study of an organization and soft systems methodologies. The third part describes a few case studies.

5.1.3 Concepts and Definitions

The following concepts are quite often used in "systems analysis literature" and we propose to define these:

1. *System*

A system is composed of interrelated elements. Thus, we can have physical systems, natural systems, human-activity systems and so on. As far as we are concerned, we will be mostly dealing in human-activity systems. Elaborating further we may say that a system is a whole consisting of two or more parts that satisfies the following five conditions (Checkland 1981):

1. The whole have one or more properties or functions that define its character.
2. Each element or the part of the whole can affect the behavior or properties of the system (as a whole).
3. There are subsets of parts which are essential parts – without any one of these parts, the system cannot carry out its defining functions.
4. The essential parts (subsets described above) of a system form a connected set. The essential parts of a system necessarily interact either directly or indirectly.
5. The effect of any subset of the essential parts of the system as a whole depends on the behavior of at least one other subset.

Combining the above conditions we may reach the following summarized version.

"A system is a whole that cannot be divided into independent parts without loss of its essential properties or functions" (Ackoff and Emery 1972). Thus, we have financial system, environmental systems, water resource system, energy system and so on.

We thus consider system as a dynamic and complex whole, interacting as a structural functional unit.

Among its various elements, energy, material, and information flow to compose the system.

A system is situated within an environment.

Energy, material, and information flow from the environment to systems and from systems to the environment via the boundaries. (This is an open system as we have defined later.)

Systems constitute entities which are in equilibrium but can oscillate and exhibit a chaotic behavior.

A holistic system is a set of interdependent and interacting parts. When we study systems, we study the systems holistically.

It follows that if a research study on school education is done by applying a systems approach, then we can only study education imparted in a specific school only if we understand the working of the educational system as a whole in the total socioeconomic system. Whether we are interested in pure academic (Ph. D or M. Phil) research on education or sponsored research, systems approach in designing the problem and problem solutions will be more desirable. Therefore, in this approach every problem will be a subsystem of a larger system. Methodologically it will be appropriate to define the system under study and various important elements constituting the systems should also be identified. Broad aspects of the larger system of which the system under study is a part should also be specified. This will help us in specifying the boundaries and the relevant environment to be considered. Various elements and their interaction to be studied to understand the system will also become clear. Thus, if we are studying the performance of specific schools, elements contributing to the performance, like teachers (numbers, quality, qualifications, etc.), school infrastructure, and school management, educational processes and systems are all relevant elements. All of these are influenced by and have influence on the larger educational system and policies. These also have influence on (directly and indirectly) socioeconomic and political environment. In systems approach explicit considerations of these are important. Wherever certain assumptions are made regarding the behavior and characteristics of the larger containing system, for a good honest study it is necessary to specify these as clearly as possible. In many conventional academic researches, most of these aspects are taken as given and excellence of performance is related to the quality of learning or quality of teachers or qualifications of teachers. Seldom are the effects of other intervening variables taken into consideration. It is necessary in modern day's research to recognize all important systemic aspects and variables and clearly specify how they are being dealt within the problem under study. It may be quite appropriate to assume certain specific characteristics for these, but they should be clearly detected and specified. Having clarified the importance of systems approach and definition of a system, we give below some more definitions. Some of the systems are called natural systems as they exist in this universe. So we have the solar system which is a natural system. Some of the others are created by human efforts; these are called humanly contrived systems. Thus, market system, educational system, healthcare system and corporate organization are all humanly contrived systems and can be effectively changed or redesigned with human effort. In addition, we give below more definitions of different systems.

2. *Open system*

An open system exchanges information with its environment. It therefore does not suffer from entropy. Those who are not familiar with the thermodynamics concept of entropy may note that entropy in our discussion is a measure of waste. Exchange of information and knowledge with and from the environment creates understanding and reduction of wastes. An open system takes enough inputs from its environment to offset outputs and material that are produced and are given to the environment. Thus, continuous inflows and outflows of goods, material, energy, and information are taking place. The steady state of the system is therefore not a static equilibrium. It is always in dynamic equilibrium.

An open system tends toward increased differentiation in functions/roles and responsibilities and therefore leads to complexities. All studies, be academic or sponsored in respect of management, sociology, economic, and social sciences, are basically studies related to an open system.

In case of an open system, the relevant environment under study should be clearly specified. Thus, in a study of a school educational system, socioeconomic condition of parents and guardians, general attitude toward education and education policies followed are relevant environment for the school education system.

How these variables interact and affect the functioning of the system under study should be clearly understood. Similarly for a healthcare system, the sanitation level of the area, socioeconomic conditions and quality of drinking water system, environmental pollution, and other related variables will interact with the healthcare system and will affect the system positively or negatively.

Thus, any study of an open system can call for:

1. Proper specifications of systems boundaries
2. Identification of necessary/relevant environmental variable
3. Understanding of interactions between elements of the system under study and various relevant environmental variables

3. *Hierarchies*

Most systems constitute a "nested system." That means there are subsystems within the system. Similarly many systems are subsystems of larger systems. Thus, a corporate organization is a subsystem of business system. Departments within the corporate organization are the subsystem of the corporate organization. Such nested systems can normally be considered as a hierarchy of systems. A hierarchical system has parallel, horizontal parts like private sector and public sector business organization, and it can also contain different divisions based on product processes or location.

Most systems studies must appreciate this hierarchical nature of systems in conducting studies based on systems approach.

4. *The state of the system*

The state of the system at a moment of time is the set of relevant properties which that system has at that time. The properties of a system derive from the interactions of its parts rather than their action taken separately.

From this definition it follows that by changing the interrelationships and interactions, the structure of relevant properties can be changed and the state of the system then also would undergo a change.

Let us assume that we are interested in an academic study suggesting the improvement of an educational system at primary school level. Here, we can suggest to change the quality of teachers in terms of educational background and training. These will have effect on the availability, budget and overall cost. These in themselves may not be adequate; school aids, teaching techniques, infrastructure, etc., and their interrelationships and their effects on the overall performance of the system have to be studied.

By changing only one aspect say entry qualification of teachers without corresponding changes in the relevant elements within the system, the desired improvement may not be achievable. Thus, for proper effective solutions, we should adopt in addition to analytical reductionist processes, methods relevant to systems approach.

5. *The environment*

The environment of a system is a set of elements and their relevant properties; these elements are not part of the system. Any change in these elements can result in the change of the structure and behavior of the system. Simply speaking the systems environment consists of all variables which can affect its properties and behavior. One has to be very careful in defining the environment while conducting a study of any problem. As all environments are related to the boundary, so once the boundary of the problem is properly defined, any variable outside the boundary which can significantly affect the properties of the system are called environmental variables. One can always question what is significant and what is not significant. Whenever significance can be assessed in an objective manner, the problem is not severe. But, in most human-activity systems, the effects of environmental variables could not very often be measured objectively. As such one has to depend on the subjective evaluation of significance, and this is a perfectly valid scientifically correct method. A diagrammatic technique called “systems map” is normally used for the specification of boundary and identification of relevant environmental variables and their degree of influence. This technique is further elaborated in Part II of this chapter.

In a research study on arsenic problem in drinking water, all aspects of neutralizing arsenic were studied; however, the solution derived can only be short lived because excessive drawing of groundwater and environmental effects are responsible for producing arsenic, and therefore, for sustainable solution, these aspects are also considered.

6. *A dynamic system*

This system is one which changes its structure or behavior or both over time. It means that its structural properties are changing over a period of time. A national economic system is a dynamic system. It is changing its characteristics over time; both its structure and behavior are changing over time. Most of the social, management, or economic systems with which we are concerned in our academic, social, management, or sponsored research are concerned with dynamic systems. Ceteris paribus (other things remain unchanged and only one variable changing) assumptions are almost always unrealistic in dealing with problems of real-world systems.

7. *A homeostatic system*

This is a stable system whose environments are dynamic. Thus, thermostat is homeostatic. Similarly, normal body temperature remains stable even when environmental temperature changes due to changes of season.

8. *Dynamic equilibrium*

Most of the problems that we study whether for research (for Ph. D or M. Phil or D. Phil) or for solving real-life organizations or social issues belong to dynamic systems. These dynamic systems are in equilibrium. Most of the real-life systems are in dynamic equilibrium. Real-life systems are dynamic and changing all the time; however, for becoming stable, all its elements are in perfect synchrony and therefore equilibrium is maintained. If any element within the system looses the synchrony, systems stability will be disturbed. Behavior of various elements of the system under study should be understood and a synchrony should be maintained in any changes proposed based on the research study. Real-life examples of dynamic systems are rotating tops, a moving train, and a moving airplane. All the observations mentioned earlier will be applicable to these cases. Rejecting the questions related to dynamic stability of human-activity system will not be appropriate in any meaningful research study of the social system.

9. *Synergy*

It basically means synthetic energy signifying that the whole is greater than the sum of the parts. Thus, the sum of the parts does not add up to the whole. Concept of synergy has a great relevance in management and social study. Any evaluation study on mergers and acquisitions must ensure that on the basis of such evaluation merger and acquisitions really produce synergy. Similarly part solutions of subproblems when applied and added together must produce synergy. In view of synergy pure reductionist solution may not be adequate for any real-life study of systems.

10. *Anergy*

This is negative synergy. If some parts of the system are in opposition of other parts, the integration of all parts is not simply the sum of the parts minus the negative contribution, and it can be more adverse than this.

Again the whole is not the algebraic sum of the parts. In many social science researches, it is necessary to ensure that solutions prescribed should not produce anergy to the system as a whole. Thus, in an exercise of allocation of funds for higher education, a higher financial allocation to this sector may deprive the lower-level, primary/secondary education. Over the years because of the reduced allocation of resources, the quality of primary and secondary education will suffer. As a result, the quality of candidates entering higher education and the performance of higher education will suffer in spite of higher allocation. Thus, it creates an overall anergy in the education system. Thus, for avoiding anergy we should encourage production of synergy in the system. The change in allocation pattern in various subsystems should be such that the total improvement of the educational system as a whole is more than the sum of the improvement of individual subsystems.

11. *Emergence*

Certain properties belong to the system as a whole and is not the property of the subsystems/parts or elements. Taken out of the system, the parts do not exhibit the property. A beautiful flower may be considered as an example. The beauty of the flower which is made up of a number of petals is not the property of the individual petals; individual petals may not be beautiful; however, the flower is beautiful. Thus, beauty is the emergent property of the flower as a whole and not of the individual petals. Beauty depends not on the beauty of individual petals but in the arrangement of petals to produce the flower.

Thus, property of emergence is a systemic property of the whole system and largely depends on the arrangement and interactions of the parts and not on the property of the individual parts. Any study of a system must therefore give attention to the emergent (property) of the system. The organizational effectiveness is the emergent property of the organization as a system and not totally dependent on the efficiency of each individual or departments constituting the organization. Property of emergence is the most important property that should be understood by all the researchers, scholars, policymakers and problem solvers in social, management, economic, and policy sciences. Quite often the emergent property which is a systemic property is treated as a property of the elements or parts. Gross domestic product is an emergent property of the economic systems as a whole, and it is not merely a property of investment policy. Confluence of various factors can converge to produce an overall growth of the economy. What combination of factors creates this emergence needs to be understood. Understanding the characteristics of an individual element like industrial growth, agricultural growth, and sociocultural changes is not good enough to study the emergent development of the socioeconomic system as a whole. In any effective study of social systems, we need to study these effects of changes on individual components, their inter relationships, and resultant emergence of the system as a whole. We should also study the overall effects of simultaneous and variable changes in the different subsystems. Emergence of qualities due to confluence of various factors should be studied and understood. Quite often we fail to grasp these systemic issues and try to solve the system problems by only taking individual components into consideration without giving attention to the interactions and interrelations among various components that created the emergent properties of the system.

Thus, attention on the growth of individual components, without attention to distributional effects and harmonious development of various components, can create dysfunctional emergence of serious law and order situation and serious complaints and dissatisfaction among various sections of the population. These are systemic properties and can seldom be tackled by tackling individual components separately.

12. *Efficiency*

In the engineering sense, it is the ratio of output to input. Efficiency is relevant to the elements of the systems and is concerned with doing things right. In a team individual players may be evaluated by their individual efficiency. In the modern world, we try to maximize efficiency. In a reductionist analysis, if all elements are efficient, the system as a whole will be efficient. In systems approach we have seen that this may or may not be true. Thus, in a football team all eleven players may be very efficient, but the team does not win games. The emergent property of the team reflects in its effectiveness which is not very good as the team members do not combine well. Our stress in research on efficiency alone is not adequate.

13. *Effectiveness*

Effectiveness is linked with doing the right things. Effectiveness is concerned with the performance of the system as a whole and a system may not be effective even though the individual members may be efficient. Effectiveness is thus a property of the system as a whole. Effectiveness emerges out of efficient combination and arrangements of the elements. This is a systemic property and in any research study should receive adequate attention along with improvement of efficiency. Thus, improvement of efficiency in tackling individual healthcare problems may be needed but may not be adequate in improving the effectiveness of the healthcare system which will depend on the proper arrangement and interrelationships among various elements of the healthcare system.

14. *A purposeful system*

A system that selects ends as well as means and displays "will" is a purposeful system. Human beings are the most perfect examples of this system. All organizations are humanly contrived systems and these are also purposeful systems. Thus, a bank, a corporate organization, a hospital and a government department are all purposeful systems.

15. *An ideal-seeking system*

This is a system which is purposeful and which on achievement of any of its goals or objectives seeks another goal or objective which more clearly approximates its ideal.

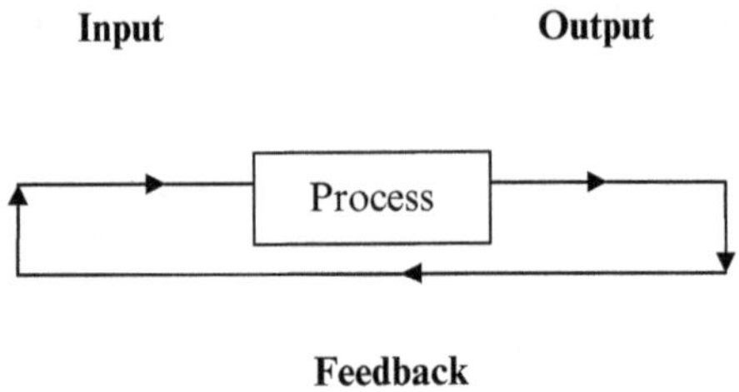

Fig. 5.1 Close loop coupling

Fig. 5.2 Serial coupling

16. *Control*

An element or a subsystem controls another element or subsystem or itself if its behavior is either necessary or sufficient for subsequent behavior of the elements or the subsystems or itself. This subsequent behavior is necessary or sufficient for the achievement of one or more of its goals. More simply, control is any method or procedure designed to influence the behavior of the system. Control is a double-edged sword. It involves ensuring doing things right and also ensuring doing right things. It is therefore relevant both for efficiency and effectiveness. Control consists of monitoring, diagnosing, and initiating corrective actions to ensure that the system moves in the charted path. In relation to control, we have to understand a few more terms.

17. *Feedback*

Control can be affected through feedback (see Fig. 5.1).

This is known as control through close-loop coupling. Control can be affected through the interaction of various methods of coupling. In engineering science apart from feedback coupling, the following two couplings are important:

1. Serial coupling
2. Parallel coupling

In serial coupling the output of one unit becomes the input of the second and the output of the second becomes the input of the third and so on. If some of these outputs are again fed back as the input of the previous stage, then it becomes feedback coupling and close-loop coupling (see Figs. 5.2 and 5.3).

Parallel Coupling Here, the same types of provisions are done in two or more parallel channels (see Fig. 5.4).

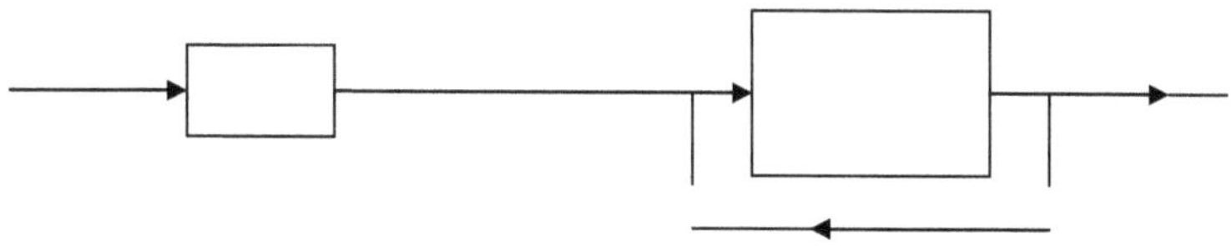

Fig. 5.3 Serial coupling – with feedback loops

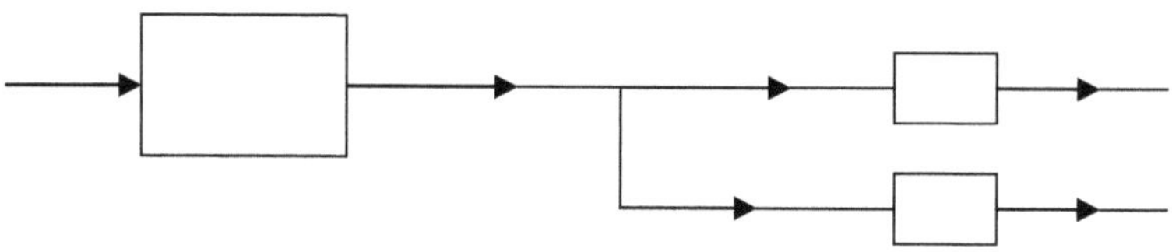

Fig. 5.4 Parallel coupling

In practice all types of couplings may occur simultaneously. In a large organization, the links among subunits typically form an exceedingly elaborate network. In this, again, some idea of effecting interaction and controlling interaction may be useful. Interactions take place because of the coupling. Sometimes interactions are transmitted through a common environment, for example, two or more branches of the same bank operating in the same urban area felt the necessity for interaction in preparing their performance budget. Moreover, some interactions may also stem from allocation of scarce resources. Even higher independent activities may draw upon the same pool of overall resources. Independent activities can be grouped into separate units.

The concepts and ideas of control and various types of control and coupling will be very useful in any study of manufacturing or service delivery systems. These can also be fruitfully applied in the study of networks and supply chains.

Further, concepts of control are very relevant in studying any socioeconomic system.

In any of our prescribed study, we should be careful to identify the control variable in the study; these aspects are related to the appropriate problem formulation discussed in detail in an earlier chapter.

Higher interacting activities should be grouped together. If interactions are kept to the minimum, then the design of the structure is facilitated. Structure and interactions are interrelated. It may be a golden rule to cluster activities in such a way that closely related activities are hierarchically near to each other. Weekly interrelated activities can be separately grouped. Unfortunately this principle is often difficult to apply in practice

In addition to the concepts above, we must also understand about certain terms in relation to systems methodology. These are given in the following section.

18. *Reductionism*

In this method the problem is analyzed and dissected to minute elements and the elements are then studied. This is the normal method of scientific study, principally in physical sciences. After studying the elements, the properties of elements are combined to understand the total problem. However, this method of analysis ignores the synthetic analysis required to understand the whole system.

19. *Holism*

In this the study of elements itself may provide an insight regarding the behavior of the whole system. So we have an approach of holism in systems analysis. The holistic analysis describes the synthetic view of the system as a whole. As contrary to the commonly held belief that the holistic thinking is a new space age phenomenon, it may be noted that this is also a very old method of enquiry. The Hegelian method (1779–1831) regarded the whole of reality as a system. As such reductionism and holism are well accepted principles for scientific enquiry for a long time, and in each stage of systems analysis, we have to use both these methods. It will be necessary before we close this section to clarify ideas conveyed by two other terms: systematic and systemic.

20. *The systematic*

The systematic method of enquiry is nothing but an orderly way of inquiry. Any inquiry having a method or plan is systematic, whereas a systemic thinking is a capacity of being able to perceive the system in a given situation. There are no clear-cut methods of achieving this insight. Perhaps an effort to look to the system as a whole may help in developing the insight.

In all normal research methodologies, we give stress on analytical and systematic processes. As explained earlier, these are necessary but not adequate in tackling complex problems, where understanding the emergence and problems of the system as a whole is equally important. Thus, for a good research study, we require both analysis and synthesis, a combination of systematic and systemic approaches which combines reductionism along with holistic integration. We therefore further define analysis and synthesis.

21. *Analysis*

To divide the whole into subparts and to study and treat the parts separately is called analysis. Thus, in "analysis" something that we want to understand is first taken apart and then an attempt is made to understand the behavior of each part of the system separately. Understanding of the subparts of the system is then aggregated in an effort to explain the behavior or properties of the whole. Analysis of a system exposes its structure and explains how it works. It provides appropriate knowledge to make it work efficiently.

Analysis generally provides knowledge about the behavior/characteristics of the system but does not provide us understanding about linkages with other parts of larger systems.

22. *Synthesis*

In synthesis the part of the system/systems that we want to understand is first identified as a part of one or more major systems. Further, in synthesis, efforts are made to understand the function of the larger system/systems of which the system studied (whole) is a part. The understanding of the larger containing system is then desegregated to identify/specify the role and function of the system under study. Synthesis is concerned with the effectiveness of the system. To enable a system to perform effectively, we must understand it. We must be able to explain its behavior, and this requires being aware of its functions in the large system of which it is a part.

5.1.4 Some Basic Laws of Systems

A system if not adequately attended to tends to deteriorates. Systems entropy tends to increase, and systems tend to become more complex:

Law of Equifinality A system can reach an equal final position starting from some initial position by following alternative routes. This principle is very relevant in strategic corporate planning. Selection involves selecting the optimal route to reach the final position.

Law of Requisite Variety A system that contains variety can only be appropriately controlled with variety of controls. The same number of controls is needed as there are a number of varieties. This important law suggests the futility to control different situations/environments by uniform policies/strategies.

In any research study, these laws should be kept in mind in terms of selecting alternative research methodologies for achieving the desired result. Similarly, tackling different variables by the same principle may not be feasible, and the researcher must be willing to use different methods for tackling different conditions. Further for conducting a complex research study, a variety of skills, approaches, and resources may be needed. These should be identified and resources acquired before undertaking the complex study.

Thus, these laws should guide the research at every phase of a complex and difficult research study.

5.2 Tools and Techniques for Systemic Research

5.2.1 Hard and Soft Systems

Before we proceed to describe certain techniques, it may be useful to differentiate between hard and soft systems.

Hard systems study involves modeling real-world problems by using simulations and computers and techniques and tools of operational research and management science. Hard systems methodologies are generally useful for problems that can justifiably be quantified. Through hard systems methodology it is normally very difficult to incorporate intangible and unquantifiable variables (like policy options, culture, emotions, etc.). These variables, even though important, tend to be ignored and have marginal effects on final solutions. Thus, it often tends to ignore the role of motivation, loyalty and group dynamics in improving productivity.

Soft systems are those which cannot be easily quantified. Particularly people systems having multiple and conflicting frames of reference are seldom tackled through hard systems methodologies. Soft systems methodologies are useful in understanding motivations, view points and interactions and also in getting insights into qualitative and quantitative factors. This methodology can deal both with the qualitative and quantitative dimensions of a problem situation. These methodologies were first promoted by Professor Peter Checkland of Lancaster University.

For conducting research study of real-world problems, it may be pertinent to mention that real-world problems contain both quantifiable and nonquantifiable variables, and both are important in arriving at a proper solution. Thus, along with scientific research methodologies and methodologies of hard system, we require application of soft systems methodologies and methods of qualitative research.

5.2.2 Steps in Soft Systems Methodology

Soft systems method is based on application of systems thinking in bringing about better understanding and insights into an unstructured complex problem situation. Some of these methods have been discussed while discussing problem formulation methods. Generally soft systems methodology consists of seven steps. The *first step* is concerned with the description of the problem situation. Here, we explore the general area of the problem that interests us. Let us take an example of a study of sustainable improvement of the economic conditions of poor tribal population in a backward area. Here, we have to first define the boundaries of the geographical areas under study and also population groups whose improvement we are looking for. We should then explore the meaning of improvement and sustainability. In exploring these issues, the following things must be understood:

Social/economic structure of communities
Processes and cultures
Overall climate in the area
Peoples' behavior
Issues that concern people
Conflicts that may surface

The *second step* is to put the above in some pictorial form. If these are expressed in the form of some diagram, it may help in further understanding.

The *third step* will be to identify and define the relevant system. Here, we may have to clearly define the concepts of improvement, culture, backward area and sustainability. In arriving at acceptable root definitions, we can consult with the local people and other experts.

The *fourth step* is to develop the model – a representation of the problem of the real world either through mathematical, logical, or graphical methods.

The *fifth step* is a checking device where we check the model structure with the real world. This can be done by unstructured discussion or structured questioning/developing scenarios by varying assumptions and conditions.

The *sixth step* consists of determining desirable and feasible interventions to bring the desirable transformations.

At this stage, the process is no longer sequential, and we suggest one method of intervention, assess its effects logically, discuss with the concerned groups and experts, modify the intervention, and proceed in the same way till we approach to solutions which are acceptable, feasible, and desirable.

The *seventh step* consists of actions to improve the situation. Again the methodology may revolve toward redefining, remodeling, and changing actions till satisfactory action programs are finalized.

It may be mentioned here that we here have sufficiently simplified the methodology of soft systems modeling. Methodological expertise can only be obtained through actual real-life problem solving. Nowadays large numbers of academic research projects are conducted by following soft systems methodologies; it is our view that no research methodology course can be considered complete without students being exposed to the ideas of soft systems methodology. Interested students and readers may supplement and complement their knowledge by referring to texts and references mentioned at the end of the chapter.

As we have seen, many techniques used in soft systems methodology are for problem structuring and getting insights about processes and systems. Many diagrammatic techniques can be helpful in the effort. In the rest of the section, we give details of some of the diagrammatic techniques.

5.2.3 *Techniques of Soft Systems Methodology*

We briefly enumerate the various techniques useful for systems analysis and soft systems study in the context of the study of organizations' social and management systems. The various techniques available have been grouped into two:

(a) Diagrammatic techniques
(b) Non-diagrammatic techniques

Here, we basically concentrate on diagrammatic techniques.

Diagrammatic Techniques These techniques are used in the analysis of human-activity systems. The techniques depend on the approach adopted for analysis. Approaches may be as follows:

5.2.3.1 The Pragmatic–Historical Approach

The human-activity system learns from its experience. As it grows, its activity set changes and the structure also changes. Organizations thus evolve over many years. Analysis of this evolution is very vital for any study of organizational problems. In order to study the organizational problem of Indian banks, it may be seen that most of the banks have structurally (formal and informal) evolved through time in a different manner and this aspect (which is often referred as organizational culture) has to be understood and studied before specific organizational studies can be taken up.

One can use descriptive verbal language for depicting historical growth; however, to obtain a quick view of the growth, some diagrammatic representation always helps. No specific method is available. What specific diagram will be drawn is left to the imagination of the analyst.

5.2.3.2 The Activity or Material Processing Approach

The basis of most human activities is the use of resources to meet ends. Usually a system takes certain materials (as inputs from outside itself) and converts them into outputs and services for which there is demand. Here the technique of drawing "flow-block diagram" is used (see Fig. 5.5).

In drawing a "flow-block diagram," it is very important to be consistent in the use of symbols and conventions. Wherever necessary, key to symbols used should be provided.

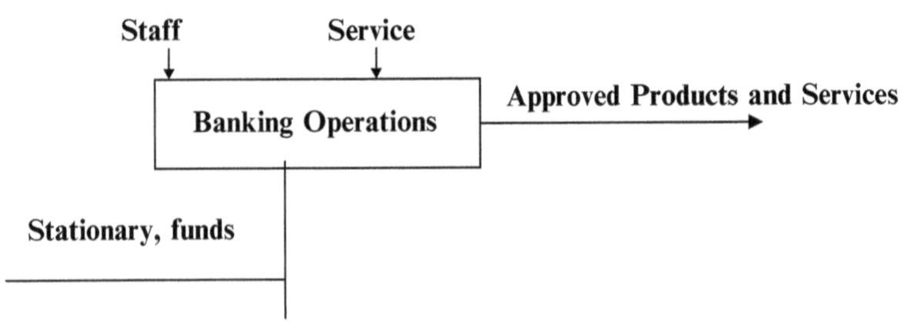

Fig. 5.5 Flow-block diagram (Note: *Plain arrow* shows material transfer or flows. Words in *rectangular boxes* (blocks) represent activities or processes. *Broken arrow* shows the use of human resources)

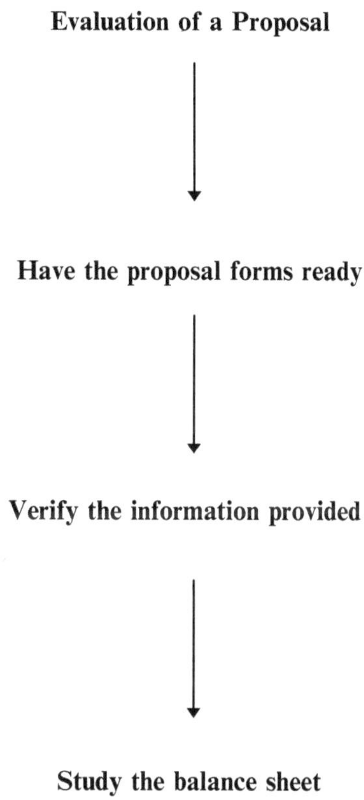

Fig. 5.6 Instruction sequence diagram

Instead of representing flows of materials, it can give sequences of activities and instructions to be taken in order (see Fig. 5.6).

The diagram above is not a flow-block diagram; the above is a process diagram. We should not mix up two types of diagrams because this can create confusion. It is particularly important to ensure that on the same diagram the same arrow representing the flow of materials and others representing control activities or simply the sequence of instructions are not used. For such purposes, different types of arrows have to be used and clear explanations or keys should accompany the use of different arrows.

The flow-block diagram is a basic analytical tool. The most obvious examples are in physical material processing, but as we have already seen, the same ideas may prove quite useful for service industries (say banks, insurance, or hotels) and for systems which process information.

5.2.3.3 The Social Structure of "Human Systems" View

Human activities are done by people. These people are grouped into human systems. Humans are related to each other in terms of authority, power, friendship, and so on

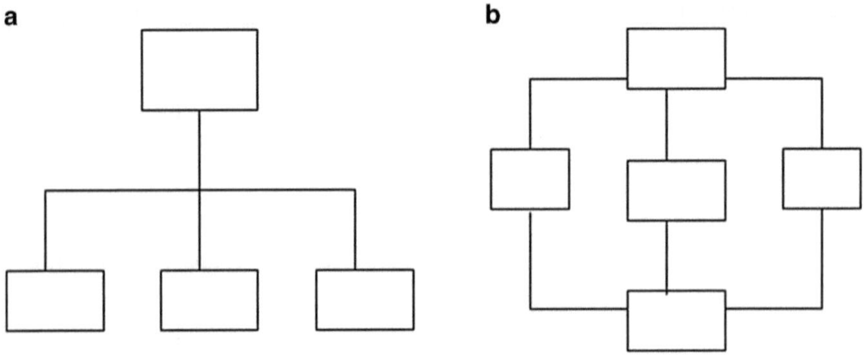

Fig. 5.7 (**a**) Hierarchy (**b**) Network

and are also connected through communication channels (informal and formal) and through the demand of the technological processes.

The total effect of all these relationships result in the formation of "social structure." In social structure diagrams, the elements of the diagrams are people (groups) and links usually represent both authority relationships and flow of information. The following two forms of a social structure diagram may be of interest:

An organization chart and family tree diagram are diagrams which represent hierarchal social structures. Hierarchal structures are related with concepts of *span of control*, *vertical line of communications*, etc. See Fig. 5.7a.

In Fig. 5.7b we have shown the network structure. Here the boxes represent the decision or information-processing nodes. These nodes are then connected to each other giving rise to a network of relationships.

5.2.3.4 The Total Systems Planning Approach

Activities and structures which are part of "human-activity" systems can be planned both internally within the organization and in relation to the external environment. We can look at the structural and functional subsystems specifically as "decision-making subsystem." Externally, the relationship of the system with other systems and influences of the environment on the system have to be studied.

The "decision-making subsystem" appraises both the internal and external situation, and on that basis, it plans for the whole system in relation to its environment.

This type of overall thinking may lead to two types of diagrams – systems maps and decision sequence diagrams.

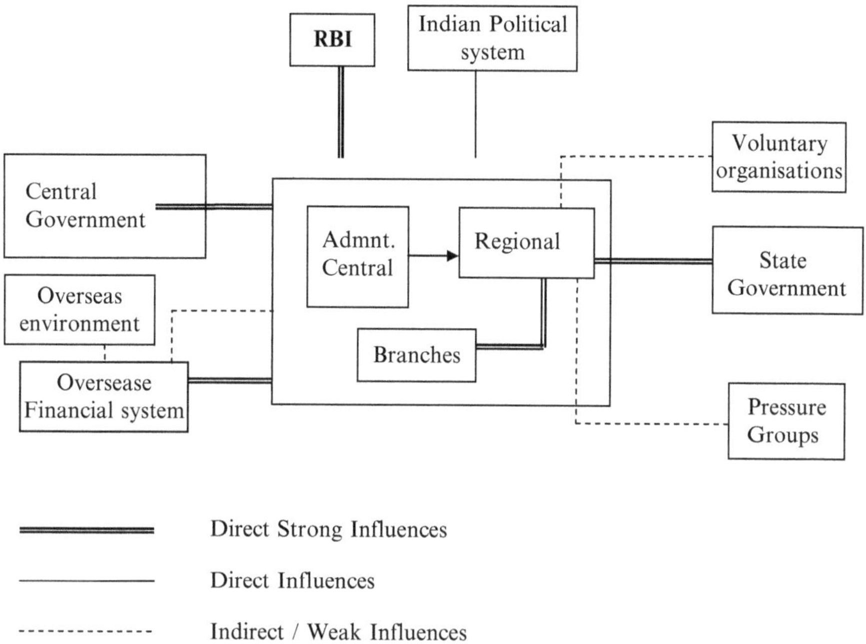

Fig. 5.8 Systems map of Indian commercial banks

5.2.4 Systems Map

Systems map are called "macro influence diagrams." It maps the influences affecting things on a macro scale.

In drawing such a diagram, we have to analyze the possible influences acting on the system. However, it is always difficult to include all influences. Some influences may be missed. It may be useful to prepare a list of all important influences. One can question the usefulness of drawing a diagram instead of listing the influences. It may be stressed here that a diagram shows the relationships of subsystems to the total system. A list does not show this (see Fig. 5.8). We have broadly drawn a systems map of a commercial bank in India in this diagram.

It is always advisable to draw a systems map in order to fix the boundaries and broad influence areas which have to be taken into consideration in studying a problem. Here, the thickness of lines indicates the degree of influence. Thus, to draw a systems map, the following steps may be adopted:

Step 1. Identify all environmental factors affecting the working of the systems understudy.

Step 2. Determine the degree of influence of the identified factors. Take only those influences which are relevant and which can affect the result of the study.

Step 3. Draw the systems map clearly showing the direction of influence by arrow and degree of influence by thickness of lines.

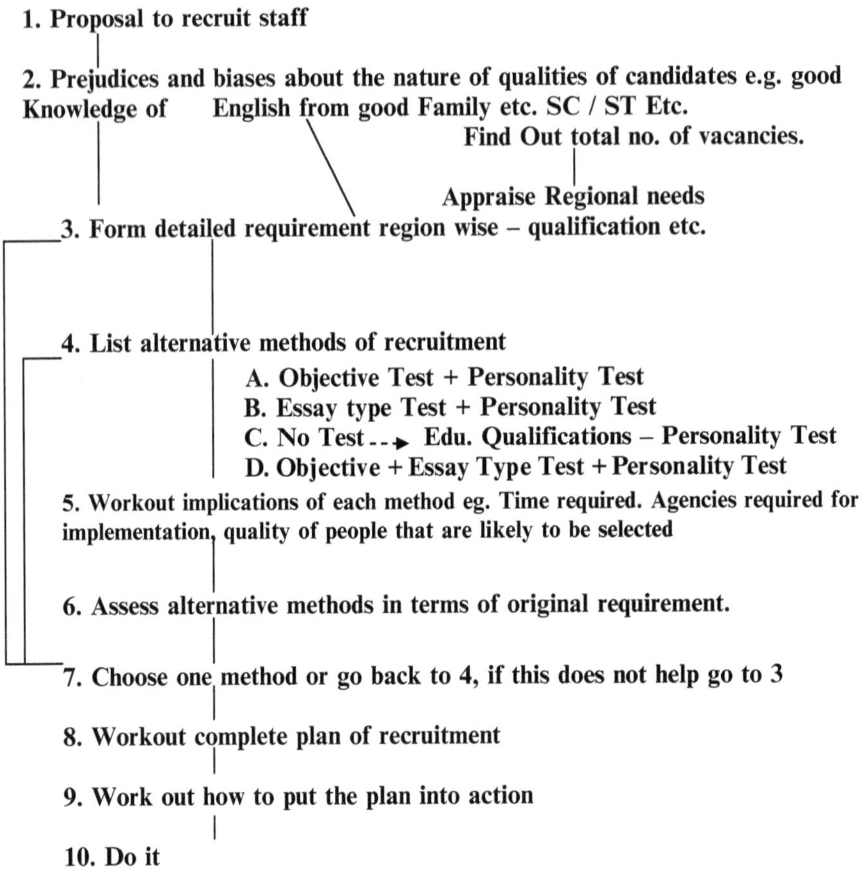

Fig. 5.9 Decision sequence diagram for a recruitment decision

5.2.4.1 Decision Sequence Diagram

A macro influence diagram or systems map is the first type of diagram that one can draw while adopting a Total Systems Planning Approach. The second type of diagram that we can draw is the decision sequence diagram. This type of diagram depicts the sequence leading to a decision or plan. These diagrams show information being processed in stages. See Fig. 5.9 where a decision sequence diagram depicts the various stages of activities for a recruitment decision. We show as an example the decision sequence diagram for recruiting staff. Here the first input is the proposal to recruit staff.

Decision sequence diagrams need not include every bit of details that are done for taking decisions, because that unnecessarily makes the diagram complicated without adding much to the understanding of the problem for the purpose of the analysis.

We have discussed about the four different types of systems diagrams for ease of reference; these are summarized below.

The ability to develop systems diagrams is invaluable in systems work in two ways. First, it concentrates the mind and assists the understanding of a situation through the process of having to order information and arrange it; and second, it can aid others to grasp quickly the essentials of a situation which one has to distill out of a mass of relevant and irrelevant details.

Trying to sort out and represent a new situation on paper seems to require imaginative new graphical ideas, whereas conveying the essentials of a situation to others requires a clear, disciplined use of particular convention. One has to use the familiar or variations of it to explain the unfamiliar. This is why the knowledge of particular types of diagrams is very useful although in any given situation the appropriate diagram is unlikely to be a pure version of any particular type.

1. The pragmatic–historical approach	←——→	No specific diagram types and the researcher is free to use his/her own imaginative ideas
2. The activity or material processing views	←——→	Flow-block diagrams
3. The social structure of "human systems" view	←——→	Social structure diagrams
4. The Total Systems Planning Approach	←——→	Systems maps: decision sequence diagrams

In addition to diagrammatic techniques, there are non-diagrammatic techniques which may be useful for analysis. We shall here discuss the techniques of developing of interaction matrices. Both diagrammatic and non-diagrammatic techniques may be used, these are mutually reinforcing in providing better insight in understanding the subsystems to be dealt with. Non-diagrammatic techniques are to be used at the end of a systems exercise.

5.2.5 *Interaction Matrices*

Interaction matrices are simple devices to understand the nature of interaction among various parts of a system or subsystem. These help to understand the problem in a specific situation. Though the solution is not guaranteed, the technique helps to develop a simple model of the system during the early phases of a study.

The following procedures may be followed in developing interaction matrices:

Step 1 Prepare a list of all the subsystems within the system, e.g. supposing we are studying the central office organization of a bank, various departments/cells in the central office may be the candidates for our listing. In case we are studying problems of rural healthcare, we have to study local sanitation, drainage, quality of available drinking water, environment and pollution, level of nutrition, economic condition and available healthcare facilities. All these interact with one another for a rural health situation.

Step 2 Arrange the components or subsystems in approximate order of importance (this order of importance is related to the purpose of the study in hand – there is no absolute ordering). Take the previous example. In reorganization of the central office perhaps according to our judgment, the department of operations may be the most important, second may be the priority sector advance, and third may be the personnel, and so on. In some other studies which are focused on personnel policy studies, the personnel department may be highest in importance. Say in healthcare, water quality, sanitation, and nutrition may be the order of importance in case of rural health.

Step 3 A simple matrix is then constructed: the procedure for construction of the matrix is as follows:

(a) All components/subsystems are listed in the same order as in step 2 both along the rows and column. The first component is in the first row and in the first column. Similarly, we have operations, priority, personnel administrative, and accounts and planning departments and each of these have subdepartments. So we have (say) OP_1, OP_2, OP_3, Pr_1, Pr_2, $Pers_1$, Adm_1, Adm_2, Plg_1, and Plg_2 arranged in the arrangement of the matrix will be as shown in Fig. 5.10.

Similar diagram can be drawn for a rural health study.

The matrix consists of rows and columns and cells which are to contain the interaction between the appropriate cells.

Before constructing the final interaction matrices, it is always useful to construct trial interaction matrices which can then be changed and modified to arrive at the final version. At this stage consultation with concerned decision-makers may be of help. As an example to determine the effect of the quality of drinking water on the prevalent diseases in the rural area, we have to discuss with public health experts.

Step 4 Having constructed the matrix, in each cell the links from a specific row to a specific column have to be indicated. For example, in the cell marked * we represent the links of OP to Pr. The links that pass in the opposition direction, that is, that pass from Pr to OP, are noted in the cell as **

In cells we can use signs or symbols, or we can use descriptions to denote interactions and their nature, etc.

Step 5 A "systems map" is drawn showing the main subsystems or components and the important links between them.

This is useful to find out whether all parts of the systems are adequately linked up. There may be discontinuities, and we may discover basic flaws in the systems structures.

Step 6 For major types of interaction in the matrix, steps 2–5 have to be repeated, till all major interactions are taken care of.

Thus, we have an interaction in respect of the flow of money, material, information, authority, etc.

	OP_1	OP_2	OP_3	Pr_1	Pr_2	$Pers_1$	Adm_1	Adm_2	Plg_1	Plg_2
OP_1				*						
OP_2										
OP_3										
Pr_1										
Pr_2	**									
$Pers_1$										
Adm_1										
Adm_2										
Plg_1										
Plg_2										

Fig. 5.10 Interaction matrix format

Step 7 Excluding all the links specified in step 6, steps 2–5 are repeated. This is a checking procedure to ensure no important link is missed.

5.2.6 Sociograms

Sociograms depict interactions among people. As an illustration consider the following example:

In a small organization consisting of seven workers, a question of discovering the appropriate supervisor from among those seven men arose. The investigator asked each worker to say which person in the group he would most like to work for. The results for the group of seven looked as below:

Person 1 named Person 3
Person 2 named Person 4
Person 3 named Person 1

Person 4 named Person 7
Person 5 named Person 3
Person 6 named Person 3
Person 7 named Person 2

The interaction matrix when drawn according to the step outlined (ordering according to the number preference obtained by each and arranged numerically where the same number of preference vote was obtained, we get: 3, 1, 2, 4, 7, 5, 5 and 6) will look as follows (Fig. 5.11).

We can construct the sociogram as shown below (Fig. 5.12).

	3	1	2	4	7	5	6
3		*					
1	*						
2				*			
4					*		
7			*				
5	*						
6	*						

Fig. 5.11 Interaction matrix (for supervision election problem)

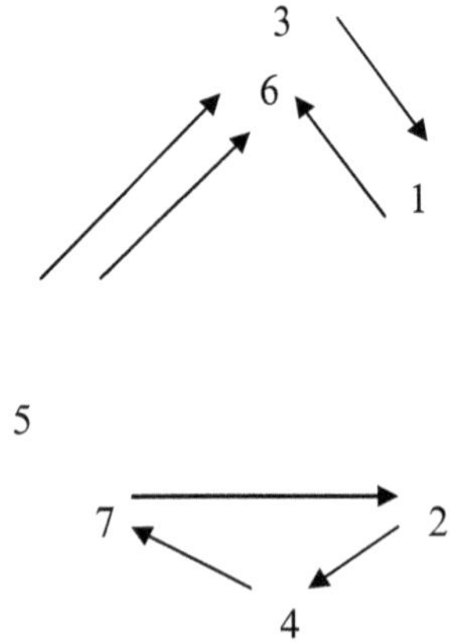

Fig. 5.12 Sociogram (*Arrow* (*solid line*) emerging from a number indicates the preference of that number)

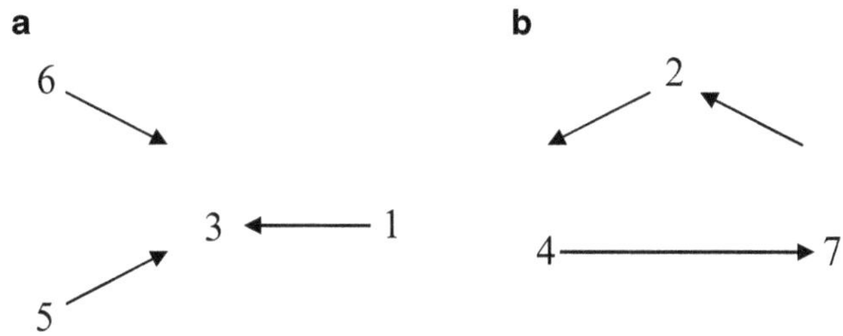

Fig. 5.13 Sociogram

To get a clearer view we can redraw the above sociogram (Fig. 5.13a, b).

It may be seen that persons 4, 2 and 7 form a clique among themselves and none of them is supporting 3. Thus, though apparently person 3 secures more preference votes, he may not be quite successful against the clique formation.

This diagram thus gives us better understanding of the situation than what we knew from simple counting of preferences. This is a simple illustration. The techniques discussed in this note may be fruitfully used in earlier stages of the study and specifically in getting better insight of the organizational processes and interactions.

5.2.7 Some Higher-Level Graphical Technique Like SODA, Cognitive Mapping and Strategic Choice Approach

5.2.7.1 SODA: Strategic Option Development Analysis

It can be used for solving complex messy problems and for strategy formulation. Thus, it can be very useful in any strategic research and in studying complex social or policy issues. For the students who want to do their doctoral research based on exploring feasible and applicable solutions to real-life organizational, managerial, and complex social problems, this technique may be found very useful. Exposure to this technique will be highly valuable to those who after the academic career want to be a part of an internal problem solving team in corporate organizations and want to take career options as consultants and advisors. In view of all these, we felt that it will not be proper in a modern textbook on higher-level research methodology to exclude an exposure to this very modern and useful technique.

SODA helps in structuring a messy complex problem; further it gives a new insight in understanding the various aspects of the problems under study and interactions of the components of the problem under study. It also helps in understanding the interrelationships of the system under study with various groups of stakeholders who will be affected by the proposed solution.

Generally SODA is complemented by the technique called Journey. Journey represents an acronym for jointly understanding reflecting and negotiating strategy. Let us take an example for the purpose of illustration. Any real-life problem of industrial location will involve the use of land for setting up industrial unit and related facilities. This will call for the diversion of the existing land from its present use for industrial purposes. The present use may be agricultural and the farmer owning the land may be completely dependent on that agricultural produce for sustainable living. By sacrificing the land for industrial use, the farmer will forfeit his/her means of livelihood. He/she will therefore be unwilling to part with the land unless suitably compensated for the loss of livelihood. Unless affected groups reach a consensus on land use or proposed diversion, the project may not at all be implemented. In India recent experiences into locating SEZ (special economic zones) in Maharashtra and locating the industry in Singur and Nandigram in West Bengal point out clearly the need for having appropriate methodologies for evolving negotiated consensus among all the affected and interested groups about the proposed land-use planning. Without such consensus the industrial development projects (just like Singur and Nandigram) may not see the light of the day. In reaching such consensus SODA or Journey may be highly useful.

In all such problems (SEZ location of industries, river valley projects, expressway construction, etc.), the aim should be to arrive at a consensus (rather than compromise). The process should generate active participation of all concerned groups and thereby these groups will have commitment toward the consensus solution arrived at.

SODA is particularly useful and applicable in the following situation:

- Consultants and researchers should be interested in working face to face with various groups of stakeholders. They try to influence the basic decision. Thus, in case of industrial location and land-use planning, the researcher has to personally interact face to face with all affected and interested groups. These groups may be affected whether positively or negatively.
- The researcher has to relate with a small number of significant personalities of concerned groups.
- The researcher/consultant will normally adopt a contingent or cyclical approach to working on the problem. The general approach is to proceed flexibly and experimentally from broad benefits to specific commitments. Thus, in an industrial location project, the researcher will present a map of future benefits of locating the industry and simultaneously will map the adverse effects of the transfer of lands and then will discuss various options of mitigation adverse effects so that consensus from the affected groups evolves over a period of time.
- Time and attention given by the researcher or consultant at this stage will save much disruption and distress later on, compared to what would have happened if the researcher concluded the location problem without going through the process of exploring a consensus.

There are four aspects to be considered in case of SODA techniques. These are (a) individual, (b) nature of the organization and social group, (c) method of conducting the consultancy or research, and (d) technologies or techniques used.

The approach is mainly based on subjectivism. Each group and its members have perceptions and subjective views of the real problem under consideration. By "cognitive mapping" these subjective views and perceptions are captured. A question arises – what is a cognitive map? A cognitive map is nothing but a model of a system of concepts used by the groups (affected groups or clients in consulting language) to communicate the nature of the problem. The model attempts to represent the meaning of the concepts by its relationship with other concepts through an action orientation. Thus, the concept of transfer of fertile land to industrial use and its effects on the loss of production and consequent loss of income have to be related to the gain of employment opportunities and other compensation along with the overall progress and economic improvements of the area through industrial development. All effects as expressed by groups are graphically represented through cognitive mapping and therefore all concerned people can see the meaning and effects of their subjective perceptions and because of this, negotiation and discussion can become more meaningful and consensus may often be achieved by flexible adjustment of action programs.

The SODA approach is aimed at producing a device that can be used to facilitate managing "messiness" of the decision situation and reach a definite consensus-based solution. Here, presenting appropriate views, analyzing relationships, and communicating through languages (verbal/non verbal) and specific tradeoffs can be attempted, and this can help in arriving at a negotiated solution. The process can be represented by the diagram as shown in Fig. 5.14.

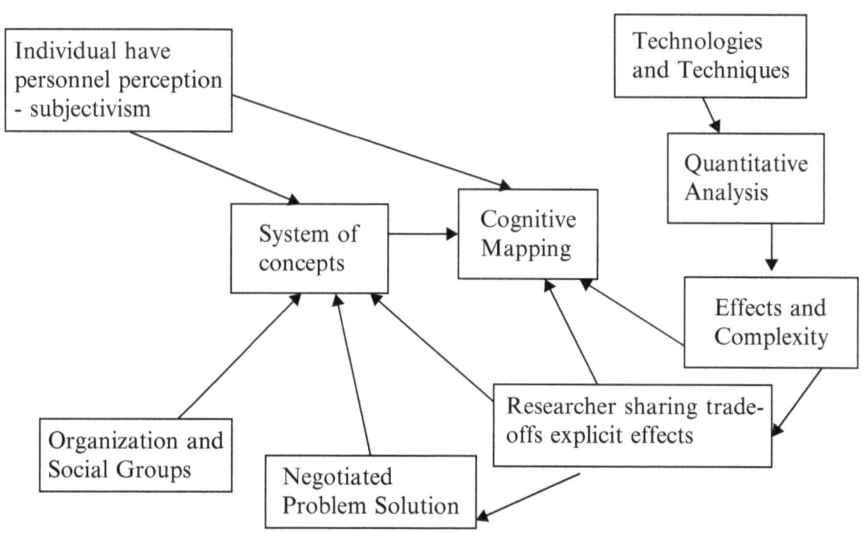

Fig. 5.14 SODA

This is a much simplified diagram of the total process. Basically perceptions of various individuals and groups are mapped; effects are analyzed both quantitatively and qualitatively. After that, tradeoffs are clearly specified in a language understood by all concerned. New concepts are often generated through mutual exchange of ideas and perceptions.

5.2.7.2 Cognitive Mapping

Cognitive mapping exists within the problem description in the SODA framework. It is nothing but a method of mapping a person's thinking within the field of psychological research or perception. Figure 5.15 shows a small cognitive map as an illustrative example (Eden 1987).

Figure 5.15 illustrates the urge of affected people for positive action to correct the problem of arsenic in drinking water. The above map can be further expanded to include more perceptions regarding possible action programs. The process of cognitive mapping thus helps to identify the people/organization to be involved in solving a real problem of the modern complex world.

The best way to develop a "cognitive map" is to obtain from the affected group a clear perception of their goals and objectives. After that steps are identified to deal with various groups and objects to achieve that goal.

Cognitive maps generally clarify goals, constraints, and options. Such maps also help in identifying actors that can help with the solution of the problem.

5.2.7.3 Strategic Choice Approach

In any real-world problem situation, if we want to resolve the problem effectively, we have to explicitly consider the various uncertainties involved. Even in solving academic-oriented problems, consideration of relevant uncertainties is very important.

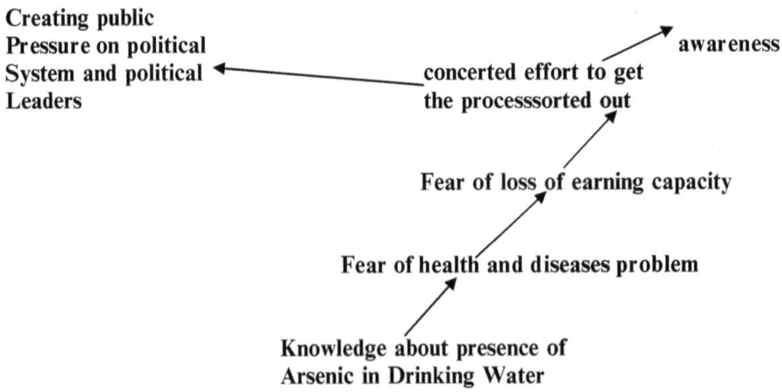

Fig. 5.15 Example of cognitive mapping for the problem of arsenic in drinking water

In the strategic choice approach, three types of uncertainties are identified. These are:

1. Uncertainties regarding the environment
2. Uncertainties about the guiding value
3. Uncertainties about choices and related agendas

Getting a clear idea about these at the beginning of any important research study will significantly help in mapping out future programs for solving the research problem. It helps in avoiding a lot of confusions later.

The strategic choice approach consists of the following steps: (1) a solution package and its action programs are designed in solving the problem. (2) The package is then given specificity by giving the details of designs and concrete shapes toward solution packages. (3) The effects of action programs are then assessed in terms of various preferences and uncertainties. (4) These were then compared with the desired outcome. The comparison is done on the basis of a likely outcome in following a specific action package. After this comparison if necessary, modifications are introduced in the action program package on the basis of the results of such comparison.

Following this method, the final package is selected. Such selection will be better than other available action packages. The final option (action) package selected conceptually in this fashion at the beginning of a study may be very useful in solving real-world problems. The public choice approach therefore will be useful in solving complex strategic problems.

Figure 5.16 illustrates the process of the strategic choice approach.

The design of option programs is based on issues and detailed shapes/structures of these problems and issues. However, a particular design and detailed shapes and structures can have effects on issues.

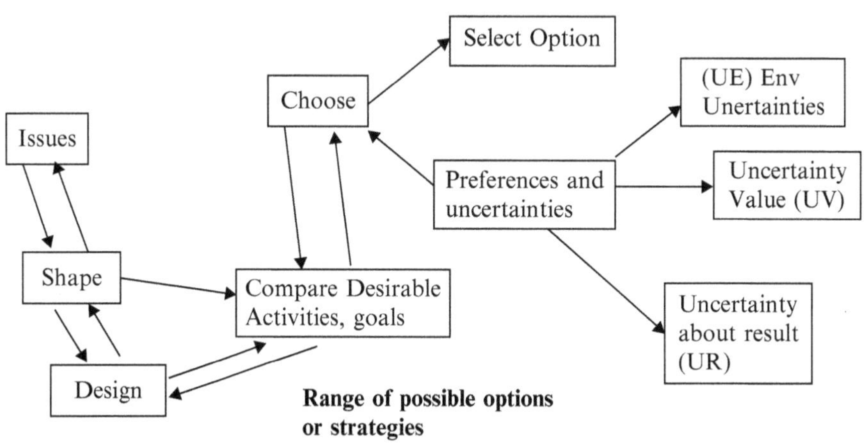

Fig. 5.16 Description of strategic choice approach

Selection is an iterative process. The process takes into consideration uncertainties involved. This is very important as all options have results in the future which are uncertain.

Selection of option cannot therefore be made sequential. Comparisons and modifications are carried out till an option likely to be successful is selected.

We have discussed a few techniques leading to a better understanding and better problem solution. These are brief descriptions; the idea is to expose the readers to these new series of ideas and techniques. Techniques are fairly straightforward, though the application will require practical exposure. Interested readers can gain more information by going through the references detailed in the end of the chapter.

In Part III of this chapter, we briefly discuss a few case studies as illustrations of application.

5.3 Case Examples

5.3.1 Case Studies

We briefly describe a few real-life case studies where soft systems methodology and combined soft and hard systems methodologies were used:

5.3.1.1 Case Study – 1

A problem of improvement of decision and information system in a government organization had to be resolved. Various decision systems and subsystems and roles and functions of different departments and subdepartments were identified. Actual details of information used, information flow, and decision problems were obtained. However, whereas some of the above were based on hard systems analysis methods, the role perceptions by different decision-makers and executives and perceptions of their information and resource needs were partly objective and partly subjective. Here, principles of cognitive mapping were found useful in mapping actions and perceived goals by different actors, and by explicit and open discussion, a consensus on an integrated picture regarding the roles, functions, decision allocation, and information needs emerged. Once the need was evident, the design of the relevant information system and related cost–benefit analysis of options were relatively logical and hard systems based. Thus, while for problem solving and getting insights into the problem we used soft systems methodology, for selecting the options of design we used a combination of soft and hard systems methodologies. All relevant aspects and impacts were considered, so it was based on the total systems intervention which included the restructuring of decision allocation, resource allocation and redefinition of roles, restructuring power, and authority structure. According to the new perception, training and cultural changes needed for making a system feasible were also prescribed. Thus, in systems approach no partial solution is acceptable. Results obtained were highly satisfactory, and since in the initial stage perceptions of all concerned executives and employees were used and understood, there was better profiling of the problem mapped. This also helped in soliciting better commitment of all during implementation.

5.3.1.2 Case Study – 2

This was a case study for improving economic conditions of backward areas which are forest infested, having no irrigation facilities and people are mostly tribal and scheduled castes and having no modern skills and attitudes. Standard solutions to such problem have been sought through a process of industrialization. The idea is to bring a large-scale industry in that area, which hopefully would be able to generate employment. The people of the area will be gainfully employed, and as economic conditions improve, education and health will improve, and the backward area will become progressive. This idea of creating a mother industry to develop an area had been adopted on a large scale for developing backward areas of an economy. By and large this strategy had failed everywhere. Basically it had failed because of a lack of systemic insight. The new industry based on modern technology would demand skills and sophistication from its employees which were not basically available in the local population; as a result, the employment generation would benefit the outsiders. Many people from outside the area would come to the area, and as a result, congestion and pollution would increase. A large chunk of local land resources would be used for the location of the industrial unit/units and to create townships for convenience of the outsiders. The local produce which used to be locally consumed were now quite inadequate to meet the demand and trade developed resulting in rising price for locally available goods and services. Poor people who did not get employment in the new factory, whose landed resources had been used for locating the industry or township, found it very difficult to survive, so instead of the improvement of the quality of life, the quality of life of the indigenous tribal and scheduled caste population deteriorates. Our research team from the study of literature and past experiences was convinced that the mother industry concept of creating large-scale industrialization was no longer a solution to the problem of improvement of backward areas and poor quality of life of local population. The team therefore had intensive participation and discussion regarding the changes that local people wanted and the way they wanted to bring about such changes. These discussions were based on previously discussed strategic choice methods and application of cognitive mapping techniques. These gave a much more clear idea of goals of the development of backward area and environmental uncertainties as perceived by the local population.

Discussions were also conducted with sociologists, technologists, development experts, and others and their perceptions were also mapped. On the basis of such two-way open discussions between the research team/experts and local population, a consensus regarding goals and available options emerged.

It became quite clear that the development of the area should be done in phases. The first phase should be planned based on the available skill locally, concentrating on productive activities which they (local people) can undertake with confidence and can perform well. Thus, stage 1 of development should be based on biomass generation and afforestation activities. By creating forest-based activities, employment could be generated and the local population would be directly benefited through employment in activities related to afforestation. They had adequate knowledge and skills for such activities. This would increase purchasing power, and demand for goods and services would increase. Slowly steps should be taken for skill improvement and education at the local level. The next step of development would be to create production activities based on forest-based products and wood-based manufacturing, production of simple tools, wooden furniture, toys, etc.

In the next stage when the local population would be skilled and sophisticated, they could then undertake activities related to production of chemicals, etc., from wood and forest products. The local population would evolve into skilled artisans and after that tiny/small/medium industrial units could be established and the local group could derive adequate benefit from such industrialization.

Thus, systems approach suggests better understanding of local needs and local capabilities. It is also necessary to understand that there is a hierarchy in the process of industrialization which should evolve in stages. The solution suggested and overall framework developed followed soft systems methodology; however, in stagewise optimization of resource, an allocation was attempted by adopting hard systems methodology. Interested readers may get further details of this case study in Bandyopadhyay and Datta[6].

Stages of development strategy for backward area development are shown in Figs. 5.17, 5.18, and 5.19.

5.3.1.3 Case Study – 3

This is a comprehensive research study undertaken as a doctoral research but rooted to a real development planning of a block (a combination of a group of villages). The process consisted of household-level planning which needed intense participation and understanding of issues of poverty and rural developments. At this stage, soft systems methodologies of systemic map, interaction matrix, and cognitive mapping were used. Land-use planning, energy balance planning and water balance planning for the generation of economic activities in the areas were undertaken.

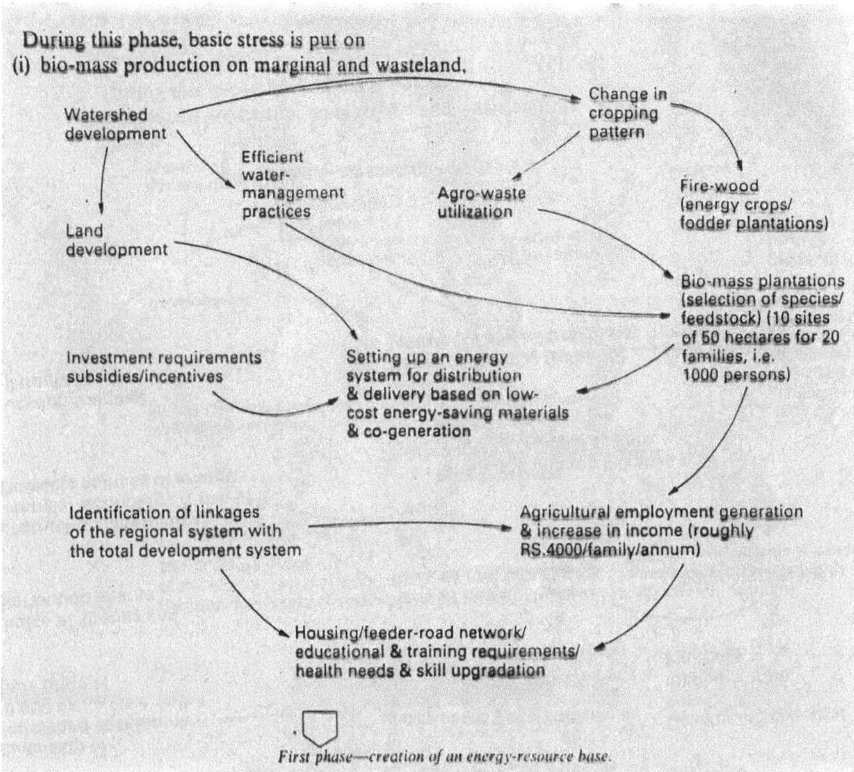

Fig. 5.17 Backward area development – first phase

Various options, their effects, tradeoffs, and uncertainties were demonstrated for the options available, and consensus regarding various aspects of balance was obtained from all concerned. The individual model of balance of resources used programming models of optimization of resource use. These required application of quantitative hard systems modeling methods.

Figure 5.20 depicts the detail of program for poverty alleviation and employment generation.

The various components and their interlinkage are shown in Fig. 5.21 where the integrated framework is shown.

These three case studies discussed here deal with real-life problems having sufficient conceptual depth to be classified as a high-level academic research. The methodologies followed in the case studies are a mix of soft and hard systems methodologies. The methodologies combine analysis with synthesis and holism and reductionism.

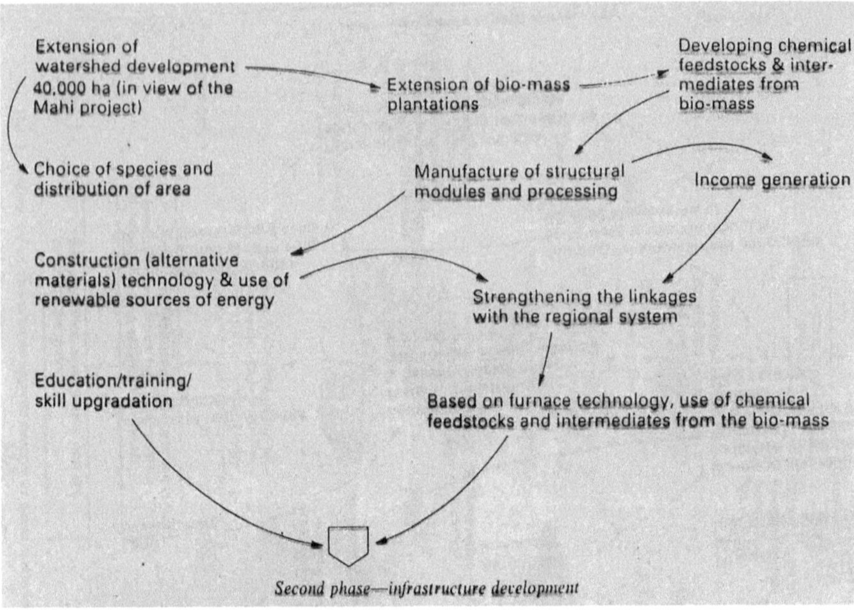

Fig. 5.18 Backward area development – second phase

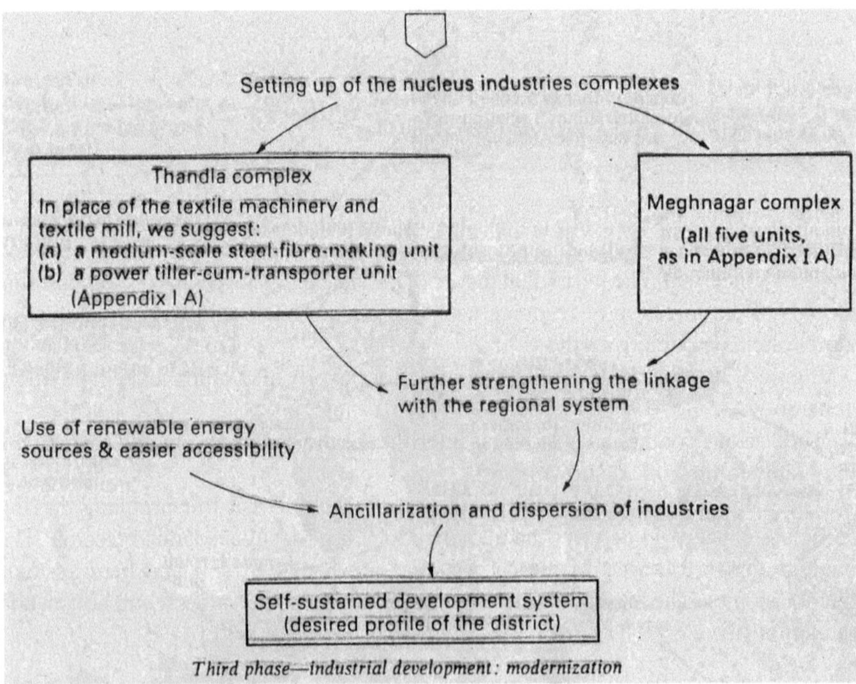

Fig. 5.19 Backward area development – third phase

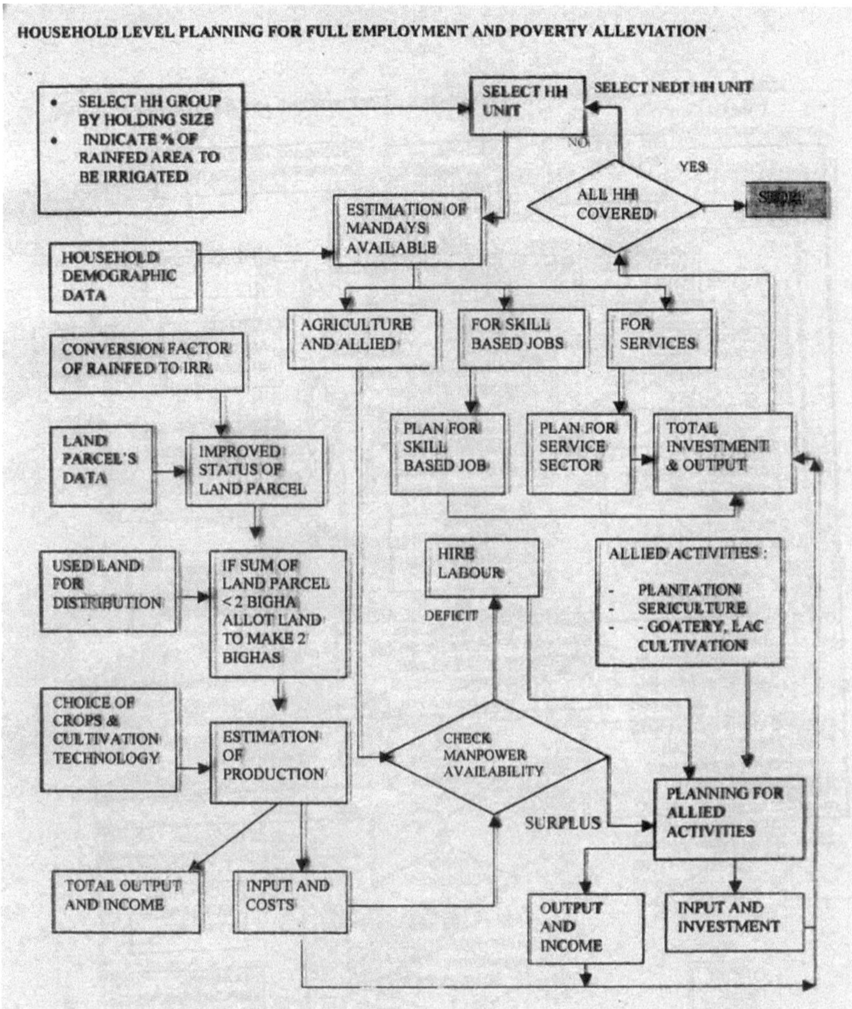

Fig. 5.20 Depiction of program for poverty alleviation and employment generation

5.4 Summary

There are large numbers of case studies undertaken by the author, and many case studies are also available in published literature describing the application of soft systems approach along with hard systems methodologies. Readers who are interested in pure academic type of researches should realize that most academic research problems should be properly defined and issues to be resolved should be adequately understood. For these discussions with guides, peer groups and experts

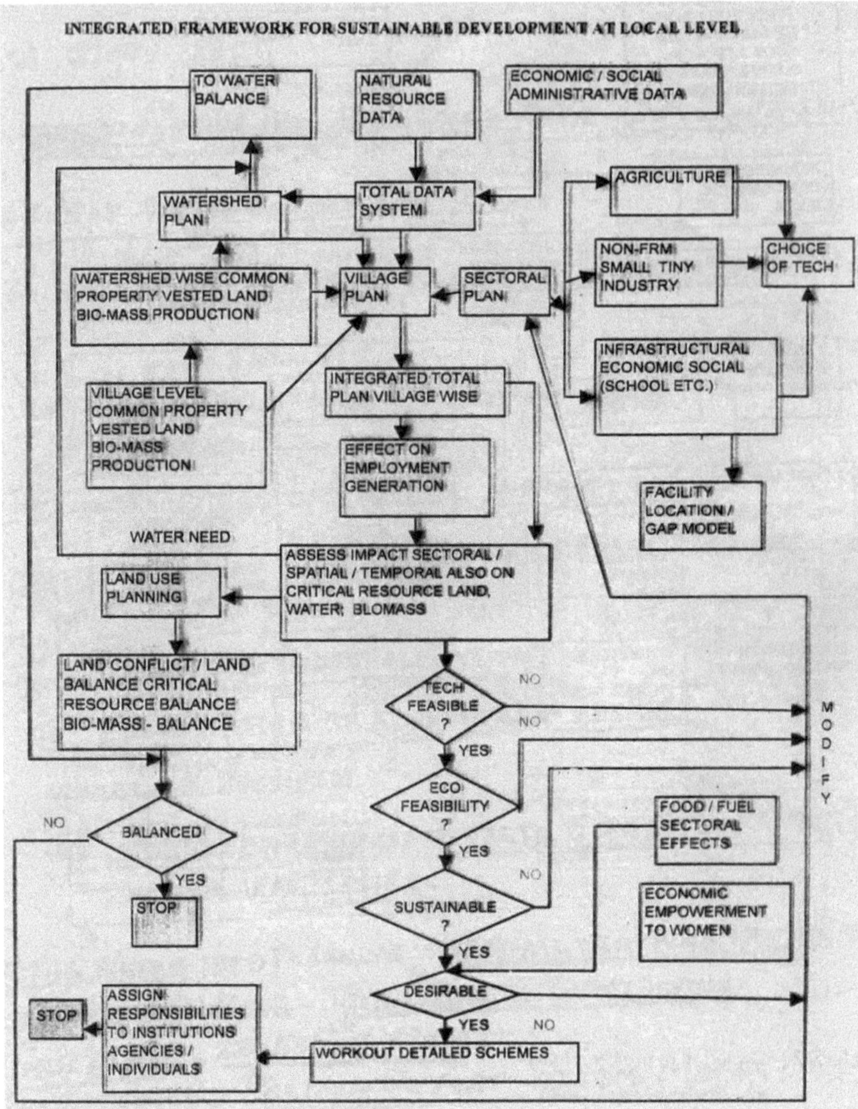

Fig. 5.21 Integrated framework for sustainable development at local level

may be useful. In doing this, the standard questionnaire method is not adequate and techniques like strategic approach and cognitive mapping can be fruitfully applied. However, more and more such research should be based on some real-world problems. Most management, social science, and organizational research should benefit immensely by following the methodologies described above.

References

Ackoff RL, Emery FE (1972) On purposeful systems. Tavistock, London
Bandyopadhyay R, Datta S (1989) Strategy of backward area development. J Oper Res Soc 9: 737–751
Centre for Applied System Analysis (1996) A sustainability energy future for India. CASAD research report, Pune
Checkland P (1981) Systems thinking, system practice. Wiley, Chichester
Eden C' (1987) Cognitive mapping. Eur J Oper Rev Res 36:1–13
Haines YY, Kindlers I, Plate EJ (1987) "The process of water resource project planning – a system approach". UNESCO, Paris
Rosenhead J, Mingers J (eds) (2001) Rational analysis for a problematic world revisited. Wiley, Chichester Ackoff RL and Emery FE (1972) "On purposeful Systems" Tavistock, London

Chapter 6
Qualitative Research and Its Application in Organizational Management and Social Research

R. Bandyopadhyay

6.1 Objectives

In Chap. 4, we have discussed the importance of problem formulation. We also discussed various methods of problem structuring. In Chap. 5, we discussed various aspects of systems approach and detailed how soft systems methodologies should be used to explore and understand complex and messy real-life problems. In this chapter, we further extend our discussion to include a detailed exposition of qualitative research methods which can be used effectively in getting better insight about the nature of the complex real-life problems. These methodologies along with soft systems methodologies and systems approach may be fruitfully used in organizational, management, and social research. Further, both qualitative and quantitative methods can be used to solve such problems. The present chapter will therefore attempt to fulfill the following objectives:

- To appreciate the need for qualitative research and in this connection to recognize the importance of qualitative research along with other methods (systems approach, quantitative methods, etc.) in solving real-life complex organizational, managerial, and social problems
- To adequately understand the basic characteristics of qualitative research and its difference from quantitative research
- To get a reasonable understanding of the various tools, techniques, and methodologies of qualitative research

R. Bandyopadhyay (✉)
Former Director, National Institute of Bank Management, Pune, India

Visiting Research Professor, University of Manchester, Manchester, UK

Present Affiliation: Hon. Director, CASAD, Pune, India
e-mail: rangband@gmail.com

D.S. Hegde (ed.), *Essays on Research Methodology*,
DOI 10.1007/978-81-322-2214-9_6

- To understand specifically various aspects of ethnographic research as an essential component of qualitative research
- To understand the need and applicability of mix of methods and in this connection understand related issues of triangulation
- To basically understand various ways of collection, recording, coding, and interpretation of data in the case of qualitative research
- To appreciate the importance, advantages, and disadvantages of case study research as part of qualitative research
- To understand the need for action research in organizational, managerial, and social studies

6.2 What Is Qualitative Research? Why Is It Needed?

Qualitative research has been described as a method of enquiry normally employed in different social science disciplines. Today, it is increasingly being used for market research and management and organizational studies. Use of qualitative research is found to be very useful in social problems, problems for decision-making in respect of development and in policy studies. Simply defined, qualitative research basically means nonmathematical (nonquantitative) data collection based on certain attributes. It therefore uses graphics, historical analysis, observation of behavior, and decision-making styles as sources of data. Qualitative analysis is necessarily more problem specific and often personal compared to standardized statistical analysis present in quantitative research. Researchers who are not comfortable with mathematics and statistics may suggest that the most important aspect of research is qualitative research. On the other hand, persons who are quantitatively oriented can condemn qualitative research as nonscientific, subjective, and full of bias. Both these views are extremes.

No research method whether qualitative or quantitative can be declared as inherently useless, wrong, or right. Both methods are useful in certain aspects and have their specific applicabilities in a research study. They fulfill different purposes. To insist that any good research study must follow quantitative methods is to insist on getting partial, half-baked solutions. Stressing on quantitative methods only, we tend to ignore/neglect many important but non-quantifiable variables and many behavioral aspects which significantly affect the ultimate research result. Thus, in a study of improvement of manufacturing efficiency, quantitative factors like working hours, quantifiable incentives, hours of training, degree of supervision, etc. are only considered. We thereby tend to neglect the effect of motivation and leadership styles and their effects on commitment and loyalty. These factors play significant effects on the improvement of efficiency of manufacturing products apart from various quantifiable tangible factors.

Similarly, to insist that only relevant behavioral aspects are important and to neglect factual aspects of facilities, infrastructure, trainings, incentives, etc. will also be very erroneous. We need to understand trend and change in relevant quantitative data; these may be quite useful.

So basically in any research study, selection of method/methods will depend on the nature of the problem and the situation under study and the nature of questions being explored through the study. In many cases, qualitative analysis will be more relevant, and in some other cases, quantitative analysis will be more important. There are many problem areas/situations where both qualitative and quantitative methods have to be used in the right combination.

Having thus briefly discussed about usefulness of both methods, it may be pertinent to discuss some distinguishing characteristics of qualitative research that make it different from quantitative methods. After that, we may also attempt to summarize areas of application where qualitative methods will be useful.

6.2.1 Distinctive Characteristics of Qualitative Research as Compared to Quantitative Research

Following are some of the distinctive characteristics of qualitative research as compared to quantitative research (Silverman and Marvasti 2008):

1. In general, in the case of qualitative research, research issues are purposefully selected according to the condition whether or not the issues selected typically represent certain characteristics or contextual locations. Thus, in studying managerial styles, decision-making behavior under different conditions and under different local pressures are selected purposefully to gain better understanding of decision-making under different situations and contexts and of methods of managing under pressures.
2. In qualitative research, the researcher is involved in the problem. It is difficult to remain neutral during the process of the study. The research process is not completely predetermined; the process evolves as the study progresses; thereby, the researcher gets more and more involved. Thus, in the case of qualitative research, the qualitative researchers are often encouraged to reflect on their roles in their research process. Such roles should be made clear while making analysis of the facts obtained through observation.
3. Qualitative research uses a wide variety of forms of data; however, its focus is on language, signs, meanings, emotions, body language and related aspects.
4. Qualitative research is generally based on holistic principles. It interprets the totality of effects and situations without studying individual components. In quantitative research, individual elements are studied in a reductionist and isolationistic fashion.
5. Holistic and subjective interpretations do not however obviate the need for rigor and transparency in qualitative approach.
6. The most important aspect of qualitative research in social science is the need for exploration. It is used for pre-/post-understanding of a problem in depth and for subsequent hypothesis generation for the problem to be studied. These exploratory studies may often be useful in puzzling quantitative research. Thus,

in an organization with highly qualified employees and good infrastructure, the market share may decline progressively. This is quite puzzling; qualitative research may explore the reason for such puzzling, quantitative results. It may find out inability to adapt to change with changes in customer expectation which is a cultural issue and lack of organizational cohesion due to leadership failure as reasons for this puzzling quantitative result. Thus, qualitative study may prima facie establish the types of hypothesis to be further tested (confirmed/ejected) by further research both qualitative and quantitative.

7. While data obtained from quantitative research are precise, reliable, and amenable for statistical and mathematical analysis, data obtained through qualitative research are usually difficult to depict and display in mathematical terms.
8. Qualitative research is more useful in understanding how and why certain outcomes were achieved (not on what was achieved). It is useful in getting answers to questions like (a) Is expectation reasonable? (b) Do processes cooperate as expected? (c) Do key players perform their duties as expected?
9. Qualitative research has the advantage of allowing diversity of responses and also to adapt to new development during the research process.
10. Qualitative research because of its evolutionary nature can be more expensive and time-consuming. Quantitative techniques are well defined; data sets are predesigned methods, are standardized, and are not evolutionary. These can therefore produce more distinct cost-effective timely results compared to qualitative research.
11. Qualitative research may use different methods for data collection and data interpretation like participant observation, historical study, ethnographic study, structured and unstructured interviews, focus groups, case study methods, and action research.

    We shall discuss some of these in detail in subsequent sections of this chapter.
12. Qualitative research stresses on knowing the why and how of social matters as compared to what, when, and where in the case of quantitative methods.
13. It normally works with a small number of cases; sample size is less.
14. In qualitative research study, a few aspects are studied in depth instead of studying a wide variety of aspects.

6.2.2 Application Areas of Qualitative Research

We have already mentioned some application areas of qualitative research. In modern, complex, globalized environment, some amount of understanding of intangible factors and qualitative dimensions will always be required. However, qualitative research is initially used to be associated with research in the discipline of sociology or anthropology. However, since 1980s, qualitative research methods started being used in many other disciplines.

Its application became quite significant in (1) educational studies, (2) social work study, (3) management studies, (4) police service studies, (5) study on nursing and hospital management, (6) study on management of change, (7) organization study, (8) women study, (9) prison life study, (10) disability study, (11) impact study on community of mega projects, (12) marketing and cultural study, (13) study on information, (14) study on decision-making, (15) communication study, (16) industrial management study, (17) labor study, (18) studies on various aspects of sustainable development, (19) political science, (20) psychology, and (21) pilot studies for carrying out larger quantitative study (Jankowiz 1993).

The list above is illustrative and not exhaustive. In short, in most areas of social, organizational, administrative, and political research, qualitative research methods are being increasingly used to get a better insight of the problems, to formulate hypothesis to be tested, and to generate evolutionary solutions.

As the application of qualitative research expanded, their methodologies also got enriched by the addition of newer methods, techniques, and instruments. Traditional, historical, participative, and ethnographic methods were aided with methods of case study and action research.

6.3 Models and Languages of Qualitative Research

In order to study the diverse methods of qualitative research, it is necessary to have some sort of classification of the various methods and languages used. On the basis of such classification, experts have suggested four types of models of qualitative research. These four types are as follows:

1. *Naturalism*

This model of qualitative research gives more stress on the factual characteristics of the object of study. Thus, in a prison study, it will study the processes and practices of prison, the routine behavior of inmates, timings of various activities, regulations, prison rules and codes, etc. It will not be concerned with emotions and feelings of inmates or prison staff, informal methods, and regulations.

Thus, naturalistic ethnography will include the study of the prison's setting, establishing rapport, and recording observation, and the attention will be to understand the inherent sociological concepts in the observed behavior and then presenting the findings. Such naturalism gives too much importance to observed facts and outward activities and behaviors; it generally tends to overlook deeper meanings of expressed behavior; in naturalism, respondents are treated as mere source of data.

Naturalism thus searches for objective reality in the physical world.

2. *Emotionalism*

Here also, the reality of the topic under study is taken for granted. In the case of naturalism, reality resides in the objective reality in physical place; in the case of emotionalism, the reality is located in the emotional life of the researcher and the respondents. Thus, in case a study of a prison where women prisoners are located, naturalism will study the objective reality of the prison life in its physical surroundings, buildings, facilities, and rules and regulations being followed, whereas under emotionalism, it is found that the researcher, over time, develops an emotional bond with the inmates (respondents). Respondents also express the reality of the emotions that they go through while in prison. Thus, while outwardly life appears routine and drab, in reality, prisoners create their own world of informal interchanges of emotion and informal give and take that makes life not that boring and of a routine as it appears apparently (This research study is described in Bandyopadhyay 2010).

The problem with emotionalism is that it tends to blur the objective social reality. It stresses on inner feelings and self-reflective confessions. To the extent possible, while appreciating the emotional aspects, the researcher should not ignore the basic realities.

3. *Ethnomethodology*

Basically, the methodology is concerned with the study of people's method of constructing reality everyday. It is concerned with social reality that gets created through everyday interaction. Thus, in a prison, prisoners have interaction with prison staff and with other inmates on a daily basis; these methodologies create a social reality separate from the emotional and natural reality described earlier.

Ethnomethodologists are thus primarily interested in understanding the way people go about doing things in their everyday life creating their own meaningful categories for others. Thus, women prisoners in Bandyopadhyay's study create their own meaningful categories for them and also for the prison staff.

Thus, prison life can have its meaning for inmates. This may be specific for a particular inmate. This impression may not coincide with the widely held global concept of prison life. Such studies and views are based on observation on specific conducts. It may sacrifice better understanding of the object under study whose behavior is based on the interaction of a large number of emotional, factual, informal, and formal realities.

4. *Postmodernism*

The subject of postmodernism is relatively vast and complex. Vast amount of literature exists on the subject. From our point of view, we consider postmodernism as one that questions every aspect of modernity (e.g., rationality, reason, science progress, etc.).

The questioning approach of postmodernism can negate many things. However, postmodernism can be useful if we accept the simple fact that allows us to realize that facts including facts of social sciences are socially constructed to serve the interest of a particular group. There is no absolute, objective, and neutral reality or fact.

Thus, any research study is a pragmatic exercise that serves different interests.

The four models that we have discussed here are methods of describing social reality. Though defined separately, these models are not mutually exclusive. Thus, an emotional and a postmodernist share the same vision for designing alternative exploratory strategies.

Given these models of reality, how does a researcher carries his/her qualitative research in the real world? The very basic aspects of qualitative research is based on pre-understanding, historical study, and ethnographic study consisting of participant/nonparticipant observation and many other methods.

Since ethnographic studies are basic to qualitative research, devoting some more attention to the details of ethnographic study will be in order. It is often felt that before undertaking any detailed ethnographic study, it may be necessary to undertake some historical study of the problem in hand which may help in improving pre-understanding of the problem under study. Thus, before undertaking any detailed ethnographic study (which may include, apart from other methods, participant observation), it may be useful to gain some pre-understanding through some study and analysis including historical analysis (Gummersson 1991).

Thus, in what follows, we shall devote one section on pre-understanding and on historical analysis. In addition, we should devote some attention to research methods and theories of qualitative research.

6.4 Methods, Concepts, and Theories of Qualitative Research

We have discussed in some detail pre-understanding and understanding of issues involved. Before going into details of actual data collection, data interpretation, methods of qualitative research, and discussion of ethnographic studies, it may be pertinent to define and clarify few concepts, methods, and theories.

As already discussed, models provide a framework for ways of looking at reality. In simple terms, they tell us what reality is like (this is called ontology), and they also indicate what is the nature and status of knowledge (this is called theory of knowledge or epistemology). Thus, defined models are like paradigms.

The concept of paradigms was advocated by Thomas Kuhn during the early 1960s. For our purpose, the word paradigm will be used to represent values, judgments, norms, perspectives, standards, frames of references, theories, ideologies, and myths adopted by the people. These things govern their actions and thinking.

In scientific research, a paradigm represents a researcher's perception of what the researcher should be doing and how. Thus, basic value premises and value judgments held by a researcher will be referred to as scientific paradigm.

In respect of paradigm, we should refer to two schools; one is called positivist school and the other is called hermeneutic school. Hermeneutic school ideas are also referred to as hermeneutics (the word hermeneutic comes from the Greek word hermeneia meaning to interpret).

It may be useful to briefly discuss the difference between positivist view and hermeneutic view.

In a positivist view, research is concerned with the description and explanation of a problem as it is seen; it generally consists of well-defined narrow shades. Thus, specific production problems, where process inputs and outputs are clearly specified, are normally subject to positivism in research, whereas research on a complex social issue say violence in society is not amenable to simple positivist paradigm. Positivism is based on traditional and statistical analysis and also on descriptive and comparative studies. In positivism, only knowledge obtained through measurement and objective identification can be considered as truthful facts.

On the other hand, in respect of certain complex social and organizational problems instead of trying to explain causal relationships by means of objective facts and statistical analysis, hermeneutics tries to use more personal subjective, interpretative processes to understand the complex social reality. Thus, under positivist approach, it is said that pre-understanding can create biases and therefore should not be encouraged. Under hermeneutic school, pre-understanding and researcher's involvement in actual problem are prerequisites for successful analysis of the problem in hand. Personal involvement is an actual requirement in understanding. In most qualitative research and ethnographic study, hermeneutic school of thought will be relevant.

Models We have earlier discussed four types of models and will not repeat them again.

Concepts These are clearly specified and defined ideas arising out of a particular model.

Concepts provide us with ways of looking at the world that are essential in defining a research problem. Thus, conducting a research on sustainable development, the concepts of sustainability and development have to be properly defined and specified so that we can then study the issues involved.

Theories Theories organize or arrange a set of concepts to define and explain some phenomenon. Thus, producing regulated green technology industrialization will produce sustainable development. Thus, a theory uses the concepts of sustainability, development industrialization, and green technology.

Relevance of appropriate theory is not often understood in the case of qualitative research. It must be stressed here that theory provides us a framework for critically understanding a phenomenon. Thus, violence against women can be better understood within a theoretical framework of violence against women giving causal and correlational aspects. Similarly, effectiveness of all organizations can be better understood under theories of organizational effectiveness. Theory also provides us with a basis of organizing unknown facts and explanations when revealed. Thus, sustainable development depends on decentralized development of rural and urban areas. It also depends on local-level commitment and participation. How these facts are to be organized to develop a model of sustainable development can be clear when we know in theory that participation and commitment lead to sustainability.

Generally, testable hypothesis for solution of the issues is proposed based on models, concepts, and theories. Next comes selection of methodologies of research and methods of data collection and interpretation leading to final results and findings. If findings are not suitable (or feasible), the hypothesis is modified and the process is repeated till a satisfactory result is derived.

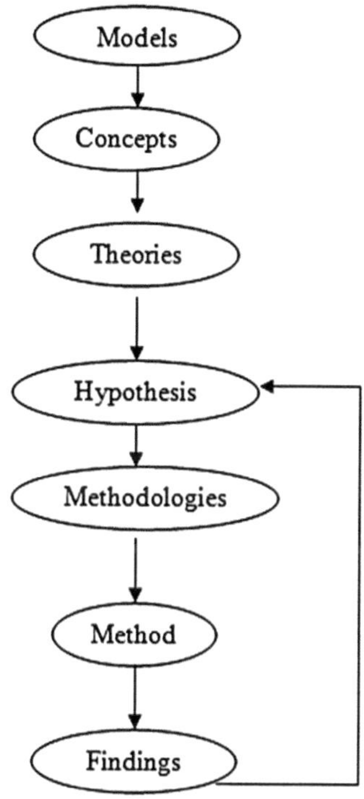

Fig. 6.1 Hierarchy of ideas

Thus, we have a hierarchy of ideas as shown in the Fig. 6.1.

Let us now briefly discuss about methods. We generally follow the following methods in qualitative research:

- Archival method
- Case study method
- Survey method
- Field experiment method

In archival method, questions are directed at people and written sources regarding issues to be investigated in the research study. This includes historical and biographical analysis (this is discussed in the next section of this chapter, Sect. 6.5). The case study method will be discussed in the later section of this chapter (see Sect. 6.10)

Survey methods are normally used in quantitative research. Focus group study and limited small-sample study may be used in qualitative research. This will be discussed later in this chapter (Sect. 6.8).

Field studies are essential components of qualitative research study. Participant and nonparticipant observations are essential aspects of the qualitative research method. However, ethnographic research methods are broader in scope, and we shall discuss this in detail in Sect. 6.6 of this chapter.

Techniques Techniques are step-by-step procedures which the researcher uses to collect data and analyze data for necessary information. Techniques can be semi-structured and open ended. Informal conversation, unstructured interviews of an individual, etc. are open-ended techniques.

Structured questionnaires and structural face-to-face interviews are structured close-ended techniques.

Any method between these two extremes are semi-structured (say partly structured questionnaire-based interview along with informal open-ended discussion).

Additional techniques may be attitude scaling. Structured observation along with field experiment can be additional techniques as well. Techniques used and sequence of use in actual field study will be discussed in detail in Sect. 6.7 of this chapter.

6.5 Historical Analysis and Pre-understanding

Any qualitative research study of organizations and social systems must include historical analysis for better understanding of the evolution of the system under study. It gives trends and provides for future directions for progress and solutions. Historical studies and analysis are relatively neglected by organizations, corporations, and social systems.

Historical review and analysis must be carried out with adequate rigor. It should not be confined only to retrospective study of the system. It should be conducted as a reflective exercise. History is always present, and new history is always being in the process of getting created through the interaction of current social, political, economic, and technological realities. History should be used as a method of interpreting the present and the future states of the system or issues under study. It acts as a hermeneutic bridge linking the past, present, and future. Study of the history of organizations and social system should not be done casually or superficially; it should be used as a serious operational tool. Historical analysis should be used as a stimulus to action. In organizations under distress, when studied for designing turnaround strategies for organizational revival, historical analysis can provide guidance and stimulus for future action.

It can help in contributing to an awakening of an organization which is steeped in slumber. It thereby raises self-confidence at a time when the overall morale of the organization or the social system is low. It helps in creating new knowledge through study of earlier processes of intellectual development. Thus, a new special type of competence can be developed, and a proper historical analysis will break the vicious cycle of dependency, despair, and failure. Historical analysis helps in understanding the roots of growth. In such a study, it is necessary to identify important milestones of changes and growth and critical events. Analysis of these milestones and critical events and their backgrounds and consequences provides new insights for future progress.

Study of history is thus used as a diagnostic instrument that helps to place the problem under study in the proper context and environment. It provides a trend and pattern. It supplies the thread and helps to create meaning in mass of data through the identified pattern.

Communication of the decision-making process and implementation of changes are facilitated if there is an overall agreement on broad historical and factual background.

Thus, for any good qualitative study of an organizational system or social system or cultural aspects, pre-understanding of the problem and issues under consideration will be useful. This pre-understanding of the problem is largely facilitated by a good historical review and analysis.

In a study based on participant observation or nonparticipant observation, the first step should be to appreciate the historical evolution of the organization and its processes, before the researcher can decide what to observe and how (as participant or nonparticipant). It also helps in deciding about other methods like informal or formal methods, structured or unstructured methods, and so on.

6.5.1 Biographical Analysis

We have discussed historical review and analysis in the early part of this section. Here, we briefly mention about biographical analysis. Just like historical review, biographical analysis can also be utilized to serve two distinct functions.

(a) Biographical analysis provides official records.
(b) Such analysis provides an account of why and how an individual or a group perceived and observed a set of events.

Especially the analysis provides records of personal experiences. These experience and observations of individuals and groups provide the researcher with an insight into the inherent values, motives, and aspirations of people.

This is called hermeneutic analysis as distinct from positivist analysis, which analyzes events as observed and existent.

6.5.2 Pre-understanding

Study of relevant literature, texts, and historical records and files and researcher's own past experiences and experiences of others in similar cases also may help in pre-understanding the issues under study. In Figs. 6.2 and 6.3, we illustrate the process of pre-understanding and understanding.

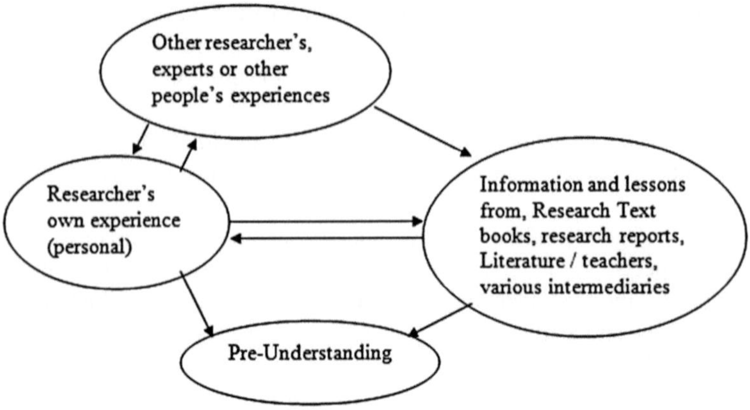

Fig. 6.2 Sources of pre-understanding interaction forces

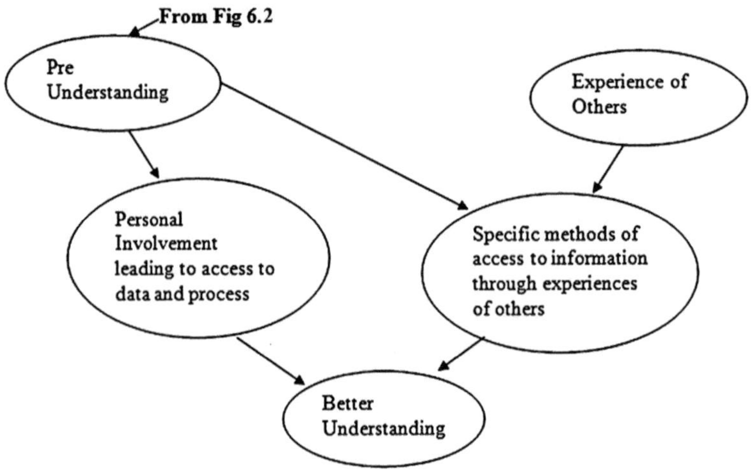

Fig. 6.3 Source of understanding

6.6 Ethnographic Study and Qualitative Research

Study of history of qualitative research reveals that the method of qualitative research is based on the central role of observation as a sociological research method. Observation can be participant or nonparticipant observation. These observations have different phases. We shall discuss all these in a subsequent section. Here, we broadly identify the basic characteristics of ethnographic study in qualitative research. Ethnography is a research strategy. This is imported originally from anthropology. Later on, it has been used in various areas like sociology, education, health, violence, women studies, etc. Though participant observation was at time central to ethnographic study, in recent time, this has become relatively less important. It has faded into background, while more general strategy of ethnography in which observation and participation are interwoven with other procedures has attracted substantial attention of ethnographic researchers.

Originally, ethnography used to study remote cultures which were generally not very familiar. Current ethnographic research is not concerned with unfamiliar cultures; it is interested in the study of certain aspects (unknown) of what seem familiar to us all.

Thus, the current ethnographic research is characterized by an extended participation in a number of fields (disciplines) employing a flexible research strategy which uses all sorts of methods. It focuses on writing and reporting experiences in the field. Today through ethnography, we study and gain insights about various types of institutions where economic/social activities are performed. Modern ethnography has different varieties like virtual ethnography, critical ethnography, and auto-ethnography.

Ethnography today (of course with certain constraints and restrictions) can be combined with a whole range of diverse research practices. These may be textual, narrative history, or even statistical methods. However, even today, ethnographic methods of observation and practice of making notes and keeping a journal during the period when research process is conducted are still quite common and are viewed as very fruitful practices in many ethnographic studies.

Currently, we tend to employ ethnography within a wide range of schools of thought and empirical areas. Thus, we use ethnographic studies for police service, law and order problem, media studies, women studies, studies of prison life, studies of social violence, education and health issues, and marketing and consumer behavior. Thus, ethnographic studies present a variety of diverse, theoretical, and disciplinary perspectives.

In spite of its diversity, ethnographic study has a few basic distinctive characteristics.

Two basic aspects are (1) field work and (2) field work report that records observations textually or through visual representation.

An ethnographer closely observes records, processes, and practices of daily life of another culture or community – this process is called field work. The observations are then described through written texts, data, and visual representation that give complex account of the various processes and cultural aspects in sufficient descriptive details.

Thus, basically, ethnography is first and foremost a study of social phenomena. Thus, ethnographic study of leadership style or decision-making system of a specific organization has to be conducted within the boundaries of the organization under study.

It is therefore rooted to first-hand exploration of a specific social or cultural setting.

Ethnographic methods (already discussed) are observation, participation, and recording and writing.

Through long-term participation, the ethnographic researcher tends to become an insider. This enables the researcher to view the world around through the eyes of other members of the organization who are also participants.

Thus, in a study of internal cohesion of a public sector organization, the researcher studied the organization over a long period and became as good as an insider. The researcher could then discover the various cliques and dysfunctional informal systems which were affecting the effectiveness of the organization, significantly. Observations of course may involve both participant and nonparticipant observations or can be both. In many ethnographic studies, both participant and nonparticipant observations are used in combination. Nonparticipant observation gives some pre-understanding and points to certain directions which are then further confirmed through long-term participant observations.

It may be stressed here that participant observations tend to be central to ethnography. It enables researcher to become an insider, and because of this, the researcher is able to access backstage areas that helps to get deeper insights into the phenomena under study.

Nonparticipant observation is not so strong. The researcher observes and records normal, natural behavior and processes but cannot become a part of the unfolding events as in the case of a participant observer.

Thus, to conduct a good ethnographic study as part of a qualitative research, the basic skill needed is the ability to observe analytically and to go beyond the apparent, visible reality. This skill takes time to develop. The observation is not merely confined just at looking at facts and processes and recording them. It is concerned with knowing what to look for and how to reflect on what is seen.

Thus, in a study of organizational cohesiveness and team spirit in a large corporate organization, the researcher initially observed a high level of cooperation and mutual understanding, suggesting a good team spirit. But over time the researcher could understand that much of the cooperative behavior was a made-up behavior; in reality, there are various conflicts and cliques which are preventing the creation of a good team. The discovery of these realities requires skills which are learnt over a period. Most participant observation-based ethnographic studies are generally long term in nature. Frankly speaking, observation as a research method means that the researchers systematically observe day-to-day events, interactions use of objects, social settings, and various conversations over a period of time. The researcher records the mundane and routine features of everyday organizational life and processes and in the process tends to discover a trend and truth that even participants themselves are not aware.

It is suggested in this connection that recording of full data by the researcher should be done as soon as possible within the proper setting or immediately after the event or positively at the end of the day. Observation by the researcher can be supplemented by interviews (unstructured/structured). Interviews may be initially based on casual conversations and later on may be carried forward through prolonged in-depth interviews.

Thus, the researcher hopefully will be able to analyze the diverse trends and forces that give the structure and form to the existing social/organizational behavior in a specific context or setting. The researcher will also be able to investigate the complex ways in which the issues arise in a particular setting. In the case of institutional ethnography, the focus is not so much on daily practices but on how these practices are institutionalized in rules, behaviors, and general relations and interactions in which individuals' everyday practices are embedded.

Virtual Ethnography Also Called Netnography or Cyber Ethnography These mostly relate to the use of the Internet and online interviewing. In a later section, we shall discuss some of these in further details.

6.7 Steps and Processes of Qualitative Research Study Inclusive of Ethnographic Study

(a) The first essential step once the research issues are identified is to obtain adequate pre-understanding and understanding of the setting of the problem, structural aspects, and other relevant issues involved. This will involve historical studies of documents and reports of the organization and environment. Here, one of the essential ways of conducting the historical review meaningfully is to identify the critical events in the evolution of the organization. This will provide better pre-understanding of the problem setting and issues involved. Thus, while studying issues related to the turnaround of a stagnant organization, the first step undertaken by the research team was to make an analysis of the growth of the organization starting from initiation and critical events (like when the organization decided to expand beyond the boundaries of West Bengal). It was also found that during its process of evolution, the organization changed gears from growth to consolidation and conservatism, and at the time the case study was done, the organization (a small private sector bank) was suffering from excessive conservatism and caution. The leadership was risk averse, the study of history and critical events helped in understanding why the organization is overcautious, while a bold strategy of expansion was needed for its survival. The historical study helped in understanding the basic causes of stagnation.

The next step is to familiarize with the organization, its present setting, and its decision-making hierarchy and processes.

Initially, this familiarization can be done through nonparticipant observation, taking a neutral observer role. At this stage, opinion of experts, neighbors, customers, suppliers, and others who have dealt with the organization in the past or are having dealings now will be very useful.

After that, in getting in-depth knowledge of the issues involved, it may be pertinent to have a relatively long-term participant observation where one or more observers become a part of the organization and observe the workings and processes on a day-to-day basis and collect relevant data and information and write field notes about such observations. Researchers conducting such participant observation should be adequately briefed and given training in the art of listening and observing and ways of developing rapport. These ensure that basic data regarding cohesion or conflict can be unearthed in due course. Depending on the size and complexity of the organization and the nature of the issues to be investigated, the nature and duration of participant observation will have to be fixed.

In the third step, it may be pertinent to integrate the data from pre-understanding, historical, and other knowledge and data from nonparticipant and participant observations. Any glaring gaps or mistakes need to be clarified at this stage. One of the ways may be to ask specific questions to concerned people regarding such discrepancies through informal, formal structured, or nonstructured interviews. However, in carrying out meaningful interviews, appropriate rapport must be established between the researcher and person/persons interviewed. During participant observation, this rapport should normally be established. In the case of the study that we referred earlier, two researchers spent about 2 weeks in various departments including the head office in observing decision-making styles. After this, the researchers came to certain tentative views regarding the reason of stagnation of the organization. Interviews were then conducted with the executives of various levels to validate (or otherwise) the tentative conclusions. Based on these observations and findings, a detailed standard questionnaire was drawn up and issued to all concerned employees, and detailed information was collected.

Thus, qualitative data collected through observation and qualitative studies were used to formulate the right type of hypothesis to be tested and to design a meaningful questionnaire for collection of relevant data. Thus, qualitative and quantitative methods were complementing each other. This mixing up of method is known as triangulation, and we shall discuss this in further detail later. Having discussed details of the qualitative research process, it may be useful to put its special characteristics in a summarized form as follows:

6.7.1 Substantial Features of Qualitative Research (Including Ethnographic Study) Are Given Below

1. Data collected is consistently subordinated to the research question to be investigated and the nature of settings and circumstances faced by the researcher while doing field study as participant or nonparticipant observer.
2. Methods of observation and data collection are not predetermined; these are subordinated to practice.
3. There is a risk involved in the process study. Processes of study cannot be planned. These are largely situational, coincidental, and individual, and therefore, success will depend on the skill and innovations of the researcher/researchers.
4. There is no prescribed method of data collection in qualitative or ethnographic study; the strategy may be to develop as many options of data collection as can be imagined and can be considered justifiable.

5. The research puts a strong emphasis on exploring the nature of a specific social phenomenon under study. It is not normally concerned with setting out to test hypothesis about the issues researched.
6. In this type of research, there is a tendency to work primarily with "unstructured" data. It basically means that the data have not been coded at the point of data collection (as in most structured questionnaire-based quantitative studies) in terms of a closed set of analytical categories. At the time of collection, the categories of data are open ended and not precoded.
7. In qualitative case study, we adopt case study research; generally, only a few cases (a small number) are investigated in detail.
8. Data analysis is done with a view to generate explicit interpretations of meanings and functions of observed and recorded human functions and processes. The result of such analysis is often verbal description and explanations; quantification if at all is seldom done. Thus, in qualitative research, statistical analysis at best plays a secondary role.
9. In the case of institutional studies, focus is not so much on daily practices but on how organizational practices and processes are institutionalized in rules, procedures, conventions, and general relations which embed the everyday practices followed by individuals within the organization.

Interviews: In the case of qualitative research, interviews are conducted (as already explained earlier) with a view to reduce errors that may crop up during the study. These approaches for reducing errors can be classified into the following classes:

1. Undertaking empirical methods which attempt to diminish or remove source of error so that minimum error can occur during interview. Thus, observations by researcher which do not fit data obtained from interview can be specifically stated to the person interviewed and then obtain necessary clarifications from him/her regarding the sources of discrepancy. This will help in removing errors during interview.
2. Different interviewers engaged in a study can produce different effects. Some of these effects when integrated over all interviews may cancel each other and may produce some basic homogeneity among the interviewing group. This will help in eliminating at least the different effects interpreted by different interviewers.
3. While interviewing, qualitative aspects should be stressed, and undue quantification and mathematization should be avoided. Thus, it is better to describe a situation of risk in qualitative terms instead of putting exact measure, say risk is 0.8.
4. Adequate care must be taken to select persons to be interviewed. Pre-understanding and participant observation can help in such identification. Thus, in the banking study mentioned earlier, once the participant observation period was over, we knew with a reasonable degree of confidence which of the 8/10 people should be interviewed to gain insight and information.
5. The interviewer must be able to obtain accurate information. The interviewer must be able to ensure that the respondents answer every question honestly, fully, and truthfully. Care must be taken so that the interviewer should in no

case vitiate the openness of the interview process by dominating the process. Interviewer's social skills should not in any way influence the opinions of the persons interviewed.

Social skills, accuracy, and relevance in asking questions and skills in probing are requisite characteristics that should be present in a good interviewer.

6. In all cases of gathering qualitative data, methods of data recording are very important.

The interviewer must be thorough and accurate in recording the responses to questions. Here, recoding the feelings, facial expressions, body languages, and psychological expressions apart from actual words exchanged in response is important. Often during interview, the help of technology can be taken. Interviews can be recorded (audio or video). These can then be played back to analyze details and contents. However, often the person interviewed may not feel comfortable in the presence of such recording devices and therefore may not express opinion freely. The most important aspect is to make the person being interviewed comfortable and free to express opinion. Thus, any recording done should be used only with permission of the person/persons interviewed.

Records of the proceeding should be written down immediately after the interview, and the interviewer must frankly record his/her impression about the various phases of the interview; delaying this process because of video or audio recordings may not be advisable. Impressions about the interview and about the response of the person or persons interviewed, his/her reaction to questions, and facial expression and body language are important inputs in putting adequate interpretation of the data collected during interview.

Once the interview data are recorded, it may be useful to conduct some content analysis of the recordings of the interviews.

The central idea in content analysis is that many words of the text are classified into much fewer contact categories. Each category may consist of one, several, or many words (words, phrases, etc.) having similar meanings. The researcher through content analysis may convey his/her feelings. It can also reveal certain trends and patterns of use of certain words/phrases to discuss certain situation. These can thus help in putting objective interpretation of the data collected during interview.

Synonyms, words conveying similar concepts like wealth and power, may help in making valid inferences from the recorded text. In this connection, it is important to ensure that the identification process adopted is reliable in the sense of being consistent.

Any classification of idea/phrases should be valid. The variable generated through classification will be valid to the extent that it measures or represents what the investigator wants to measure. For example, in a qualitative study of organizational performance, expressions used by the person interviewed about the relative factors affecting performance are valid variables to be noted with care.

The content analysis should be stable, reliable, and valid. The same recordings analyzed in different periods of time through content analysis should produce some consistent interpretation; in that case, the content analysis is considered stable. For this, coding of different data and phrases should be reliable and invariant and consistent. Inconsistency in coding can arise (1) due to ambiguity in the process of coding by following different coding rules – e.g., one coding based on expression of exclamations and another based on expression of despair. These two types of coding can create confusion in interpretation. Coding can be erroneous because (2) records are not error free.

6.8 Focus Group

We have discussed the process of conducting the qualitative study. We may like to illustrate the processes further by discussing one or two cases in detail. Here, we give a brief description of focus group interviews.

Before discussion of focus groups, it may be useful to mention generally about group interviews

The main advantage of group interview is reduction of cost. These interviews are basically low cost but rich in data. The group members may stimulate each other and support each other in remembering relevant and critical (critical to the study in question) events. Thus, a group interview can produce valuable and rich data which may not be possible to obtain through the process of interviewing individuals separately.

This characteristic of group interaction is fruitfully utilized in focus groups interviewed:

The hallmark of focus group is the explicit use of group interaction to produce valuable and rich data and insights that would normally be less accessible without the interaction taking place in a group.

Focus groups are therefore used as a valid method of data collection because of its inherent merit. However, it can be used in combination with other methods like large-scale surveys, participant or nonparticipant observation, and single interviews.

Thus, focus groups will be useful for the following situations/conditions:

- Where one wants to orient oneself to a new field of qualitative/quantitative research
- Based on better insights of the problems and issues involved, the researchers are willing to develop meaningful hypothesis
- When the researcher/research team wants to develop a meaningful schedule and wants to design a good structured questionnaire
- Where it is considered desirable to get interpretation of participants in respect of earlier studies done on the problems or issues under study

Focus group interviews are more common compared to group interviews. It is suggested that focus groups should be used instead of single interviews only when there are beneficial effects other than saving time. The benefit of saving time may not be feasible because considerable effort may be needed to understand group dynamics and interactions.

Additional benefits apart from saving time should justify focus groups.

Interaction among group members and dynamics of group members can produce an emergence of knowledge that may throw special light in the interpretation of issues at hand, and in such situation, focus group interview is always advisable.

In actual research study, focus group interviews are often used to improve understanding of the problem and in generating hypothesis. In a study on the effect of the Internet and cyber cafes, it was felt that a focus group interview should be used as a starting point of the study before deciding the detailed structured questionnaire and hypothesis to be tested.

In the modern days of the Internet and electronic communications, electronic ways of data collection and interview should also be discussed. The next section is devoted to this aspect.

6.9 Online Qualitative Research

At the end of the first decade and at the start of the second decade of the twenty-first century, to neglect the use of the Internet for qualitative research will not in any case be a practical and prudent proposition. Digital and technological revolutions have technically affected the quality and characteristics of qualitative research.

The following aspects of qualitative online research may be noted:

- Qualitative online research is a growing area. Many of the established methods of qualitative research can be carried out online.
- Today online interviews can be arranged in a synchronous form. This basically means that the researcher gets in touch with the participants in a chat room. He/she (researcher) can then directly exchange questions and answers as both participants and the researcher are online at the same time. This is closest to face-to-face interview and visual exchange. This type of synchronous form of online interview has most of the elements of a face-to-face interview.
- However, online interviews can be organized in asynchronous form also. The researcher sends questions to participants and participants can send their answers after some time. The researcher and participant are not online at the same time as in the case of synchronous form.
- It may be pertinent to mention here that qualitative online research offers some advantages compared to real-life, real-world research studies. It saves time and inconvenience of transcription; however, as against the above advantages, online qualitative research faces a lot of other problems. It faces the technical problems of accessibility and appropriate identification of the right type of participants.
- While conducting online qualitative research, it may be difficult to verify truthfulness and validity of the data obtained. This may involve issues of ethics.

6.9.1 Use of Computers in Qualitative Analysis

Apart from what we have discussed above, it is necessary to appreciate that we can use computers effectively to conduct qualitative research.

- Computer programs can be developed for analyzing texts (content analysis). At the beginning of the research study, we should clearly decide about the use of computers and the way to use its programs. In that case, relevant program for analysis can be developed to analyze data where the same becomes available.
- Available programs are developing fast, but they have similar features and capabilities which may or may not suit the needs of a specific research. It is therefore essential to do some advance checking and planning for selecting the correct and suitable computer program for this purpose.

Available programs may not do the analysis the way the research study demands, and as such, their impact on the way their users do their research is rather limited.

In view of this, it is crucial to reflect on the way the researcher should use the software. The use of software should be subordinated to the style of the research by the researcher and not the other way round.

It may be stressed that with preplanning, proper matching of the software and computer programs can be achieved for a specific research study. Thereby, the use of computers can be made more useful and specifically useful for the research study in question. We have discussed various aspects of qualitative research and ethnographic studies. We have briefly discussed the research process involved, interviews, data collection, data interpretation, and data recording. We also discussed the aspects of focus group interviews and essentials of online qualitative research. Lastly, we have briefly sketched the profitable use of computers for analysis of qualitative research.

In what follows, we shall discuss the essentials of case study and action research. We shall then discuss the process of triangulation. At the end, we shall attempt to specify the quality of a good research and steps to be taken to ensure good-quality research.

6.10 Case Study Research

One important component of qualitative research is the case study research. In survey research which is basically a quantitative research study, we generally use standardized measurements and sampling procedures with a view to (1) improve reliability of observation, (2) facilitate replicative studies, and (3) permit statistical analysis of data and make scientific generalization.

In case study research, the basic idea is that one case (or a small number of cases) will be studied in depth using methods that are considered appropriate (there is no standardized method). There may be a variety of specific purposes and research questions to be explained through case study research; however, the basic objective of the case study research is to develop as full an understanding of the case under study as possible. Comparing case study method with survey method, we say that the goals of case study research are (1) to capture the frame of reference and the definition of the situation of a given information or participant and thus to avoid standardized measurement procedures, (2) to examine in detail the various processes of the organization, and (3) to enlighten these factors peculiar to a specific case that provide greater understanding and insights about various crucial factors of a specific situation.

Case study method is very feasible. A variety of information collection methods can be utilized in a case study.

Some experts have identified three different classes of case studies: (a) intrinsic case study; case is of general interest. The case is of interest in all its particular aspects and ordinary qualities. So when an intrinsic case study is attempted, no further attempt is needed for generalization to go beyond a single case. (b) The second class of case study is called unstructured case study. Here a single case is studied in depth to reverse prevailing generalization. (c) The third class is called collective case study where a number of cases are studied to validate or otherwise some general phenomenon.

Case study research is useful in the following situation:

- When specific aspects are to be answered. Thus, when we want to know whether financial incentives lead to creativity, case study method may be found useful.
- When we want to get answers to questions why and how of a particular phenomenon. Thus, when we find increase in turnover in executive levels, by conducting case study research, we can find how and why the increased turnover is taking place.
- Case study research will be useful for understanding unique and rare situations and thereby help us to learn something new.
- Where we are to deal with large number of variables and a variety of complexities. In such situations, a survey method will be too difficult and costly. Through case study, we can generate appropriate understanding of the problem.
- For exploring before formulation of hypothesis or propositions.
- Testing the validity and applicability of a theory for a particular situation (prespecified).
- For comparing and contrasting different situations, case study research may be convenient and useful.
- Where new research areas are to be investigated, to gain understanding is important, and case study research provides requisite insight and understanding.

6.10.1 Debate for and Against Case Study Research

Critics of case study research have described it as anecdotal and of limited scientific value. It is often dangerous to generalize from a few or limited number of case studies. Thus, case studies fail to provide general solutions and are therefore of limited and temporary value.

As against the above view, it can be argued that case study helps in indepth study of a specific situation, it is holistic, and therefore it generates greater insights. The main advantage of case study research is the opportunity that it provides for a holistic view of the processes involved. Thus, when a specific organization is not performing adequately, the case study research will identify specific external environmental factors that are affecting its performance. Similarly, it will also identify lack of internal cohesion, presence of clique, and opaqueness in processes in the internal organization that are affecting its performance. It will also identify leadership gaps (if any) and input/resource gaps internally; thus, a comprehensive case study is quite holistic, and it creates the necessary indepth systemic understanding which is not normally possible through reductionist quantitative study conducted through survey method. The basic issue is that all problems cannot be solved by case study research.

6.10.2 Factors to Be Considered for Selection of Cases for Case Study Research

The following factors need to be considered for undertaking a case study research:

- *Target population* for investigation; if the number and variety are too large, a case study cannot be very effective. However, if the target population is relatively small and homogeneous, a case study research can be an appropriate method.
- *Accessibility* of population is another important factor.
- *Time for specific study* is an important factor in determining a research method. In the case of survey research, the time required is generally very long. In case of nonavailability of adequate time for such research, conducting a few indepth case studies may be preferable within the available span of time.
- *Resources available* for the study are another relevant factor.
- For deciding the number of cases to be studied and manner of conducting case study research, the *theoretical framework* that has to be validated and the *variables* that are to be studied are important considerations.
- The next important factor in respect of case study research is *selection of the firm for conducting the study.*

Within the firm, care also has to be taken to select the departments and subdepartments to be studied and the selection of individuals for interaction and indepth study.

- Qualitative researcher in general and case study researcher in particular should be very *good listeners* and should have *ample of patience* to remain undisturbed in spite of adverse conditions and hostile responses.

- In any qualitative case study, the researcher's ability to read between the lines is very important. There should be the ability to understand not only what is being said but also what is being meant.

In this connection, it may be proper to say that to study any particular aspect there is no upper or lower limit of the number of cases to be studied. The researcher has to decide the number of cases to be studied. The researcher has to decide the number of cases to be studied based on the problem, research objectives, and availability of resources.

6.10.3 Skills and Approaches Needed for Case Study Research

The following are the essential skills and approaches for conducting a good case study research:

- Ability to conduct indepth, unstructured, or semi-structured interviews
- Ability to interpret records/history
- Capability for penetrative observation
- Flexible approach to data collection and in conducting the research study
- Ability to train assistants in participant observation and in conducting indepth interviews

In this connection, it may be stressed that whatever we are talking here about case study research is equally applicable for any other type of qualitative research. Further, it may always be better to do a pilot study before starting the real data collection.

6.10.4 Data Collection

Data collection process is crucial. Relevant and probing questions have to be asked to collect appropriate and useful data. In case of a single case, comparing findings for validation may not be possible. In such a case, multiple data sources from the same organization under study can be used for comparison.

In most case studies, it is difficult to adhere to a prefixed, preplanned timetable for data collection process. Data collection must be flexible and adaptive. Further while interpreting data, researcher must be very careful not to allow personal biases to creep in data interpretation.

In case study approach, one has to create a proper balance between rigor and flexibility.

The detailed observation entered in the case study method enables us to study many different aspects. It is necessary to examine these aspects in relation to each other. Processes have to be viewed within their total environment. Researcher's capability of understanding such interaction should be fully utilized. Case study research thus offers us an opportunity which is relatively greater than other research methods in order to obtain a holistic view of a specific research project.

6.10.5 Design of Case Study Research

From the point of view of design of case study research, we can have four types as follows:

Type 1. Single case study – In this, case design has to be holistic and there is a single point of analysis.

In the case of *type 2 case studies*, again we have a single case study, but a number of sub-cases are embedded in a single design.

In this, we should design for one case study with holistic approach but having multiple units of analysis, say a case study of one bank with an analysis on the number of bank branches.

In the case of *type 3 designs*, we deal with multiple cases but each being dealt with holistically.

In the case of *type 4 designs*, we have multiple cases and each case has sub-cases embedded. In this type, we have similar selection as type 3 except that we have multiple points of analysis.

6.10.6 Case Study Design Principles

In designing any case study research, we must have some theoretical framework which is validated and resolved as we go through the research cycle. Generally, there are four stages in the research cycle. These are:

- Drift
- Design
- Prediction
- Deconstruction

Initially, we drift from one idea to another. This is common to most research studies. After some time, we settle down to some specific ideas and theories and design the research study based on these ideas and theories. In designing case study research, we design the strategy for data collection and decide the research questions to be answered. Tentative explanations to various observations are also decided at this stage.

Major areas of the research are generally suggested and unfolded during the drift stage. During the design stage, the researcher accesses and refines the major areas. Thus, in a case study of organizational collapses at drift stage, one can identify ideas, like mismanagement, lack of cohesion, competition, excessive greed, fraud,

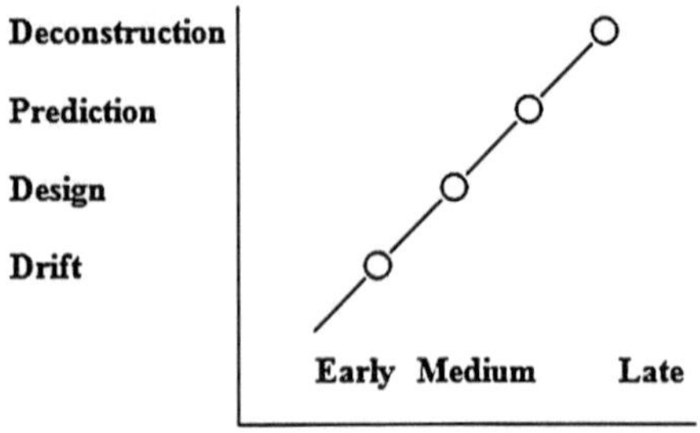

Fig. 6.4 Stages of research

and many other areas. At design stage, organizational efficiency and financial frauds due to excessive greed and unethical practices may be marked for detailed study subordinating other areas identified during drift stage.

Prediction stage in the research generally appears toward the end of major study areas, where a reasonable understanding of various factors is obtained, and it may be possible to make reliable and plausible prediction of likely results of the study. If such prediction does not answer the questions for which the study was conducted in the first place, the entire research process and design is deconstructed, and new cases may be investigated; new situations may be encountered to test the validity and generalizability. Thus, the process of research is cyclical.

The curve in Fig. 6.4 depicts the stages.

Whatever ideas have been discussed here in respect of case study research are also applicable in the case of other research projects under qualitative research.

We shall conclude our discussion of case study research, stressing that there are useful areas of application for case study research, but it should be used with caution. Any generalization should be carefully considered. However, it is very useful as exploratory study and in designing large survey research based on the indepth understanding during case study research.

6.11 Action Research

Action research is a form of case study research as one can do action research only in one or a few cases.

According to Gummersson (1991), action research is the most demanding and far-reaching method of doing case study research. Following are worth noting:

1. Action research or action science always involves two basic goals: (a) to solve a problem for the client or the sponsor and (b) to contribute to the science of management. Thus, one can conduct action research in introducing planned management of change in an organization thereby solving the problem of dysfunctional control. One can also do an action research to form teams in rural areas and create awareness in the people regarding issues of development thereby enriching the principles of participation and team formation in management of

rural development. The second action research is more involved in concepts and theory formation and their validation in practice. The first action research is involved in solving a problem specific to an organization. It may be seen from the examples above; we generally combine academic and consultancy aspects in an action research study.

2. During the action research project, the researcher and the client groups learn from each other and develop their competence. Thus, in the case of introducing the planning system, all executives and employees learnt about planning, and its utility in improving control. Similarly, the researchers learn about specific details of the organization and learn to modify suggestions and prescriptions accordingly. In the above example, the researcher learns about the difficulties in organizing teams in rural areas and in making them effective. The rural people learnt about the benefit of various aspects of rural development and benefits of participation in the development process. Both groups learnt and as a result their capabilities improved.
3. The understanding developed during action research process is holistic. An action research must focus on the totality of a problem but still makes it simple enough to be understood by all involved.
4. Action research requires cooperation between the researcher and the beneficiaries of research or the client personnel. Constant feedback must be exchanged between parties involved. It also involves continuous adjustment of research methodologies to new information and new events. Thus, action research evolves and adapts based on participation and cooperation.
5. Whenever any planned change of processes and system are to be introduced for appropriate management of change, action research will be useful in understanding, planning, and implementing change in management system and structure.
6. Any change and proposed solution to problems that are introduced in action research must be within the bounds of ethics acceptable to the researcher/research group and the client group.
7. Participatory research is a part of action research. Here, all managers, executives, and employees become integral parts of the total action research team. This totally rejects the myth that only professionally trained experts can legitimately take part in action research. Thus, in a qualitative research involved in turnaround strategies for an organization, a series of steps in terms of action research were undertaken. Solutions were jointly derived by the research group, managers, executives, and employees actively participating in the process, and they were all involved in implementing the solutions. Thus, action research sets in motion a process of learning and change in the concerned organization. It ultimately helped in the process of changing values as the learning process proceeded. This often resulted in a "paradigm" shift, and it completely shook/broke the status quo. It therefore did not take existing values, norms, and constraints as given; it changed them thereby facilitating double-loop learning. In single-loop learning, systemic constraints, norms, and values are given as non-changeable, and improvements are effected within the boundary of given systems, norms, and constraints. However, when these constraints are also considered as changeable,

we bring a process of change based on the principle of double-loop learning. A good action research helps in double-loop learning. In the turnaround strategy discussed above, we had double-loop learning.
8. For successful action research, a good pre-understanding of the organization and systems under consideration is absolutely essential. Thus, it is necessary to have appropriate pre-understanding of the corporate, environmental and other relevant conditions of the specific business. This is vital and critical for effective action research.
9. As explained, a positivist paradigm deals with system as it exists. Hermeneutic paradigm goes beyond the existing system and tries to develop the system as it should be. Action research should normally be governed by hermeneutic paradigm, although certain aspects may be dealt with in terms of positivist paradigm. As noted earlier, paradigm basically connects the underpinning values and rules that govern the thinking and behavior of the researcher.

6.12 Triangulation

We have earlier mentioned about triangulation. Triangulation basically means combination of methodologies within the study of the same phenomenon.

It therefore collects data through different methods. Thus, the researcher or research group collects different types of data of the subject matter of the study. In an organizational study, a researcher/research group collects data through historical review or by preliminary observation and through structured or unstructured interviews. Data collected through various means becomes important because the process of triangulation helps in improving accuracy of judgment.

Data collected through different methods may not always be consistent. In that case, further validation may be needed. Thus, data obtained through participant observation and through answers to structured questionnaire may not be consistent. The inconsistency in data can be removed by further informal or formal interviews.

When different methods are used for data collection and data interpretation, we may come up with different results and contradictions. Further research (observation, interviews, reinterpretation, etc.) have to be conducted to remove such contradictions. Thus, in a research related to time allocation to different areas by the chairmen of banks, questionnaire study got certain allocation pattern. On actual observation and on keeping proper records of time devoted to different activities by chairmen, the results that were obtained were totally different. Thus, according to questionnaire study, it was found that the chairmen of banks spent substantial part of time in priority sector and rural banking issues. However, on keeping record, it was found that over an extended period of 9 months, chairmen of banks have spent less than 1 % of their working time on issues related to priority sector and rural banking. When these discrepancies were found, further round of structured and unstructured interviews were conducted to remove contradictions and to note real facts.

Triangulation or use of multiple methods to approach the same study may be useful even if we do not get the same/consistent result. It leads us to better understanding or to new questions that can be answered by later research. Thus, in the example of the time allocation by chairmen of banks, it was found that an unrealistic impression was created that new priority sector banking was affecting the quality of conventional, traditional, and industrial banking. Results, however, reflected noncommitment of the top executives to priority sector issues, and therefore, it was necessary to investigate through further research what should be done to give the priority sector the priority of time allocation that it deserved.

Thus, triangulation can produce more complete holistic portrait of the object under study. Given the availability of resources and time, method of triangulation is considered desirable.

In conclusion, it may be noted that different methodological perspectives complement each other in the study of an issue and this is conceived as the complementary compensation of weaknesses and blind spots for each single method. Today, the processes are slowly establishing an insight that qualitative and quantitative methods should be viewed as complementary rather than as rivals. Figure 6.5 depicts the complementary nature of qualitative and quantitative methods as revealed through a process of triangulation.

6.13 Evaluation of Quality of Qualitative Research

We have discussed various aspects of qualitative research. It may be pertinent now to consider essential aspects of evaluation of quality of qualitative research.

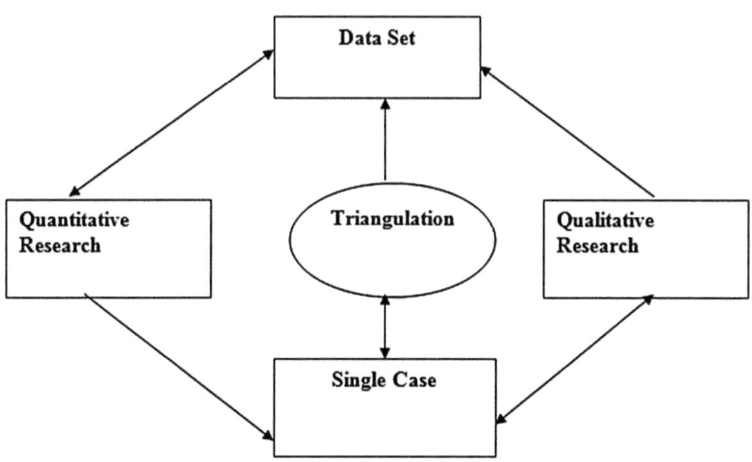

Fig. 6.5 Complementary relations between qualitative and quantitative research via method of triangulation

6.13.1 Quality Defined

Quality can be defined as conformance to requirement. Alternatively, we can define quality as fitness for use. When research results are implementable for better outcomes, the research quality is considered adequate.

The requirements of research need to be specified with clarity and without any ambiguity. Norms and values need to be specified clearly. But in all real-life problems, organizational processes are seldom clearly specified. They are often unspecified, unexpected, and ambiguous. Under such conditions, perception of quality may differ resulting in unclear and often ambiguous specifications. Here, there may be differences in perception (perception gap) between those who conduct the research and those who assess the research. There may be a tendency to concentrate on measurable/quantifiable factors, ignoring intangible, difficult to measure factors. However, such factors may be very important and crucial in affecting the overall effectiveness of research results. If we concentrate on defining quality on the basis of fitness for use, we run into the problem of identifying the user. We must have a clear understanding regarding fitness of whose use. Quality of research is then to be decided by the perceived usefulness of the research to the identified user group.

In an organizational research, there may be difficulty in identifying user group, certain research may benefit employees being profit neutral, and some other research may benefit employers affecting working conditions of employees. In the first case, if the user group is an employee, research quality is adequate, but if the user group is an employer, the conclusion may not be valid.

Thus, quality prescription is often problematic. Generally, academic and scientific approaches to business management and organizational research are largely a mixture of different paradigms. We have already discussed positivist and hermeneutic paradigms in this connection.

Research reports are generally drawn up in traditional, orthodox positivist ways. Such research reports are very common; they represent the conventional, traditional knowledge propagated in universities and academic institutions. As opposed to positivist paradigm, there is hermeneutic paradigm. In the case of hermeneutic paradigm, the researcher concentrates on understanding and interpretation. Efforts are directed to take a holistic view. Here, distinctions between facts and value judgment are less. However, there are large elements of subjectivity. Here, the research/research groups are themselves individuals, and they allow both feelings and reasons to govern their actions.

However, in actual practice, a strict application of hermeneutic approach is rather very rare. Basically, this is due to relatively less appreciation and knowledge of the approach among academicians.

Where we talk of action research, the situation is quite different. An action-oriented researcher however has to apply both positivist and hermeneutic knowledge in conducting effective qualitative research of good quality.

6.13.2 Key Questions

Where any research study is based on a mix of positivistic and hermeneutic paradigms, the following questions become important in assessing quality:

(a) *Replicability* of research: Can we replicate the result of the research in a similar condition or a similar problem? Without replicability, the usefulness of the research is too restricted.
(b) *Validity*: Do the research results reflect conditions of the real world? Can the prescriptions be applied in real-world problems? This is the criteria of validity. Quite often in conducting research, practical constraints are ignored; thus, in reality, the solutions obtained will not be valid and of much use. Thus, when all relevant constraints are considered, research results even denoting marginal improvement will be valid and useful.
(c) *Criteria of relevance*: Apart from the results which may look attractive, are the results relevant for similar cases that are considered important? Thus, a research may suggest significant improvement in teaching effectiveness with significant changes in infrastructure and socioeconomic attitudes. However, given the present situation of lack of infrastructure and prevalent socioeconomic approaches to education in rural areas, such solutions will not be relevant.
(d) *Criteria of generalizability*: How much of the results can be generalized? Without generalizability research, benefit is very limited.
(e) *Criteria of credibility*: Research results must be credible and should look prima fascia feasible and be reflective of reality. We have to ask the question "Are there sufficient details in the way evidences are produced, so that the methods can be judged as credible?"

6.13.3 Summary of Quality Evaluations

Having thus classified the five criteria of replicability, validity, relevance, generalizability, and creditability, we propose in what follows to summarize basic questions to be addressed for assessing quality research:

1. Can we draw valid conclusions from the study?
2. What is/are the paradigms used in the research study? Are they specified clearly, and are there evidences of understanding of the paradigms followed?
3. Is the research credible in terms of feasibility and reflecting reality?
4. Is the research valid?
5. Practical research should be easily accessible. Is the research accessible?
6. What are the basic contributions to theory or practice or both made by the research?
7. Can it be applied in changing conditions? Basically, are the results dynamic and adaptable?

8. Is the research creative and promoting new ideas and innovations?
9. Does the research clearly demonstrate sincerity, pre-understanding, and honesty?
10. Does the researcher demonstrate commitment and integrity?

6.14 A Few Case Examples

While discussing individual aspects of qualitative research, we mentioned some real-life examples. Here, we give a few more real-life case examples. Each case is briefly described from start to end.

6.14.1 Case "A"

This case deals with a doctoral (PhD)-level real-life study concerned with improving decision-making system of a large steel manufacturing organization. The study was also concerned with development of a framework for assessing information value in an organizational decision-making context. The researcher used both quantitative and qualitative research methodologies in conducting various aspects of the research study. However, most of the methods used had a large degree of qualitative research elements. Initially, some time and efforts were devoted in knowing the historical evolution of the organization. Steel industry in the UK was initially in the private sector. It was later on nationalized by the Labour Government. Steel industry during the early 1950s just after the conclusion on the Second World War faced a seller's market as there was tremendous demand of steel and steel products for post-World War reconstruction. By mid-1960s, this period of reconstruction was nearing completion, and the steel industry market slowly moved from seller's market to buyer's market. There was a slackness of demand for steel and steel products globally. The question was how, during this period of adjustment, production efficiency should be improved to reduce costs significantly to remain competitive in the buyer's dominated market having a large number of competitors.

This required, apart from understanding the growth history, a complete pre-understanding of the specific organization, its decision and information system, its method of resources use, its style of leadership, etc. Initially, the researcher tried to know as much as possible through nonparticipant observation. During this phase, the researcher obtained opinion of experts, ex employees, and market experts and technologists. The researcher also tried to draw up comparison with other global steel making organizations.

Once the researcher had reasonable pre-understanding of the industry and also of the specific organization under study, the researcher wanted to gather in-depth knowledge through participant observation process. The researcher spent approximately 18 months as a participant observer of various departments, various decision-making nodes, and actual day-to-day production processes and methods.

After interpreting information obtained from historical review, pre-understanding, nonparticipant, and participant observations, the researcher was in a better position to design a meaningful structured questionnaire for various executives and employees. Once the data from questionnaire survey was obtained, they were compared with earlier qualitative data and perception. In certain cases, there were conflicts and contradictions. Thus, it was followed by informal/formal interviews with concerned executives, where such contradictions were resolved to the extent possible. Here, focus group interviews were also conducted.

Integrating information from (1) historical review and pre-understanding phase, (2) nonparticipant observation phase, (3) participant observation phase, and (4) survey and further formal interviews included focus group interviews; main research questions were explored and tentative solutions were derived. These were then tested for validity, replicability, and credibility with academicians, steel technologists, decision makers, and other concerned groups. These resulted in the development of a framework for assessment of information value. The research also identified specific steps for improvement of quality and effectiveness of decision-making at various level of organizational decision-making.

The framework developed was based on both qualitative and quantitative research methods.

6.14.2 Case "B"

This was an action research case study where the turnaround strategy for a distressed organization was formulated and implemented to very successful effects. Again, in this case, we went sequentially through processes of historical reviews, pre-understanding of the organization, and nonparticipant observation. Then, we followed the process of participant observation and focus group interviews. The research team participated along with the management teams, i.e., implementing some of the solution that emerged out of the research study. This was the process of action research, at the time of implementation. Some of the recommendations were made more effective through appropriate modifications. Some were found unsuitable and rejected. This action research process of formulation, implementation, and modification continued till we got a newly designed strategy and system that will fulfill our objective of the study in respect of effective turnaround. Thus, the process of action research provided an opportunity for learning and evolving.

6.14.3 Case "C"

The third case was concerned with ascertaining whether the allocation of efforts and times by senior and top-level executives is in alignment with the declared policy objectives of the banks after nationalization in 1969. It was claimed that substantial proportion of time and effort of executives were getting allocated to rural sector and priority sector issues, and as a result, banks were neglecting conventional business of income-generating sectors. To verify the validity of that perception, the research team studied the records and files and also spent some time as nonparticipant observer in banks of different sizes. After getting some insight and pre-understanding, it was felt that the prevailing perception might not be exactly correct. It was therefore necessary to verify these perceptions further. Methods adopted were (1) participant observation, (2) maintaining a diary of time spent by executives of banks for a period of 3 months, and (3) sending a detailed questionnaire to all senior and top-level executives. On the basis of (1) and (2), the allocation of time was calculated that however varied significantly with the data obtained through questionnaire survey as in (3).

Therefore, these discrepancies were further discussed in focus group interviews with executives. This resulted in mitigation of discrepancies. It also helped in change of perception as it was seen that though perception was that a substantial amount of time was spent in rural and priority sector issues; in reality, only less than 1 % of time and efforts were spent in these sectors. This change of perception resulted in more equitable distribution of time and efforts to these important sectors resulting in improvement of decision-making and performance of these sectors. The research methodologies followed were partly quantitative and partly qualitative. Thus, method of triangulation was effectively used in this research study.

6.14.4 Case "D"

This case example is related to rural development issues. Here, again both quantitative and qualitative methods were used. This was related to development of a rural block. A block is a cluster of a number of villages. Generally population of a block may vary from 60000 to 100,000). We were concerned with the development of Chhatna block in the state of West Bengal, India. This is a block which is relatively underdeveloped, having significantly tribal population. The research work was done at doctoral level (PhD research) but was done at action research mode. The researcher spent time in acquiring reasonable historical and geographical knowledge of the district of Bankura in general and of Chhatna block in particular. Technically, the reasons for present economic and social conditions were identified tentatively from historical review, talking to knowledgeable people of the area and experts. Based on this pre-understanding, the important areas and villages of the block were visited. Discussions were conducted with the local leaders, politicians, the administration, and common villagers. Based on this, the researcher prepared a framework for collection of data. Perception and views were shaped further during participant observation. Researcher spent about 6 months in the block as a normal resident of the area and participated in the normal activities. This helped in getting an insight about the lifestyles followed, cultures, festivals, spending behavior, development initiatives needed, etc. Based on these ideas, focus group interviews were conducted with selected groups representing all sociocultural and economic sections. This provided a clear picture of aspirations and problems of local people. Researcher then prepared a plan for local-level development and had constructive discussions with local people. The plans formulated were discussed threadbare with all concerned. Suggestions and modifications were introduced. Thus, a development plan for the area was formulated through a process of local participation in action research mode. Some of the ideas started getting implemented. Here, the most important aspect was establishing rapport with the local population. Researcher has to win confidence of the concerned people regarding his/her sincerity and integrity, and only then real issues would be discussed openly without inhibition. The resource allocation within the plan framework was quantitative. Participation, discussion, and historical reviews were basically qualitative. A good blend of methods through triangulation was achieved.

6.15 Concluding Remarks

Based on our conceptual and theoretical discussions and supported by our case study examples, we can summarize the steps for a good qualitative research study as follows:

1. Understand the organization – get an overall impression of the organization and the issues to be studied.
2. Generate pre-understanding and understanding (historical review, preliminary visits, focus group interviews, discussion with knowledgeable persons and experts, etc.).
3. Go through a brief period of nonparticipant observation – during this period, try to build rapport.
4. Follow with participant observation. The period of duration varies with organization and issues under study. In this period, get involved; conduct informal interviews and also some formal structured interviews if needed.
5. Record data on a daily basis; the use of modern devices (audio, video, cameras, etc.) can be subject to the approval of the persons concerned. Interpret the data so recorded.
6. Conduct survey research if considered desirable based on the subject under study after designing the structured questionnaire.
7. Tabulate and integrate data obtained from various sources.

8. Compare the data obtained through various sources. Identify discrepancies and contradictions if any.
9. Remove contradictions/discrepancies by further talks, validations, interviews, discussions, etc.
10. Derive results and conclusion from analysis and interpretation of data collected from various sources.
11. Discuss validity, reliability, and creditability with concerned persons and experts.
12. Modify results, conclusions, and interpretation if called for after step 11.
13. Arrive at consensus solutions feasible for implementations.
14. Implement the solutions and suggestions.
15. Monitor the implemented outcome. In case the desired outcomes are not forthcoming, repeat steps 4–15 till satisfactory outcomes are achieved.

It may be pointed out that in spite of great progress in quantification and quantitative research methods, the need for in-depth qualitative research because of the complexity of the modern globalized world has further increased. It is therefore advisable that all researchers/problem solvers in analyzing and in dealing with all managerial, organizational, and socioeconomic and policy problems must be familiar with the various methodologies, concepts, philosophies, techniques, and tools of qualitative research.

References

Bandyopadhyay M (2010) Everyday life is a prison. Orient Black Swan Pvt. Ltd., Hyderabad

Gummersson E (1991) Qualitative methods in management research. Sage, London

Jankowiz AD (1993) Business research projects. International Thomson Business Press, London

Silverman D, Marvasti A (2008) Doing qualitative research a comprehensive guide. Sage, Los Angeles

Van Maanen J (1985) Qualitative methodology. Sage, Beverly Hills

Chapter 7
On the Role and Significance of Contextualization in Economic Research

Dinesh S. Hegde

7.1 Introduction

It might be worthwhile to recall a familiar story about a shipwreck and the three survivors marooned in a small island, hungry and waiting for rescue. One of them was a physicist, the second a chemist and the third an economist. Lo and behold! All of a sudden, one of them notices a can floating ashore and picks it up only to find to their utter relief and joy that it is a can of food. Now, the problem was how to open the can. The physicist said, if only he had a prism, he could make the sunrays focus on the lid and open the can. The chemist said, if only he had some chemicals, he could make a reaction happen and make the lid come off. But, with no access to prism or chemicals, they both felt helpless and looked at the economist expectantly. The latter said, 'let us assume there is a can opener!' Surely, societies, their polities, economies and peoples are far more complex and so are their interactions, be they cultural, social, political or with respect to trade, commerce, science and technology, what with the vastly divergent role of the state and institutions. In order to understand this complexity, therefore, simplification and abstraction become necessary which in turn entail assumptions. But the question rarely asked is how far and at what cost? It is time, one raised such a question, especially in the light of the monumental failure to foresee if not predict the USA and European financial crises in the recent times. Not long after the crisis erupted, the Queen of England expressed her dismay in an address at the London School of Economics in late 2008 and asked why nobody noticed it and how everybody missed

D.S. Hegde (✉)
Former Professor of Economics and Dean (Academic), National Institute of Industrial Engineering, Mumbai, India

Present Affiliation: Visiting Faculty, IIM Raipur, India
e-mail: dshegde108@gmail.com

D.S. Hegde (ed.), *Essays on Research Methodology*,
DOI 10.1007/978-81-322-2214-9_7

it. To her utter surprise, the response to the Queen by Professor Luis Garicano, the then Director of Research, was one of sheer helplessness, but revealing nonetheless. He said, at every stage, someone was relying on somebody else and everyone thought they were doing the right thing. More astonishingly, yet another incidence took place three years later. On 2 November 2011, students of an introductory course in economics at Harvard University walked out of Professor Gregory Mankiw's class after giving him a protest letter citing reasons of bias, espousing a limited view that perpetuated problematic and inefficient systems of economic inequality. They highlighted, among others, the need to include a critical discussion of pros and cons of various simplifying models.

Needless to say, the two instances cited above speak volumes as to the extent to which relevance has been relegated to the backstage and the scarce attention, if any, paid towards exploring possible alternatives. It is against this backdrop that the paper attempts to address the very important issue of relevance with a focus on contextualizing analysis for better understanding of problems, events, processes and phenomena, enriching analysis and balancing quantitative precision with qualitative narrative-descriptive complexity. In so doing, some fundamental assumptions and judgments are critically examined in addition to highlighting the need to sound caution on perils of disparate data sets being subjected to empirical investigation.

The obvious question that arises here is what do we mean by contextualization? It refers to comprehending things, events, processes and phenomena occurring around certain historical happenings, work settings, organizational settings and geographical and social settings of countries and their peoples and in particular their internal dynamics including power relations, their influence in public policy and its processes, agenda and implementation so that analyses are located in such contexts. Notwithstanding that the main objective is to make advances in inquiry and knowledge, contextualizing, therefore, assumes significance whether the research study is on poverty, traffic, productivity, work ethos, entrepreneurship, gender, ethnic, land reforms, civil rights, racism, health, environment or market regulation. Also significant are power relations and their influence over public policy, its processes, agenda formulation, implementation and the like. In this way, when events, processes or phenomena under study are placed in the appropriate context, our understanding of complex issues in their entirety is likely to improve a great deal. In other words, rigour if combined with relevance has higher potential by way of contributing useful knowledge or its advancement, rather than quantitative accuracy per se. To begin with, some recent trends are taken up for discussion and how gaps in understanding them have led to cynicism. Some specific contexts discussed, among others, are estimates of poverty and air traffic in India. This is followed by a description of emerging technologies, some incremental and others of leapfrogging variety, and an analysis of their implications. Lastly, a few spillover/spread effects of such new technologies are also highlighted. The sections are structured accordingly.

7.2 Yawning Gaps

What is noticeable conspicuously for a long period now is that most analyses have been carried out in the straightjacket frameworks of static, comparative static and dynamic types, in our thinking as well as analysis, and in this journey, we have largely gone along with assumptions of rationality of the economic agents (who as consumers maximized their utility and as producers maximized their profits) and efficiency of markets. That such a tendency has come to prevail for so long springs hardly any surprise! Few would desire to move from the comfort zone, for after all, it served the purpose well amidst the continuing prosperity of the developed Western economies for five to six decades following the end of World War II and the dominant thinking that developing economies could replicate this experience if only they followed the leaders. The differing sociocultural contexts, pressure on land given the huge populations and their densities in the developing countries tend to be glossed over in making such inferences. One should only recall the vocal and often violent protests against industries, mining and SEZs to gather evidence of this nature, thus casting serious doubts on the wisdom of such a partial and simplistic approach to growth and development strategies. Likewise, it does not occur to us until the damage is done that a policy of subsidizing biofuels while mitigating the energy problem goes to hamper food supplies. Again, we monetize bad debts of banks to farmers, power, aviation and others and then complain about inflation, worsening fiscal deficit. Yet, time and again, we fail to see that the subsystems within the system are interconnected and disturbance in them either induced or autonomous does cause disturbance in the other subsystems and finally in the entire system depending upon the degree of interdependence or backward and forward linkages and their relative strength in terms of the ripple effects. In all this, there appears to be a general amnesia, as it were, in not recognizing the serious limitation of partial equilibrium analysis and reductionism. Is the reluctance due to the comfort zone within which things have served us well in the past and should only be expected to do so in future as well? Or is it due to a diehard belief that assumptions are in any case required for the purpose of simplification and abstraction and variations can always be explained away by being exceptions not falling within the ambit of the ceteris paribus assumption?

Thus, given this dominant paradigm as advanced by Thomas Kuhn's *The Structure of Scientific Revolutions*, it follows that the underlying belief and philosophy were no different with regard to applied econometrics as well. Historical contexts, institutions, organizations and values, not being amenable to quantification, have conveniently been excluded. The results of such studies, by and large, fell neatly into place or at least appeared to be so. Almost routinely, sign, size and significance of the coefficients of the regression equations were reported and the hypotheses accepted or rejected. The objections raised by Karl Popper in his *Conjectures and Refutations* (1962) as to 'acceptance' of a hypothesis and his advocacy of 'falsification' as a criterion for scientific knowledge, failing which a more appropriate recourse to 'non-rejection', seem to have been forgotten. If at all, there were problems, they could invariably be explained in terms of possible data-related and/or model-related problems. Rarely, one reflects beyond the surface, even when the estimates and forecasts tend to be way out of line with reality and of little use. Nevertheless, the curve-fitting exercise has continued unabated. Often, variations could be seen by way of non-linear models; introduction of lags, continuous functions, etc.; causal relationships established; and the paths worked out to suggest damped, explosive or fluctuating tendencies. In a dynamic context, expectations were introduced. Also came to be widely used are time series models to reflect the viewpoint of letting data speak for themselves! Thus grew the copious literature including numerous Doctoral and M.Phil dissertations. Over the years, the trend has only perpetuated itself so much so that one is reminded of Schumpeter's (1964) prophetic apprehension as to the latter half of the twentieth century being characterized by thoughtless empirical work as against the excessive word-mindedness of the previous half. He had also cautioned about the pitfalls of economists having knowledge of history but without a sense of history. The latter has already been dealt with in Chap. 1 of this volume, with illustrations from the abolition of Corn Laws and the unwarranted frequent usage of the word struggle.

One may wish to consider, for example, the poverty estimates in the country over the decades. Going by these estimates, the proportion of population living below the poverty line varies between 1/4th and 3/4th, depending upon the criteria adopted (per capita minimum caloric consumption, expenditure, access to basic goods, etc.). Rarely considered are the barter exchanges and other nonmonetized transactions that commonly take place in rural areas. In fact, they cannot even be termed as exchanges as more often, they take place arising from economy of affection among neighbours, relatives and friends. Thus, frequently, a portion of home-grown pumpkins, gourds, jackfruit, sweet potatoes, tapiocas and other fruits and vegetables is shared among these people.

Further, we may take the case of demand elasticity of electricity with respect to GDP at 1.5 or its counterpart for air traffic at around 0.6. The former implies power generation had to grow at 9 % to meet the needs of the economy growing at 6 % in the 1990s, as was repeatedly harped upon then. Towards the end of the decade or thereabout, the Power Ministry lowered the target from 9 to 7 %. Of late, we keep hearing about the sector having to grow at about 6 %, suggesting in effect an income elasticity of demand around 0.8 in the face of the economy growing between 7.5 and 8 %. Clearly, it was a case of gross overestimation! As to the air traffic, it is a case of gross underestimation, as it has been growing at around 16–18 % in the last few years as against the forecast growth of around 4 % based on the estimated income elasticity. One wonders what the missing links might be! Could it be that the composition and structure of electricity demand (as between agriculture, industry, services and households) and its pattern had changed? Likewise, in the latter case of air traffic, could it be that proliferation of no-frill airlines and/or changing lifestyles induced higher growth in air traffic? Also, cases are not infrequent where demand elasticities are estimated without even converting incomes data to constant prices. Needless to say, such large deviations between forecasts and actuals undermine credibility in the eyes of practitioners who tend to become sceptical and even cynical about the so-called academic exercises.

7.3 Some Recent Trends and the Larger Perspectives

At this juncture, it is pertinent to recall here what Koopmans had stated in his *Three Essays on the State of Economic Science* (1957) by way of criteria of a good theory – rigour, relevance, comprehensiveness and immediacy. Arguably, the great success of Keynes's General Theory was precisely because it fulfilled these criteria to a large extent. The Western economies could pull themselves from the Great Depression of 1929–1933 and experience unprecedented development with substantial growth in incomes, employment and quality of life spread over the next five to six decades, needless to mention the enormous amount of scholarly works that ensued including the well-known growth models and empirical literature. Little wonder, it came to be known as Keynesian revolution! Incidentally, it is significant to recall how carefully Keynes formulated his consumption function, savings function and investment functions making frequent references to psychological propensities, psychology of savings, psychology of investment, psychology of the community, psychological characteristics and the like. Such behavioural aspects seem to be forgotten long ago. Subsequently, however, there has been some excessive overindulgence with it on the part of many a country including many developing ones as well, justifying fiscal profligacy and the so-called consumption story almost to the point of bankruptcy. Indeed, it was not infrequent for students to raise doubts during lectures as to the virtues of savings, investment and factor productivity in the growth context. It simply did not carry conviction with them in the face of the grand American consumption story driving the growth trajectory. It was all so overwhelming not only for students but also professionals, analysts, mighty media and policymakers. Perhaps, it has now begun to dawn upon them that behind all this were reckless borrowing, feeding consumption and speculation and that bulk of such demand arose from neither needs nor wants but from aspirational consumption, compulsive buying (for its own sake), self-aggrandizement, acquisition and/or greed. A detailed account of this phenomenon can be obtained from several issues of the economist over the last few years and also in the recent work of Seaward (2005).

At one end of the spectrum, we have ivory tower academicians engaged in theories, models and testing with little regard to their relevance, based on assumptions which are sometimes described as being fat with excess content. The readily available user-friendly software packages have further lent momentum to this trend.

At the other end of the spectrum, there are professional consultancy outfits, some private, some public and yet others autonomous bodies, and individuals providing quick fix practical solutions which might be relevant but falling far short of rigour and comprehensiveness. Such solutions are, by and large, partial and short term in nature and do not address the long-term and systemic perspectives. As a consequence, we find firms implementing enterprise resource planning (ERP), moving towards strategic business units (SBUs), etc., without an understanding of what impinges their performance in the first place. A case in point is the all too-familiar training/facilitation issue, for unless people who man the organization and its processes are not taken into confidence and trained in tune with the change and its requirement, the expected results are unlikely to materialize. It has been the experience of many an organization that IT integration sans people integration hardly makes the intended impact. Without the latter in place, one often finds firms with ERPs, SBUs, TQM, TPM, etc., being present more in form than in content! As has been widely seen, the first reaction of people occupying positions high or low would invariably be fear of possible loss of job, besides resistance to change which needs to be overcome first and foremost. Otherwise, one ends up in situations where the left hand does not know what the right hand does! For instance, it is not uncommon to observe Section Heads sending their daily reports manually, despite the prevalence of software packages like ERP in companies and Integrated Port Management Software (IPMS), etc. Admittedly, there is a lot to be desired in terms of contextualizing.

As between these two extremes of theory and practice, we find numerous empirical studies, some providing evidence in favour of or against the hypotheses formulated, others inconclusive and calling for further work, extensions, etc. In most such works, however, it is scarce to find the underlying paradigm being critically examined in their undue haste towards quantitative analysis of data using readily available software packages. At times, even the adequacy and accuracy of the data sets do not seem to get due attention and yet elaborate tables tend to be produced and size, sign and significance of the coefficients get interpreted. The possibility of the data not being independent of theory or that a grounded theory might emerge out of empirical analysis is rarely considered. In this context, it might be worthwhile recalling Schumpeter's prophetic apprehension that if the first half of the twentieth century saw excessive word-mindedness, the second half would be characterized by thoughtless empirical work. Admittedly, the end result is there for us to see, by way of more and more output being churned out with scarce regard for theory and relevance.

It is thus seen that the question is not one of profit maximizing, satisficing or strategic behaviour. Although the latter two have gained greater acceptance in managerial economics over the years, they fail to take cognizance of faster pace of technological changes, tastes and preferences. In the section that follows, the rapid pace of technologies, both incremental and leapfrogging types, and of consumer behaviour and their implications are discussed. In addition, reference is made to influence other factors such as the increasingly larger human co-operation, institutionalism and sociocultural and historical backdrops/legacies.

7.4 Revisiting Assumptions in the Changed Context

Over a fairly long period of time, we have been in the habit of taking the assumptions for granted as they have served us well in the past and hence should be expected to do so in the future as well. That this expectation can be more than tweaked has rarely been considered. Besides, assumptions are needed after all, for the purpose of abstraction and simplification! It is time, however, we revisit the comfort zone in the light of the developments that have been taking place over the last three decades, culminating in what is now being called the new economy. The features of the new economy are described briefly in the following two paragraphs.

Viewed from the *technology front*, what has happened is not just incremental changes but leapfrogging progress with widespread spillover/spin-off impacts across industries, sectors and economies. Let us consider, for instance, the IT revolution. It has long ceased to be one of higher speed in computing and spread far and wide to communications, electronics, banking, travel, tourism, education, printing, publishing, entertainment, government and other services in addition to numerous IT-enabled services in manufacturing, BPOs, KPOs, etc. Also witnessed in the recent periods are the onset of several state-of-the-art technologies not only enhancing speed but also involving significant strides in material substitution, savings in energy, labour and other input costs, not to speak of recovery, recycling through application of cleaner technologies, better practices, etc. Two such examples which can be cited are a state-of-the-art agrochemical plant in the Union Territory of Dadra and a direct reduction process-based pig iron plant in Dolvi, Raigad, in Maharashtra. While the former has total manpower strength of 29 employees including 16 officers and above rank as against the 300 plus in the older plant, the latter has a little over 2,000 compared to the several thousands in others in the category. More significantly, there is also the adoption of cleaner technologies in such plants thus drastically reducing the end of pipe treatment costs including the associated energy costs. Added to such developments are the reinforced effects of part automation in production, introduction of PLCs, automated packaging and the like. In the recent times, we have many more such developments. They are cloud services, robotics and remote-presence robots enabling presentations at meetings/conference/seminar presentations without physically being present, digitally networked environs, 3-D printing, nanotechnology, fuel cells, artificially intelligent personal assistants or predictive intelligence softwares, use of magnetic tape for mass storage data, smart weapons, smart grids, smart cities, driverless cars, internet of things, etc. Indeed, they are simply mindboggling with an unimaginable gamut of widespread impacts!

On the *consumption front*, it is no longer the old story characterized and driven by needs and wants predominantly, with the sole exception of the Giffen goods. It is self-evident, for quite some time now, that aspirational consumption has gained stronghold and is on the rise with the active state and other institutional promotion of mall culture. In fact, it no longer comes as a surprise that semiurban and rural areas including urban slums provide huge markets for white goods, electronics, beauty products, etc. So, tastes and preferences do change and, of late, have been changing at a faster pace. So much the worse, if they can be induced! Steve Jobs is often quoted these days to justify the merit of product designers deciding what consumers want in the face of the latter's ignorance! Surely, it has been so far so good, at least for the time being. It is not just Apple, but also Skype, Facebook, Twitter, Amazon, WhatsApp and several others testify to this. What the future will hold can only be left to one's imagination, stretched even to a wild one at that!

Clearly, therefore, neither technological progress nor tastes and preferences as envisaged in much of the previous century and least of all, their being constant can hold any longer. Such assumptions may have carried conviction during those yesteryears/decades, given the more or less stable pace in respect of either technology or consumer tastes and preferences over a fairly long period of time, say 30–40 years, as was the case with automobiles, aircrafts, chemicals, electronics, etc. Thus, it was reasonable to assume that technology as given, as in the Cobb-Douglas production function. It is, however, no longer so! For a detailed discussion on the subject, see Hegde and Nilakantan (2004), who have attempted to reformulate the model using a sigmoid function.

7.5 Spillovers Across Sectors

Up to now, we have discussed about the technological developments taking place within sectors like steel, chemicals, energy, IT, ITES, etc. There are still others gathering pace, which need our attention. Together, they hold immense possibilities not only within the sectors where they take place but also across several other sectors by way of ripple effects.

Such developments originate in a certain sector or industry and, in addition to revolutionizing that very sector/industry, are capable of bringing about immense impact in other sectors/industries as well. For instance, if fuel cells get commercialized and their usage generalized, the consequence would be large-scale ramifications in automobiles, grids and even individual households which, as is claimed, can then produce their own power requirements combining fuel cells and nanotechnology. So would be the implications of 3-D printing with immense potential for cottage industries in several sectors. Similar types of ramifications can be imagined as a result of intensifying alternative sources of energy that are of renewable variety like wind, solar, biofuels, etc., changing drastically the scarcity value of oil and foreign exchange. Digitally networked environment is yet another speedy and significant development with far-reaching implications for theory of the firm, market signals, organizational command hierarchy, reductionism and development of theory and policy. Cloud services are yet another recent development with immense potential for significant reduction in costs of IT infrastructure, its maintenance and use on real-time basis. This and robotics and 3-D printing are expected to usher in the 'third industrial revolution', according to a recent issue of *The Economist* magazine

(April 21–27, 2012)! Other significant developments in this category are arms and ammunition with expiry date with high prospects of peace, magnetic tapes for massive data storage as a least cost and loss-minimizing option, remote-controlled robotic presentations, shale gas discovery as a game changer, smart grids/cities, etc. There could be a sea change in scarcity values across the board, reduction and even pre-empting of waste, efficiency in resource use and finally ramifications on environment and geopolitical dimensions.

In a similar manner, impacts alongside can be envisaged with respect to consumption as well. Imagine a situation where the youth of a country take increasingly to a monk's hairstyle or dressing style of Steve Jobs! Demand for beauty products and formal dresses would then decline drastically. Again, if superfast bullet trains become a reality, demand for air travel may decline, and, in effect, derived demand for jet fuel, employment and expansion plans of the aviation sector, etc., may be severely impacted.

In the new economy, therefore, these secondary or spillover impacts combined with the primary impacts of changes in technology and tastes and preferences already discussed in the previous section may have a reinforced effect in a variety of industries/sectors. In the face of such developments, contextualizing and modifying theories and models become all the more inescapable.

7.6 Conclusion

It clearly emerges from the discussion that there exist gaping holes in the practice of continuing with unrealistic assumptions which, in effect, raise some methodological implications. Further, it goes on to show that assuming technology or tastes and preferences as constant is no longer tenable, especially in the light of their ever-increasing pace, variety and also the direct and indirect impacts which tend to have widespread ripple effects across several sectors. So also is the case with the assumption of efficiency of the markets. As a result, some serious issues with respect to theory, modelling and empirical work arise on the very grounds Koopmans had espoused and Schumpeter had cautioned. Thus, it is not merely a question of causal versus time series models, static versus dynamic models, linear versus non-linear models or partial versus general equilibrium analysis. Much more is involved if only we develop a sense of history in addition to according due recognition to the role of institutions, values and attitudes in addition to learning from practice and experience, thereby gaining insights to establish a connection with basic principles. Only then, we might be able to grapple with the changing context and to address the problems being faced in a more meaningful way as also strike a balance between rigour and relevance. It hardly needs to be overemphasized that such a possibility would be nearer, greater the adoption of a judicious mix of positivist and phenomenological approaches rather than an either or orientation.

References

Hegde DS, Nilakantan K (2004) Implications of emerging technologies on econometric modeling: the case of production functions. In: Nachane DM et al (eds) Econometric models: theory and applications. Allied Publishers, New Delhi

Koopmans TC (1957) Three essays on the state of economic science. McGraw-Hill, New York

Schumpeter J (1964) History of economic analysis. Oxford University Press, New York

Seaward BL (2005) Quiet mind, fearless heart. Wiley, Hoboken

The Economist (2012) The third industrial revolution, April 21–27

Chapter 8
On Using Experimental Designs

V.K. Kool and Rita Agrawal

8.1 Introduction

Experimentation is an important method of data collection as much in the behavioral sciences as in the natural sciences, and in order to conduct an experiment, we use what has been termed the experimental method. By definition, the experimental method is that method in which one or more variables is/are manipulated by the experimenter in order to see its/their effect on another variable. The variable which is manipulated is known as the independent variable, and since changes in the second variable are dependent on the variation in the independent variable, this latter is known as the dependent variable. Thus, to take an example from the natural sciences, one might want to study the effect of altitude above sea level on the boiling point of a substance. In order to do so, one creates conditions in which the boiling point of the substance is recorded at different altitudes above sea level. The latter, that is, altitude above sea level on which the boiling point is said to vary would be then called the independent variable, while the boiling point itself becomes the dependent variable. To take another example, this time from the behavioral sciences, one might be interested in studying the effect of different training programs on the performance of employees in an automobile manufacturing unit. What would be the independent variable? The independent variable would be the one that is being manipulated by or is in the control of the experimenter, namely, the different training programs. Since performance would be a function of these different training programs, that becomes the dependent variable.

V.K. Kool
Professor, SUNY Polytechnic Institute, New Palt, NY, USA

R. Agrawal (✉)
Professor and Director, Faculty of Management & Technology, Harish Chandra Post-graduate College, Varanasi, India
e-mail: ritaagrawal49@gmail.com

D.S. Hegde (ed.), *Essays on Research Methodology*,
DOI 10.1007/978-81-322-2214-9_8

To this point we can draw parallels between experiments in the natural sciences and those in the behavioral sciences. But a variety of differences can be pointed out, and it is these that in fact create the essence and the complexity of experimentation in the behavioral sciences. First and foremost, the subject of research, namely, the substance whose boiling point is to be measured, is lifeless. As such, no matter who conducts the research, it does not matter, and nor does the lifeless subject have moods, attitudes, personality, etc. Also, since it is without life, we can divide our total amount of solution into ten or, maybe, twenty or even a hundred portions, and each portion would yield the same result, all other factors being kept constant. In contrast, the subject of the research in the behavioral sciences is a living organism and even more so is a complex function of emotions, motivations, personality, etc. Can we divide our human subject into ten or even two parts? These and many other similar factors, inherent in any subject that has life, call for the utmost caution while conducting research and especially experiments in disciplines such as psychology, sociology, anthropology, etc. It is much more difficult to obtain reliable, valid data unless due controls are exercised by the experimenter. It is primarily for this factor of control that stringent experimental designs have been created so that we may be able to establish cause-effect relationships, much akin to those obtained in the natural sciences. An experimental design can be likened to the architect's blueprint which is not only prepared after considerable thought but is also dependent upon the needs of the user of the building. So also, a variety of experimental designs are available from which the researcher can pick and choose depending upon his needs and the needs of the research problem.

In a scientific research, an important consideration is the way experimental conditions are created by a researcher. This step is followed by the application of appropriate statistical methods. Whether we are conducting an experiment in biology, physics, or social and behavioral sciences, initial research efforts demand how each treatment condition will be set up and, in most cases, would be compared with another condition. For example, we may want to investigate the following:

(a) The effect of radiation on the levels of growth of cancer
(b) The effect of an amount of money earned by people on their levels of happiness

We need to develop a strong argument that radiation is linked to the growth of cancer or that money makes people happy. If there are plenty of cases that we observe corroborating such conclusions, we take the first step in developing a rationale, called a hypothesis, that is, worthy of verification. A number of steps are generated from this point onwards, and each step is carefully planned to meet the standards of a robust experimental design that an experimenter wants to use for demonstrating a firm conclusion.

8.2 Steps in the Designing of an Experiment

Given below are the steps that are generally pursued in designing an experiment to test a hypothesis:

8.2.1 Begin with a Hypothesis

Generally, we begin with a hypothesis which, in statistical terms, is called the null hypothesis. Thus, in the above example, the null hypothesis would be that exposure to radiation or not will not cause any difference between the groups (null meaning zero difference between the exposed and unexposed groups). The job of the experimenter is to demonstrate that the radiation-exposed and unexposed groups are indeed different, and by employing an experimental plan, she shows how to reject the null hypothesis. In short, the goal of an experimental hypothesis is to reject the null hypothesis. The reader will notice that what we commonly observe leads to the formation of a hypothesis, but to meet the rigors of scientific testing, we need to present our hypothesis in the form of an experimental hypothesis. This latter hypothesis takes the form of a statistical hypothesis when we apply it to the parameters of a population. For example, money affects the levels of happiness if income decreases, but after a certain level, too much money might become a source of unhappiness (where to invest, how to keep it safe, etc.), too. In other words, if we prove statistically that money is a source of happiness, the same hypothesis might not yield any difference (null hypothesis) now because the characteristic of the population (those with too much money) has now changed. In other words, the experimental hypothesis is not the same as the statistical hypothesis, the latter being restricted to rejecting the null hypothesis, albeit they both complement each other in an empirical investigation.

8.2.2 Is a Hypothesis Ready for Testing?

A basic criterion for developing a hypothesis is that procedures should be available for testing the hypothesis. After satisfying this condition, the next step is to identify an experimental condition, called the independent variable. Since it is a condition that is manipulated by an experimenter, we must first determine that whatever we are taking as our independent variable is in fact capable of being manipulated by the experimenter. Thus, for the above example, namely, to find the effect of different doses of radiation on the growth of cancer, we have to determine in the first place that we can indeed vary the dosage of radiation. Simultaneously, the experimenter eliminates the effects of other conditions that contribute to the growth of cancer, such as exposure to heat, smoking, and so on, because these factors have the potential to cause cancer and we would never know if the cancer occurred because of radiation alone or something else. Those variables that have potential effect on an experiment but are not in the domain of an independent variable are called extraneous variables or nuisance variables. They must be eliminated or kept under control to enhance the trustworthiness of an experiment.

8.2.3 Where to Locate the Effect of the Cause in an Experiment?

The effects of an independent variable must be measured in some form. For example, increases in radiation doses would be linked to an early (or delayed) onset of cancer. In other words, an experimenter is interested in finding out the cause-effect relationship, that is, finding the impact of independent variable on the dependent variable. Typical examples of dependent variables in the case of radiation experiment are loss of weight, speed, activity, latency of response, or virtually any performance that is triggered by the radiation. Because experiments require a lot of hard work and time, the appropriateness of a dependent variable is critical in research. A good hypothesis is not likely to be supported if the selected dependent variables are unrelated to the independent variable.

8.2.4 Whom Do We Test? The Size of the Sample

A cardinal rule of an experiment is that the sample in a study must be drawn randomly, that is, each subject or unit must have equal chance of selection. Once a procedure for a random allocation is established, subjects are assigned to the conditions of an experiment. For example, how many doses of radiation do we need to include in the study? To what extent do the subjects differ in their health condition to account for the variance in the case of cancer study? What are the chances of making an error owing to the smaller size of a sample?

8.3 A Survey of Experimental Designs

The selection of a design of an experiment is guided by many considerations: time, number of subjects, human and fiscal resources, tolerance of magnitude of statistical error, and several others. While discussing the entire gamut of experimental designs would not be feasible in this small chapter, we will offer to the readers a wide range of designs and demonstrate how such designs contribute to the success of a study.

8.3.1 Designs Without a Control Group (One Set Designs)

At a very basic level of experimentation, a researcher may simply be interested in testing the effect of an independent variable. It is assumed that the independent variable is likely to show an impact (e.g., the doses of radiation will cause cancer). There are many situations in which due to the paucity of time and money or the exigency of a situation, a quick appraisal is necessary. It is fairly common in social programs to assume on an a priori basis that the program will cause the intended effect. When a program lacks a cogent theory or model, it is considered pragmatic to offer something that is better than nothing. Box 8.1 presents two examples of one set designs. While the first simply tests the effects of the independent variable, the second goes a step further. Since we want to be sure that the changes in the dependent variable have been caused by the effect of the independent variable alone, we pretest the subjects which would then be used as the baseline data. Thereafter, the independent variable is administered upon the subject, and observations on the dependent variable are taken afresh. A comparison of the pretest data with the posttest data enables the researcher to conclude that the differences between these two sets of data, if any, are caused by the effect of the independent variable. In other words, the degree of control exercised by the researcher is greater in the second design than in the first.

Box 8.1: One Set Designs

A. Independent variable (exposure to radiation) → Posttest effects (effect of radiation)

B. Pretest on the dependent variable → Independent variable (exposure to radiation) → Posttest (effect of radiation)

8.3.2 Design with a Control

In natural sciences, however, it is mandated that the results should be validated by demonstrating that in the absence of the independent variable, it would not be possible to reject the null hypothesis. Under such conditions, the experimenter creates another group, called the control group that is not exposed to the independent variable. It is imperative that the subjects in the two groups be randomly assigned, and while one will receive the placebo treatment, the other will be exposed to radiation (Box 8.2). The addition of the control group helps control another extraneous variable, namely, the variable of time lapse between the exposure and the independent variable and the measurement of its effect upon the dependent variable. It also helps ascertain whether the seen effects are due to the administration of any variable or due to the particular variable whose effects are under scrutiny.

Box 8.2: Designs with Two Groups: One Experimental and One Control Group

Pretest independent variable		Posttest	
Experimental group	Test	Exposure to radiation	Test (compare with pretest)
Control group	Test	No exp./or exp. to placebo	Test (compare with pretest)

8.3.3 Solomon Four-Group Design

One problem with the above experimental designs is that there is no assurance that the effects are caused by the independent variable alone. For example, in a speech therapy program, the young babies who participate in this program (an independent variable) might show improvement in comparison to those babies who were kept in the control group, but there is still no assurance that their improvement is in fact due to the program. It is well known that speech development among babies is not uniform and some babies catch up at a later stage of development. It means that the program was, in reality, ineffective, though the layout of the experimental design erroneously pointed out that the independent variable was a significant contributor to the development. In order to make sure that the independent variable is indeed effective, it is important that we include more groups in the study to demonstrate the impact of the independent variable.

A popular but more time-consuming and expensive method is the Solomon four-group design in which the experimenter measures the effect of the independent variable by including or excluding it under different conditions. Box 8.3 presents a summary of the conditions of this design. This design is effective because it has the potential to identify the role of any pre-existing condition which may contaminate the results of the experiment. This is a serious concern, and we will discuss it further in the section describing threats to internal validity.

Box 8.3: Solomon Four-Group Design

Pretest		Independent variable	Posttest
Pretested	Test	Exposure to radiation	Test the effect of radiation
Pretested	Test	No exposure	Test the effect of radiation (?)
Unpretested	No test	Exposure to radiation	Test the effect of radiation
Unpretested	No test		Test the effect of radiation (?)

(?) = Under these two conditions, no radiation was administered, but the same testing (e.g., blood test, tissue damage, etc.) will be conducted to rule out if variables other than the independent variable caused the effect

8.3.4 Experiments with Several Treatment Levels

In the above scenario, we restricted our discussion to comparison between two groups: pretest versus posttest scores or experimental versus control groups. The independent variable is of one fixed value, for example, the amount of radiation. Suppose we were to vary the treatment levels by exposing several groups to different amounts of radiation. In this case, we would be able to investigate not only whether radiation has any effect on cancer growth but also whether the rate at which the growth of cancer is accelerated because of the changes in the intensity levels. This effort of an experimenter is an extension of the same design but yields additional information regarding the variation of the effect of radiation. By employing analysis of variance (ANOVA) techniques, a statistical method that goes beyond comparing means and relies on accounting within and between variances of scores, a researcher can compare different treatment conditions causing varying levels of cancer. Box 8.4 shows a typical layout of a randomized experiment involving more than two groups.

Box 8.4: Several Treatment Levels of One Independent Variable

	Group A	Group B	Group C
Amount of radiation	Low	Medium	High

Note: Subjects should be randomly assigned to each group, and thereafter exposure to radiation can be observed for the dependent variable in each group

8.3.5 *Designs with Two or More Independent Variables and Treatments*

Consider the possibility of unequal effects of radiation among children and adults. Using a randomized design in which both children and adults are exposed to different levels of radiation, we may form and retain or reject three null hypotheses in the same experiment:

(a) Both children and adults are similarly affected by radiation (in this case age is the independent variable # 1).
(b) Changing radiation doses does not increase levels of harm (in this case dosage of radiation is the second independent variable #2).
(c) Adults and children suffer harm similarly when the intensity levels of radiation doses change. Now, here we gain additional information, that is, how the treatment levels of radiation doses are equally (or not) influencing children and adults. This type of design is called a two-factor design that involves investigation of one variable having an influence on another variable. Such an effect is called the interaction effect in a two-way analysis of variance test, and its 2×2 layout, with two treatment levels of radiation and two age groups, is given in Box 8.5a.

Box 8.5a: Two-Factor Design (2 × 2 Factorial)

	Levels of radiation	
	High	Low
Children		
Adults		

In this example, the experimenter is free to increase the levels of treatments in each independent variable, but it will still be called a two-factor experiment because the number of independent variables remains the same (Box 8.5b).

Box 8.5b: Two-Factor Design with Three Treatment Levels (3 × 2 Factorial Design)

	Levels of radiation		
	High	Medium	Low
Children			
Adults			

When an experimenter includes one more independent variable, for example, gender, the design becomes a three-factor study (see Box 8.5c below).

Box 8.5c: Three-Factor Design (2 × 2 × 2 Factorial Design)

		Levels of radiation	
		High	Low
Children	Males		
	Females		
Adults	Males		
	Females		

8.3.6 *Designs with Repeated Measures*

In many experiments, it is not possible to randomly assign subjects to different groups often because of the paucity of subjects. It is also mandatory to study the same subjects over a period of time in longitudinal studies. In both these cases, designs known as repeated measures designs are used. The designs are so named because the same subjects are tested repeatedly during a given period of time. Such a design is also useful when an experimenter is interested in evaluating the stability of scores. For example, if you are interested in studying the effect of a spiral rotation that causes an illusion to move in the opposite direction after it becomes still, you may need to test the same subject at rotation periods of 15, 30, and 60 s. Why do we need to test the same subject repeatedly? It is because since we already know that the base rate of this illusion differs from one subject to another, using this experimental arrangement, we can test the hypothesis, whether the aftereffect of perception of movement in the opposite direction would be seen for a longer duration (dependent variable) with increases in the exposure time from 15 through 60 s. Since there is only one independent variable with three treatment levels involved in this study, the design is called a "one-factor treatments-by-subjects" or one-factor repeated measures design (Box 8.6). The same design will become a two-factor repeated design if we add one more independent variable (e.g., subjects with a brain injury)

Box 8.6: One-Factor Repeated Measures Design

	Spiral rotation time		
	15 s	30 s	60 s
Subject # 1			
Subject # 2			
Subject # 3			
...			
...			
...			
Subject# n			

The above design becomes more complex as per the nature of hypotheses tested in a study. With more than two factors involved, the experimenter may require repeated measures on the same subjects on either one variable or on both variables. For example, if we add brain-injured subjects (independent variable #2) and test both males and females (independent variable #3) repeatedly, an extension of the design in Box 8.6 would be a three-factor design with repeated measures on two factors. Such mixed types of designs are very useful as they allow us to investigate several hypotheses at a time, including the interaction effects as discussed earlier.

8.3.7 Latin Square Design

Let us go back to the spiral aftereffect example. If we expose subjects to the rotating spiral in the fixed order beginning with 15 s and then to 30 and 60 s, respectively, the latter conditions after the 15 s exposure may cause a cumulative effect on the subsequent conditions and therefore contaminate the results of the experiment. Given this scenario, the experimenter will be tempted to ask the following question: "what if we systematically assign each subject in a different order of the spiral rotation exposure?" Box 8.7 summarizes a simple arrangement of subjects under the three spiral exposure conditions of this experiment. By counterbalancing the treatment levels (15-30-60, 60-15-30, and 30-60-15), the experimenter can now investigate the cumulative effect of the exposure arrangements

Box 8.7: Latin Square Design

Order of presentation	Spiral rotation time		
	15 s	30 s	60 s
First	Group 1	Group 2	Group 3
Second	Group 3	Group 1	Group 2
Third	Group 2	Group 3	Group 1

The above design becomes very complex when a researcher finds that the order of presentation plays an important role in the study. In Box 8.7, you have not seen the following arrangement: group 3 followed by group 2 and group 1 as compared to the first order of presentation: 1, 2, and 3 for 15, 30, and 60 s.

8.4 Multivariate Designs: Experiments with Two or More Dependent Variables

The experimenter is often confronted with a situation in which the effect of the independent variable is expected not just on a single variable but on two or more dependent variables. To take an example, industry experience might be showing that employee performance is greatly affected by leadership style. But we may also be led to suppose that leadership style affects not merely performance but also the level of commitment shown by the employee. Moreover, there is enough evidence from both industry experience and empirical research to show that the level of employee commitment also decides performance. To empirically prove hypotheses such as the above, we require a more complex set of experimental designs known as multivariate designs which use MANOVA for their statistical analysis. The basic difference between the designs discussed above and the ones that follow is that the researcher takes observations on more than one dependent variable with each manipulation of the independent variable(s). Two typical layouts are presented below, one with one independent variable (Box 8.8) and the other with two independent variables (Box 8.9).

Box 8.8: Multivariate Design with One Independent Variable

Factor 1 at three levels: level 1, level 2, and level 3		
Observations being taken for two dependent variables, X and Y		
Level 1	Level 2	Level 3
Democratic leader	Autocratic leader	Laissez-faire leader
X^1(performance)	X^2(performance)	X^3(performance)
Y^1(commitment)	Y^2(commitment)	Y^3(commitment)

X stands for observations for performance and Y stands for observations for commitment. Thus, in the same experiment, we are able to test for the effects of leadership style on performance and commitment simultaneously. This becomes important because were we to limit ourselves to observations on just either one of the dependent variables, we would not be able to understand whether the changes are due to just changes in the independent variable or because of the intercorrelation between the two dependent variables. It also leads to considerable parsimony of time and effort because in a single experiment we are studying the effect on two variables, which would otherwise have required two experiments. But, more important than parsimony, we are able to avoid losing out on a lot of information because experiments on single effects do not take into account the correlation between two dependent variables.

8.4.1 Example of a 2 × 3 Factorial Design with Effects on Two Dependent Variables

Since both performance and commitment would be affected by factors other than leadership style, the researcher might be interested in studying the effect of not just leadership style but also the nature of reinforcements being given in the company on both performance and commitment of the employee. We might take into consideration the three types of leadership style mentioned above and two types of reinforcement, namely, monetary reward and praise.

Box 8.9: Factorial Multivariate Analysis with Two Independent Variables

Factor 1:	Level 1	Level 2	Level 3
(Leadership)	Democratic	Autocratic	Laissez-faire
Factor 2	X^1(performance)	X^2(performance)	X^3(performance)
Level 1			
(Monetary reward)	Y^1(commitment)	Y^2(commitment)	Y^3(commitment)
Level 2	X^1(performance)	X^2(performance)	X^3(performance)
(Praise)			
	Y^1(commitment)	Y^2(commitment)	Y^3(commitment)

All the experimental designs discussed above, for example, the single-factor randomized group design, the factorial design, the repeated measures designs, and the Latin square designs, lend themselves to multivariate designs. Though complicated in terms of statistical analysis, these designs provide much more information than several experiments conducted with measures on single dependent variables. Many a time, the single dependent factor experiments may all end up with nonsignificant results, simply because of the covariation between dependent variables which would be revealed only when they are considered in the same experiment.

8.5 Experimental Designs as a Bridge Between Conceptual and Statistical Validity

An experiment is conducted to determine a cause-effect relationship that is established by the manipulation of an independent variable. It is assumed that the effect of an independent variable will be found on the dependent variable. An experimental design is a tool that helps to establish the proposed conceptual framework of a relationship between the independent and the dependent variables. Further, the variations in a design, such as the Latin square design, help the experimenter to determine the strength of the relationship between the two variables. For example, if the aftereffect of a moving spiral has a cumulative effect, then its longer exposure should generate its afterimage of a longer duration. Therefore, the role of a powerful experimental design should not be underestimated.

It is a common practice in the statistical treatment of data to determine if our results are significant at a minimum chance level of 95 % or higher (0.05 level of significance). This is the minimum value that is conventionally targeted to reject the null hypothesis. Now, what happens if we get statistically significant results but, conceptually, the independent and dependent variables do not relate to each other in a meaningful manner? Suppose we put one leg of an individual in fire and the other in ice, based on an average of the two extreme temperatures, we could predict a very tolerable temperature for the survival of the individual. The statistical average of the two temperatures makes sense, but does it make conceptual sense? Can we say that the average of the two extreme temperatures would decide the temperature that would be tolerated by the individual? Similarly, we may find a result to be statistically valid, but, conceptually, it may not make any sense. In other words, if the results are statistically valid, it may or may not mean that the conceptual validity is also strong. A powerful experimental design acts as a buffer to show that we have found out what we were looking for. By employing a pertinent experimental design, the experimenter tests her hypothesis in different ways (conceptual validity), and through the statistical methods that we follow for each design, we offer statistical validity in rejecting the null hypothesis.

The reader will notice that we have used the concept of "validity" in a generic way. In fact, validity is simply about measuring something that we intend to measure. If we are measuring mechanical energy in sound waves, we should be measuring the same phenomenon. In behavioral research, if we are measuring intelligence, we should measure intelligence and intelligence alone and not personality. A validity issue that emerges out of its impact on the relationship between the independent and dependent variables is called internal validity. The goal of an experimenter is to employ an experimental design that reinforces the relationship between these two variables or in other words provides internal validity. Additionally, when an experimenter makes an attempt to extend the results to other populations of subjects and settings, she would be exploring the extent of external validity of her experiment.

8.6 Threats to the Validity of Experiments

There are a number of situations and factors that may damage the nature of the relationship between the independent and the dependent variables, and we may falsely believe (or not believe) that the effect was caused by the independent variable. In the radiation example, while the experimenter might conclude that the doses of radiation caused cancer, other factors, if not properly controlled, might also cause the same effect. In a teaching program, if the students are doing well, it might not be because of a new teaching method but owing to the raised level of the motivation of students who took the challenge to try this new method of instruction. In spite of a rigorous experimental design and a robust statistical analysis, there are chances that the criterion for validating the findings of an experiment may still remain elusive. Broadly speaking, such threats to the internal validity of experiments fall under three categories.

The first category consists of factors that are not directly related to the independent variable, for example, the age factor. The levels of development may change with time. In a learning program, children may mature and catch up faster than their predecessors who had joined a program earlier at a younger age. Speech, motor, and intellectual development in children does not take place at a uniform rate, and hence a program that is designed to accelerate their growth may falsely get the credit, but instead, children's natural growth tends to contribute, albeit belatedly, to their growth. Further, owing to some historical reasons, a program may look good or bad. For example, an agricultural program for boosting crops may look bad because of the cyclical nature of the low-yielding crop in a particular year. Another factor that tends to obscure the internal validity is what is known as regression to the mean. It means that those who perform well for a long time might not continue to perform at the same rate. A pilot who makes several very smooth landings will probably fail to do so in the next attempt. Basketball players know their diminished rate of success after making several perfect free throws.

Finally, a faulty instrument or the way in which a subject is tested may blur the relationship between the independent and dependent variables. A poor measure of performance may nullify the positive contribution of a teaching program. Moreover, the conditions in which the subjects are tested might cause problems. While we may perform well privately, the same performance may suffer at a public stage, and therefore making a dance program look bad. We react to situations, and it is not uncommon that a potentially effective program turns out to be unsuccessfully because of reactive conditions in which the dependent variable is being tested.

8.7 Concluding Remarks

In this chapter, we have presented some basic information on the layout and usefulness of experimental designs. The main concern in employing an experimental design is the ingenuity of an experimenter in tying the independent variable with the dependent variable. Further, we attempted to show how experimental designs and statistical validity help to enhance the conceptual framework of an experiment and why the purpose of experimentation might be defeated owing to the several threats that contaminate the relationship between the independent and dependent variables. In those scenarios in which true experiments are impossible to conduct, for example, where there is no possibility of the randomized assignment of subjects, the researcher has no choice but to adhere to the quasi-experimental techniques such as a time series design. Having its origin in economics, this latter method has become very popular in many social sciences in recent years, especially when manipulation of an independent variable and sample distribution poses a problem to the researcher.

References

Keppel G, Wickens TD (2004) Design & analysis: a researcher's handbook, 4th edn. Pearson, Upper Saddle River

Kirk RE (2013) Experimental design: procedures for behavioural sciences. Sage, Thousand Oaks

Winer BJ, Brown DR, Michels KM (1991) Statistical principles in experimental design. McGraw-Hill, Columbus

Chapter 9
Questionnaire Design for Survey Research

Omer Bin Sayeed

9.1 Questionnaire Design

9.1.1 Introduction

Social science methodology is greatly facilitated by sharp and incisive methods of enquiry and a variety of refined techniques of questionnaire-based researches. The tools and techniques of measurement are systematically adopted to evolve perception-based assessment or indices covering a wide variety of themes of researches in the form of questionnaire data. The questionnaire data comes from various sources; some of them are intimately psychological, whereas others are *matter-of-fact* surveys. Broadly classifying these questionnaires, they belong to three major categories. One of them is to assess personal dynamics, which are hidden but measureable with the sincere intention of subjects and their honest answering. Such subjects tend to show strong inclination as to who they are and would like to get assessed themselves for creating some awareness for a purpose, for instance, using a personality inventory for counseling purpose or generating feedback based on the scores obtained by managers individually or in a group.

The second category of questionnaires belongs to social/organizational subsystems of various types in which the subject is the target of processes as well as occupies an identity of an observer with some background conditions within which he is embedded. He carries along with him an amalgamation of perceptions containing events, happenings, fantasies, and true to life perceived actions he has

O.B. Sayeed (✉)
Former Professor of Organization Behaviour and Dean (Research), National Institute of Industrial Engineering, Mumbai, India

Present Affiliation: Adjunct Professor, OB/HR, IBS Hyderabad, Hyderabad, India
e-mail: omersayeed@gmail.com

D.S. Hegde (ed.), *Essays on Research Methodology*,
DOI 10.1007/978-81-322-2214-9_9

observed. He keeps on synthesizing these events and gives some meanings to them. The process of giving meaning is though subjective, yet a group of people giving way to data and associated meanings in a similar way creates authenticity for such processes. Questionnaire response thus codifies the meaning of such processes in quantitative terms or in terms of inferences made around a theme of research being investigated by the individual researcher.

The third category of questionnaire might be short enough, carrying a short-run effect, and it is intended to know, in a nutshell, a given political or social process in the form of an opinionnaire. Such opinionnaires will be brief in their format and would tend to reflect one event or a set of happening or multiple events that did take place or are likely to take place in a context. For instance, preferences for a given political party or leadership ratings of community/political leaders are assessed through such opinionnaires. In short, opinionnaires' quantitative assessment is generally made through rating scales and frequencies, percentages, means and standard deviations, pie charts, and histograms that are selectively used to highlight a set of alternatives answered by the general public or by a target group.

Whether it is a social context or an engineering assessment of a framework or work mapping of one sort or the other or some method of personal evaluation involving superiors and subordinates, a set of well-defined attributes/dimensions of instruments/questionnaires aid the researchers. The measurement tools providing with a framework or hinting upon the outcome of measurement largely aid in inferring what is hidden from the naked eyes. The perceptual assessment (observed, interpreted, and responded to a suggested framework being the perceptual process) thus becomes the main crux that goes deep into the inferential processes used by the researcher. Based on these inferential processes, we try to conclude whether a system is described in a matter-of-fact way or in an evaluative way, weighting some of the characteristics against a standard criterion or a benchmarked factor. We try to assess whether a process is healthy or sick, an organization is effective or ineffective, and roles of incumbents in an organization are efficacious or inefficacious. And also through questionnaires/instruments aided by observational data, we assess the extent to which psychiatric diagnosis should put the candidate into psychiatric illness category or healthy person category. All such critical attributes of inferences drawn from the questionnaire help the researcher in using his/her model of research and taking a stand as to its implications for research and/or practice in social, organizational, or management systems or subsystems.

It is also necessary to think whether without a structured questionnaire it is possible to measure the targeted features of a study in an organization or in a social subsystem. Many consultants well versed with their environment due to long experience of action research-based studies seemingly make right inferences, subject their analysis to a logical conclusion, and convince the organization or system managers to implement proffered/suggested changes. In fact, their hunches even without quantitative data have helped organizations in managing their system and processes more effectively. It is easy to guess that such management consultants must have been applying a "virtual design approach"; perhaps it is visualized in their minds and executed intelligently due to their long-drawn management insights. A relevant example is Mintzberg's (1973) theoretical understanding of organizational structure and role descriptions he arrived at due to organization-based experiences and without applying systematic and exhaustive questionnaire-based approach.

While the above cited example is more obvious in view of organizational experiences and the power of conceptualizing a variety of models of work systems of an organization, however, the rigor of research demands quantitative basis for developing an organizational or a social system or a management-based model to explain as to how it works. It is also besides the fact that if quantitative baseline is created, personal biases would have less chance to creep into the conceptual arguments. Hence, application of questionnaire methodology becomes imminent in organizational, management/engineering centric studies and also in social system researches. The final outcomes of quantitative researches which are based on questionnaire data ultimately serve the purpose of being verifiable all the time; the amount of deviation that has taken place due to interventions made in the target group is also self-evident.

The rigor of research thus demands objective assessment and verifiability of such thought processes which can be measured. Rigorous research is seriously interested in defining an objective framework of the study which can give way to a set of variables to be considered for the survey/questionnaire design of the study. The major difference between theoretical conceptualization (e.g., hypothetically building a theory) and questionnaire-based study is that there should be strong explanatory power for the social or organizational phenomenon in the case of conceptual studies, while the same conceptualization can be attained bit by bit if questionnaire design/survey researches are being focused on diverse aspects of a phenomenon and gradually built up a model of the social/organizational system under study.

9.2 Design of Instrument/Questionnaire

9.2.1 Framework

Once a well-defined research frame is sought for by the researcher, whether he is novice or well experienced, he would like to search a tool for measurement of the type of variables he has chosen or develop one for collecting data from the target group. It is typically seen that in well-researched areas a variety of instruments/questionnaires are available or at least these researches tend to provide some insights about the variables and as to how to measure them. In gray areas of research, where partial or inadequate conceptualization of variables exists, one needs to develop a research tool unique to the target group. Hence, before one develops an instrument, it is necessary to comprehensively view the conceptual scheme of research and operational definitions of variables chosen for the study and where it is applicable. In other words, an integrated approach in building the research tool is extremely desirable.

On the other side depending on the type of literature resources for obtaining a questionnaire or instrument, a researcher may like to explore the field of literature. Sometimes, if not always, articles/books provide a well-designed questionnaire as an appendage or give some clues for measuring certain variables the researcher is interested in. In almost all social science disciplines (psychology, sociology, public administration, political science, anthropology, etc.) and allied management sciences like industrial engineering, supply chain management, project management, etc., some questionnaire resources are available. The discipline of psychology generally advanced itself on the principles of objectivity and empiricism; it relied heavily on a variety of measurement techniques. Thus, it gave research centric direction to standardize a variety of psychological processes and helped developing compendia of instruments, standard enough to measure directly several processes or subprocesses of the human system specifically and a variety of sociopsychological experiences in general. Box 9.1 provides a few useful source books for questionnaire-based researches, which can be used profitably in management and social science disciplines.

Box 9.1: Source Books/Compendia of Questionnaires/Surveys

Carlson JF, Geisinger KF, Jessica L, Jonson JL (eds) (2014) The nineteenth mental measurements yearbook. University of Nebraska Press, Nebraska

Cook JD, Hepworth SJ, Wall TD, Warr PB (1981) Experience of work: a compendium and review of 249 measures and their use. Academic press, New York

Pestonjee (1988) 2nd handbook of psychological and social instruments. Concept Publishing House, New Delhi

Sarupria D, Rao TV, Madhavan P (1996) Measuring organizational climate. Academy of HRD, Ahmedabad

Pfeiffer JW, Jones JE A handbook of structured experiences for human relations training, 11 vols. Contains some Instruments generally used for classroom feedback.

Pfeifer JW, Jones JE (2013) Annual for HRD facilitators (several volumes). This series of books published annually contained a section on questionnaires that can be applied on a variety of personal and organizational situations and also often used in classroom discussion and feedback purpose.

Pareek U (2002) Training instruments in HRD and OD, 2nd edn. Tata-McGraw-Hill, New Delhi

It needs to be reckoned that instruments/questionnaires are not systematically standardized in multidisciplinary fields of engineering or related areas due to not meeting specific needs of surveys, and after having examined their efficacy or practical implications in certain specific areas, such questionnaire has been ignored. Even in financial and economic studies, questionnaires are not readily available due to two reasons. Firstly, these disciplines rarely placed emphasis on perceptual or perception-based studies. Secondly, numerical indices and ratios based on financial and economic data can easily be casted for research purposes and may be unique to a given work-related context. However, in an interdisciplinary type of researches, there is a chance of having a mixed approach, whereby financial ratios/economic variables are taken along with some perceptual measures for determining implications of economic/financial outcome of the measuring phenomenon under study. Many journals which emphasized interdisciplinary or multidisciplinary frameworks in management field gave emphasis to measurement tools and techniques combining financial analysis with HR-related dimensions.

In the event of non-availability of a desired questionnaire or a survey (sometimes survey is defined as a questionnaire), the researcher has to think in the direction of developing an instrument/questionnaire unique to his type of study. Quite often, doctoral-level researchers as well as others look forward to using standard questionnaires which are available in questionnaire databases or compendia of such questionnaires referred to above and then generate survey/empirical data of a specially targeted sample for interpretation. Further, for specific engineering process-based research studies in supply chain management, inventory control, project management, man-machine studies, and related interdisciplinary areas, questionnaires/surveys are generally not available. A researcher in these disciplines is compelled to work, from start to finish, using self-defined but discipline-linked dimensions or without earlier research support and develop a measurement tool. In fact, his conceptualization may have full support within a research framework, yet he is forced to think how he would like to uniquely measure the variables for evolving and establishing innovative approach in his studies. In many situations, the result is not short of redesigning of existing questionnaire or getting the clues from already designed questionnaires. In certain unique situations, if the variables turned out to be non-measureable through conventional approach and by way of perceptual dimensions, he looks forward to defining variables of the study or attributes of variables by simple frequency counts/occurrence of a given process or an event as part of the measurement technique. Sometimes, a grounded theory framework is used for evolving the variable set, and then he moves into the direction of verifying or refining the variables of the study through discussion in the relevant focus groups using multistage or onetime Delphi assessments or techniques. It is possible that in this way he may take support of the theory, reconceptualize the study parameters, and emerge with some sort of well-defined items of the questionnaire. In view of the complexity of the research design, the process of building a questionnaire could prove to be a lengthy and time-consuming process, yet it seemingly holds a good strategy to verify a theory conceptually if the research variables are yet to be defined.

9.3 Steps Involved in Developing a Questionnaire

9.3.1 Operational Definitions

The researcher begins with operational definition and tries to make it as objective and as understandable as possible. Operational definition if not making sense to others will fail to generate the right sort of variables for the study under way. Good operational definitions are generally drawn with some rationale and some sort of research backup. Certain operational definitions written by one self may even generate a set of variables, but respondents not in a position to answer those means useful data cannot be generated obviously because of the inadequacy of the variables being measured. This generally happens when highly philosophical or esoteric statements are created to map up operational definitions. Hence, with good research backup, variables are more easily defined and connected to existing literature, making them empirically verifiable and perhaps forcefully tuned to expand the base of the theory for which research is designed. Otherwise, it would be termed as an isolated piece of research, even if it may perhaps ignite some researches here and there. Interests in these areas tend to fade away faster due to inadequate and inappropriate framework of study holding attention temporarily as a new concept. Hence, it is necessary that the research frame should give way to appropriate operational definitions of *theoretical dimensions*, which would finally culminate into *specificity of variables' (items)* definitions that would be measureable.

9.3.2 Questionnaire Items Based on Research Literature

Based on the past literature, also one can produce items/statements on the variables drawn from the operational definitions. In addition, the hunches developed while collecting information on the research theme or during the process of literature review can also be included. It is expected that the item (statement) sets produced at this stage should be large enough so as to reasonably tap the universe of the items defined as providing holistic comprehension of the defined phenomenon. The evidence for decency and sufficiency of items written by the researcher comes from extensive literature survey and the gut feelings that enough number of items in the item pool is obtained. Perhaps at this juncture, sharing of preliminary pool of items through an initial seminar might considerably help the researcher in building his confidence in the measurement tool as well. Some investigators may think it appropriate to run some sort of Delphi Seminar as well. The comments from knowledgeable experts irrespective of the personal biases they have might help the researcher to either look for additional sources for items or eliminate some of the items from the item pool.

9.3.3 Validation Process

The next step is now obvious. The field experts of a given discipline would vouchsafe for the intrinsic value and relevance of such variables being measured and whether these are conceptually authentic. In other words, such variables do have their unique identity and are measureable raise a fundamental question. If the researcher is able to answer it in affirmative, then only the next step of measurement is decided. If it so happens that expert judgment, coming from more than one expert does not provide evidence for the existence of such variables that they are not measurable rethinking about the variables themselves become significant. At this stage, the researcher should garner some quantitative evidence by way of a rated score on each of the scale items for assessing usefulness and viability of the items identified. For instance, Chattopadhyay (1972), while developing his inventory entitled Organizational Environment Inventory for Hospitals (OEIH) (Sarupria et al. 1996), also developed a rating scale intended to evaluate relevance and criticality of the items in measuring hospital environment. For the purpose either fully semantically anchored rating scale can be used or any of the Likert of validating any Inventory/scale items or Likert-type scaling formats would also serve the purpose would also be useful. After collecting preliminary data from experts, Means and SDs can be calculated for evaluating the degree of consensus among experts who have rated the OEIH with reference to certain criteria predefined by the author of the scale. At the end of the exercise, such items/dimensions of the survey are retained that tend to show lesser degree of variability (or greater consensus) among judgments obtained for the purpose. Some of the variables and/or dimensions are liable to be dropped for want of consensus among expert ratings. It is specially noticed that many researchers do fail to follow this step that forewarns against accepting variables/dimensions by one's logic alone rather than through some sort of expert consensus. It seems to be a sort of research snag where researchers become more vulnerable and later are found defenseless on the issue of adequacy of questionnaire design and the measure developed.

It is also obvious that these steps strengthen one's research framework due to obtained consensus on the variables/dimension and pave the way for a more logical study of the phenomenon being measured. Hence, it is recommended that most of the rigorous studies that claim rigor in their research framework should not bypass this step lest they be questioned and blamed for inadequate or wrong conclusion drawn from their work. Without further explanation, it is obvious that an *inadequate questionnaire* provides erroneous or questionable results of the study more than a well-designed but simple questionnaire clearly asking questions on issues that need to be authentically tapped for assessment.

Sometimes a different approach for defining the dimensions/variables is also used. A group of experts in the field of interest, 7–10 in number as a focus group/expert judges/Delphi round table conference members, is given written items, and they are asked to put them into a set of piles already labeled as dimensions. Consensus is drawn then as to how many experts correctly classified various items accurately. The higher the percentage consensus obtained for each dimension, the greater is the relevance and acceptability of that dimension. In this way, some of the dimensions are characterized as invalid or nonviable ones and thus eliminated from the research study.

It is also to be reckoned that questionnaire design is considered to be more efficient if it establishes construct identity through standard statistical technique such as factor analysis, which establishes orthogonality or relative independence of the dimensions that comprise a *set* of items (uniquely different from other *sets* of items) and strongly loaded on the defined dimensions. On the other hand, the grounded theory framework has also provided an additional basis of establishing validity by way of believing in intrinsic and involved assessment of the dimensions which stand as hallmark of the capability of the questionnaire for further data collection. Irrespective of the validity techniques to be considered, questionnaire capability in terms of the extent to which it has been subjected to validation process is significant and important for authentic and precise data generation at a later stage.

9.4 Developing the First Form of the Questionnaire

As a next step, a tentative set of items are randomly placed together in the first form of the research questionnaire. Depending upon the nature of a wider spectrum of a questionnaire's adequate or near adequate number of items, whatever may be the case, item are to be pooled together. Hence, the number of items in a given questionnaire could be as less as 10 or as huge as over 300 statements. At this stage, items need not be classified as belonging to different dimensions and placed together. The pool of items needs to be randomized and assembled together. If it is not done so and items are placed under various dimensions or subscales, it may invite personal biases of respondents, and the task becomes extremely easy for the respondents to choose a single type of response or rating value of the scale on the basis of dimension heading or label. Thus, the respondents may not answer the items discreetly mainly due to the *mental set* caused by the label of questionnaire dimension. The psychological state of mind of respondents requires to be controlled and adjusted in such a way that he is in a right mood and flow of thoughts to answer the statements independent of dimension labeling. Hence, it is logically assumed that the final item pool with randomly placed items would evoke more definitive, discreet, and discriminative responses than the items placed under a label predefined by the researcher.

As a convention emphasizing rigor of the questionnaire to be established, it is generally proposed that a set of items/questions taken from the total pool of items should be positively worded and other set of items should be negatively worded. It is argued that such a composition in the questionnaire would make respondents more alert and break their *mental set* while they answer the questionnaire items. In fact, this seemingly appeals to our logic, yet there is a danger of confusing respondents by negative and positive statement occurring in a particular sequence. This is generally outmoded by high reading levels of respondents undoubtedly, yet for the low reading level respondents for whom questionnaire is basically intended, it may affect the accuracy of responses. In order to tackle this problem well, the researcher has to think about the alternative solution. The best solution, nevertheless, is to provide all statements of the questionnaire in a positively worded fashion, so that the confusion does not prevail and respondents proceed with their inner assumption and spontaneously activated mode of answering the statement in a responsible and ethical way.

9.4.1 Structural Elements of Questionnaire

Three distinct parts of a questionnaire are generally recognized. These are instructions to respondents, body of the questionnaire that includes scale of measurement or response categories, and lastly brief interpretation. The instruction part often contains brief description of what is intended to be measured by the questionnaire or what is planned to be achieved through the questionnaire so that respondents are sensitized to the issue of answering the statements properly. In the case of clinical/training instruments intended for counseling/training purposes, respondent's involvement is expected to be maximum; hence, answering accuracy is ensured, whereas in organizational or social or engineering studies, one's involvement may go down due to personal biases, fears, and preconceived notions nurtured by most of the respondents. In such situations, it is significantly important to indicate what the questionnaire has intended to measure, and what benefits will it carry, and then request respondents if they could provide with their honest answers. It is also imperative that while avoiding elaborate explanation about the technicality of the rating scale, it should be made clear how to respond to the scale placed just below the statement or alongside the statement. This helps in putting the respondents in the right mental frame while he answers the statements one by one. Sometimes, the type of rating scale and its connection to items are not clearly understood by many respondents. It is therefore necessary to provide example(s) within the instruction sheet so as to evoke proper answers from respondents. The example should only serve the purpose of creating readiness and right mental frame for the respondents rather than influencing his judgment as thought of by the researcher.

The next part of the questionnaire consists of series of questions/items randomized and placed together with serial number of the statement. A short questionnaire/instrument consisting of 10–40 items is more useful and better than a long questionnaire, the appearance of which makes the respondent to be afraid of the daunting task of answering sensitive questions. Since respondents' ease and comforts are important while he answers, personal verbal assurance should also be given besides what has been assured in the instruction part of the questionnaire. Such concerns for ensuring receipt of accurate responses would surely testify and confirm the theoretical constructs and would approximate the expected pattern of results matching with other results in a similar context so as to confirm better generalizability of the research findings.

The third part of the questionnaire being the brief interpretation about the intended explanation of results need not appear in survey studies. However, in instruments created for the purpose of generating feedback for the respondents, such as when Fundamental Interpersonal Relations Orientation-Behaviour (FIRO-B), Myer-Brigg Type Indicator (MBTI), etc., are administrated in a training environment, it is expected that results will be shared verbally or a written report of the profile of the respondent is shared in groups or given to individuals separately for individual consumption. In the survey type of questionnaire or the questionnaire intended for a thorough behavioral assessment of organization as done by the Organizational Development (OD) consultants, assurance is given that the results will be shared for the group with group-based scores for the benefits of the respondents. Such assurance creates a climate of involvement on the part of the respondents, ensuring greater authenticity and accuracy of the responses. Following the pathway of OD consultants, a researcher can stimulate the would-be respondents by assuring them that the findings of the study would be shared on its completion.

As part of the process of answering statements, research questionnaire need not be scored immediately while a training instrument or a psychological instrument is intended for immediate interpretation either for training feedback or for counselling advice. For the research purpose, statements with negative connotation need to be reverse scored. It is done deliberately to get the correct score for each dimension of study if *intuitive scoring method* (e.g., grouping the items/statement by their semantic similarity as a intuitive scoring method) for obtaining the scores is used. In this way, one can get the corrected scores for subdimension (may comprise 10 items each) and also get the composite scores (comprising 50 items) for the complete set of items.

It has been typically seen that irrespective of the size of pool of items, global or overall scores are also obtained. It appears to be a poor practice to have only total score and fail to try subdimension scores. It is expected that a larger pool of items is not always unidimensional; there will always be some degree of multidimensionality shared among the items. Hence, using subdimension or subscale scores is most desirable for advanced statistical analysis. In many behavioral science researches, the preferred technique of scoring is that of intuitively judged summated item scores belonging to a given dimension, and then scoring is attempted either arriving at average score or total score for the dimension. Average score for each dimension is most preferable as these become comparable across several dimensions than the total scores obtained for each dimension. In comparison with intuitively judged dimension scores, it is to be acknowledged that factor-based scoring procedure attempted after proper labeling of factors is also regarded appropriate.

9.5 Establishing Validity and Reliability

The best technique for validating a multi-item index for any type of questionnaire-based assessment is to get construct definition verified by an appropriate method of factor analysis. Before that, it is necessary to decide how many dimensions our questionnaire is made up of. Initially, it is not known to us how many dimensions there will be for a pool of items. The situation is different if dimensions are obtained by intuitive grouping of items as it is done either by oneself or by experts. On the other hand, factor analysis provides a basis for grouping of items based on inter-item correlations or covariances, whereby a set of factors are obtained. An interpretable factor structure, representing internal structure of items, stands for construct definition of the questionnaire dimensions. In quite a few situations, the factor structure remains undefinable, whereas in other diverse situations, based on similarity of items, they become definable allowing us to combine variables' scores into dimension scores for further use. Factor structure being interpretable allows two types of scoring, i.e., *factor-based scoring method* or *weighted factor scoring method*. The former method requires sorting out items representing dimensions, and for each dimension summated scores are calculated. The latter method is based on weighting original scores by factor score coefficient for the purpose of obtaining a weighted factor score for each of the accepted dimensions.

In yet another situation where theoretical dimensions are well supported by a theory, the verification obtained by a factor analysis on such items indicates that semantic labels independently given to the intuitive dimension and the factor labels given after finalization of factor structure clearly suggest the establishment of construct validity of the inventory of items or scale or questionnaire whatever may be the case.

Establishing factor structure of questionnaire items after a theoretical base straightaway confirms it, and the future researchers proceed on the assumption that the questionnaire has necessary factorial validity. Thus, they can consider the scale a standard one for current and future uses. At times, across the culture, some of the questionnaire data may not yield similar results, necessitating verification of factor dimensions. In such conditions statements need to be modified partly to suit the cultural requirements of a given country or nation. One cannot simply take questionnaire usage for granted and equally applicable across the globe.

All along the line, questionnaire dimensions or total score should also indicate consistency of score pattern obtained from a sample specifically drawn for a purpose of assessment. This sort of initial analysis on the questionnaire data must have internal consistency estimates Cronbach Alpha split-half reliability using odd and even item scores, and possibly repeat reliability. Reliability analysis thus fulfills a purpose of strengthening belief among recipients of questionnaire results that responses of individuals are *worthy of trusting* as the reliability coefficient obtained from the sampled data is sufficiently high. Another significant point regarding Cronbach Alpha and its applicability in various types of measures though undeniable, yet we observed studies which used noncontinuous measures, applying alpha reliability. Especially in scales and subscales where continuous measurement is in use or factor dimensions are used to develop composite scores for a set of items, Alpha reliability is more appropriate. In any case, Cronbach Alpha should reasonably be high for accepting the dimension as more reliable. An exception to the rule is that if the questionnaire is newly constructed, perhaps one can even tolerate alpha coefficient as low as .60, whereas for the tested or well-established instruments/questionnaire items, alpha reliability should invariably be as high as .70 and above.

Prior to the above analysis or if factor analysis is attempted at a later stage, then item validities need to be established within the domains of intuitive dimensions or factorial dimensions of the study. This sort of analysis is mostly of primary nature. If it is done systematically, it may positively aid the right type of factor structure to emerge as well. As mentioned earlier, item validities for a continuous scale of measurement are conducted by developing corrected item-total correlations in general. However, point biserial correlation analysis is often used for assessing the amount of relationship between the item and the total scores obtained for the set of items under questionnaire study provided that item scores can be dichotomized appropriately at the midpoint of the score and with a purpose to check discriminative power of items as against the total scores one item at a time.

It needs clarification here that there is a difference between simple item to total correlation and the corrected item to total correlation. Simple item-total correlation is calculated by relating each item's score with the overall score, whereas corrected item-total correlation subtracts the item score from the total; a new total is obtained to which the actual score of a given item is correlated. This exercise is thus repeated to obtain corrected item to total scores for all items in the scale or subscale. Afterwards, item validities (corrected item-total correlations) are to be scaled from lowest to highest with a cutoff point (either median or mean value) above which items will be retained. Below the cutoff value of corrected item-total correlations, such items will be eliminated. If a much rigorous approach is to be applied, probably one can have a higher cutoff point, which would allow only those items which had substantial discriminatory power contributing more to the total score of the dimension.

9.6 A Practical Approach in Designing Survey Questionnaire

Methodologically, a practical/pragmatic approach has also been accepted in the literature for generating questionnaire items. This method uses a well-defined construct of a theory and proceeds with the assumption that those involved during construction of a questionnaire for measuring a theoretical construct are well versed with the concept as practicing professionals/students/managers and also as knowledgeable persons. They become a resource group competent enough to generate a pool of items together for the study. This focus group comprises of knowledgeable and experienced individuals who can be of value for writing/defining the statement in two ways adopted for the preliminary collection of items. The first method mainly depends upon in-depth open-ended interviews conducted with the focus group members. A good amount of experience at the level of interviewers may ensure that the grounded theory input in the form of spoken statement is reliable, diverse, yet consistent enough across the members of the focus group chosen for the purpose. Generally, a focus group comprised of 15–20 experts/knowledgeable individuals is sought for the in-depth interviews though a relatively large group is more desirable. One can even think of a group of 30–40 persons, who would perhaps generate more useful information required for an efficient pool of items than a small group of 10–15 persons.

While interacting with the chosen focus group members on a *one-to-one basis*, it needs to be ensured that the members are sufficiently provoked to the extent that their thought process gives way to effectively relating with the topic of the study in question, thereby allowing the interviewer to record the information. This sort of central information relating to the phenomenon or the construct to be measured would largely provide a frame of reference to the researcher for suitably framing questionnaire items/statements. As a researcher, it may rarely happen that alone one could think of a large pool of questionnaire items. Perhaps, an exception is Pareek's (2002) uncanny ability as an OD consultant/teacher with intimate knowledge of psychology and organizational behavior, who was thus able to turn out more than 100 instruments/questionnaires single-handedly. Many of his devised instruments mainly intended for classroom feedback in training sessions and also for giving feedback to MBA-level (Master of Business Administration) students are now extensively used by researchers in generating research data. Quite often, such questionnaires are used without modifying the items or looking into the relevance of semantics or the social context in which these questionnaire items are applicable. Even many seasoned researchers never questioned the definition of constructs provided by Pareek (2002). On the other hand, with a close look at the pool of questionnaire items, one can notice that some of his scales do not seem to show enough construct validity acceptable for a given research. For instance, Organizational Role Stress (ORS), Motivational Analysis of Organizations-Behaviour (MAO-B) and OCTAPACE instruments never yielded a clear factor structure statistically validating the construct definition intuitively proposed or defined by Pareek (2002). Contrasting the above findings with some other scales, like Role Efficacy Scale, Conflict Management Scale suffered least with conceptual contamination.

A word of caution will be in order here. If a self-generated set of items are intended for training but used for research purposes, it is imperative that they be verified for clarity, focus, and relevance. It is also imperative on the part of the researcher to partly modify the statements and do a pilot survey to verify occurrence of conceptual confusion or semantic contamination perceived by the respondents. It is better to perform a factor analysis, eliminate those items that do not fit into the factor structure, and have a repeat run of factor analysis for duly verifying the constructs/dimensions of the questionnaire/instrument. If the results are consistent and semantically acceptable, one can finalize a short list of items for the final study. Of course, other parameters of the preliminary analysis such as establishing item validities through an appropriate statistical technique and Cronbach Alpha need to be considered as equally applicable as part of the routine testing of the questionnaire.

9.6.1 Essay Writing Method

Another alternative for developing a questionnaire/instrument depicts essay writing method applied in a group of partly or fully knowledgeable individuals who understand the concept in their own ways and are willing to describe it in words. In order to initiate this task, the participants of such groups should be provided with an open-ended question/a brief descriptive note on the conceptual measure to be developed and allow them to write an essay comprising of one or more pages as per their practical understanding. There is no rule to fix the size of the group for this work. However, it may be noted that a sizeable group comprising 40–50 individuals with relevant background is better and provides extensive description of the concept even though in some ways concepts and ideas are repeated across the group members. At the end of such a session or multiple sessions, a detailed verification for weeding out the repetitive or out of focus descriptors written by the participants is needed. Only those descriptors satisfying certain criteria of the concept or idea will be retained for further work.

A word of caution is in order here. Semantic confusion might be much more with this exercise, the reason being the differing ways of expressing the descriptors of the concept. At this stage, language skills of the researcher might help in cleansing the irrelevant statement and separating out the relevant statements from the irrelevant ones, having a bearing on the central theme of questionnaire measure. While doing editing of statements, researcher's biases need to be kept in check for preferring certain items over the others. At a later stage, one can think of adding a few statements generated by the researcher himself on the basis of grounded theory approach. If his statement complies with the participants who wrote short essays and thus tended to manifest strong item validities all along the line from content and context points of view, it is fully accepted. Otherwise, such items need to be eliminated.

9.6.2 Preparing Statements/Items

The next step in the sequence is to settle down on the items the researcher has identified for further work. Various items are to be prepared focusing on the referent variable, concept, construct, etc., on which so many essays were written by participants. For example, if the items are on Human Resource Development (HRD) climate, the items written should be more focused on Human Resource (HR) techniques, interventions, and strategic features rather than the general perception of HR environment or HR management per se. All sorts of processes associated with HR climate that defines HRD techniques and their impact should be brought into focus. Items might refer to HR climate with differing angles and perspectives experienced by the participants. The assumption is that if such a scale is prepared or designed, it will be positively responded by those who have similar work experience in the organization. If it is organizational commitment, statements/items should be connected to a single concept, namely, organizational commitment (as a referent to the organization contrasted with the job referent), from a diverse perspective originally perceived by the respondents. If the above is followed properly, the first version of the questionnaire/instrument will be ready for further exploration into two technical aspects to question whether items are relevant and whether these items can be easily reflected upon and answered by the targeted sample.

9.6.3 Verification of Validity of Item Contents

Apart from reflecting on the statements by oneself, what is more desirable is its content verification from the language point of view. Hence, a sound theoretical semantic assessment by a few experts of the discipline in which such a questionnaire has been created is most desirable. For instance, if it is a sociological concept, a technology expert or industrial engineering discipline man will not be able to judge item relevance and overall adequacy of the questionnaire. Similarly, a psychological inventory designed to measure self-actualization as a concept cannot be adequately vetted by a non-psychologist. Akin to this, a questionnaire design for valuing a given manufacturing process needs to be evaluated by an engineering/technology expert of similar branch of knowledge. Nevertheless, for inter- or multidisciplinary studies, considerable experience of evaluators may be of greater value and thus provide adequate and accurate results. For instance, a questionnaire on virtual team efficacy in project management may be equally effectively vetted by a sociologist having considerable work experience in group dynamics and also by a project manager with enough experience of managing such teams over a long stretch of time. In fact, quantitative evaluation can be appended to enhance validity verification as an additional check (readers may like to refer to the relevant section of this chapter that deals with validation process and may like to apply the technique for enhancing rigor of the research questionnaire).

9.6.4 Scaling Techniques

Scale of measurement provides a quantitative basis for judging variability among responses. Questionnaire data producing extremely varying responses is not accepted. Similarly, an item that gives too much of the response variability is likely to be adjudicated/evaluated as an inadequate statement.

At this juncture, a researcher, keeping in view the above considerations, would like to decide whether a discrete scale or nominal (yes/no type) will be good enough to generate useful data or a Likert scale with 5-point semantic anchoring is desirable. In other words, a judgment is to be reached whether a discrete scaling pattern would be better or continuous scaling format would be more desirable. Sometimes a continuous scale, for instance, with 6-point semantic anchors, a midpoint is not provided results into more or less a discrete type of scale. Such scales due to non-availability of midpoints can also be treated/converted into discrete scales. On the similar lines, using continuous scaling methods, 7-, 9-, and 11-point scales with or without semantic anchors can also be created. For instance, for a partly anchored 9-point scale, score 1 is labeled as lower point or what it means, the midpoint (i.e., 5) is labeled as the average value of the scale, and the end point (i.e., 9) is provided with a label. In such scales, respondents can easily position themselves due to low to high grades of the scale values. It is typically seen that where respondents are not compelled by the forced choice scaling technique, they are more comfortable to choose easily one of the multiple points of the scale as it applies to them or to their jobs. Perhaps this may add some degree of error and may enhance error component of the score. However, there is no way to have a check on this except closely assessing the normality of the scores measured by a variety of statistical tests or trying parallel two different scaling formats and finally selecting the one which excels in measurement.

A moot point that significantly contributes to questionnaire design is also to consider the uniform scaling pattern throughout the questionnaire irrespective of single or multiple sets of items that are placed in the questionnaire. Ease of respondents, in answering the questionnaire, therefore, is one of the goals of efficient questionnaire design. If the questionnaire becomes cumbersome due to several branching offs within the sets of items and take number of bypasses from a set of questions then it makes the work of respondents a bit complex either due to the nature of target group or complex nature of assessment. Hence, a good questionnaire designer is supposed to address this issue and make his questionnaire design more efficacious from answering, scoring, and statistical analysis points of view finally tapping accurate data from respondents.

9.7 Case Example # 1: Questionnaire Design by Theory

9.7.1 Development of Organizational Health Index

A questionnaire was developed in the area of HR/OD using available literature, expert hunches appearing in technical papers and books, conceptualization based on one's experiences as a consultant in a variety of organizations, etc. More specifically, the statements designed to measure organizational health of a large bank were prepared after a systematic analysis of organizational variables, studied and operationally defined by a large number of authors. The collection of a set of variables/items that assessed various features of organization gave us an idea that organizational health index (OHI) as a questionnaire or as a summary index of positive perception of people about organization is measurable. The organizational climate scale (OCS), available in the literature, comes very close to OHI, yet there was a need to distinguish between the two constructs on sound logical lines. Initially, an attempt was made to define OCS as perceived index of organizational description, whereas on the other side, OHI is to be conceptualized as a value-laden construct of organizational perceptions concerned with salient features of various organizational characteristics. Quite often, OD experts interchange these two constructs while providing an assessment of organization as part of their first critical evaluation of organization and its various features. Sometimes they use organizational climate as descriptive account of organization and sometimes use it as an evaluating index for introducing a change process in the organization. Thus, climate of an organization is generally defined without valuing/weighting components, whereas organizational health is a value-laden assessment of what is happening within the vicinity of an organization. It can also be said conceptually that OC stands as a background condition like a neutral descriptor of the organization, while organizational health is either a positively or negatively defined feature of it. To distinguish both concepts further, it could be said that each organization would have an organizational climate, yet it cannot be characterized as healthy or sick. Hence, climate is simply reduced to the level of describing organization in terms of certain characteristic features of the organization.

9.7.2 *Conceptualizing Variable Set*

There is a good amount of published theoretical work on organizational environment or organizational climate, but practically no empirical work on organizational health and various aspects of it. The theoretical work on organizational climate of institution/colleges has been done extensively by Stern (1968), Taguiri (1966), Halpin and Crofts (1963), and several other researchers. Instruments developed by these authors are also extensively used on educational, administrative, and manufacturing organizations with a wide variety of settings.

9.7.3 *Initial Attempt*

The index of organizational health was prepared after analyzing Fordyce and Weil's typology of healthy and sick organizations. Fordyce and Weil (1971) have analyzed organizational factors relevant to OH conceptual criteria to track down or infer about healthy style of functioning of organization from the organizational processes observed as defining attributes of health or sickness of the organization. This sort of typologies or benchmarked criteria is generally based on the hunches backed up by the practical experiences in organizations. Such typologies can also be used to develop an instrument or a set of questionnaires. For example, ILO's Quality of Work Life Survey is a suitable example of such theoretical-measurement linkages.

Incidentally, it will be of some consideration to note that Christie and Geise (1970) have analyzed personality characteristics of individuals as depicted by

Machiavelli and developed an instrument which measured Machiavellianism. Christie and Geise's work, as one example among many, is suggestive of utilizing known and accepted typologies of organizations for constructing an entirely new instrument that measures organizational health. As further support to the above argument, Myers-Briggs Type Indicator (MBTI) is clearly based on the personality types developed by Jung (1971) himself. Deep psychological thinking on the part of Myers and Briggs with the application of the measuring tool paved the way for assessing personality types comprising 16 types which are relatively independent yet interdependent within their close segments.

The case example of OHI which measured the degree of organizational health and sickness has been originally based on the attributes listed out by Fordyce and Weil (1971). However, some of the items less than 15 have been borrowed from the Organizational Health Survey (Reddin 1989), which is seemingly based on similar typological analysis of organization. The scale seems to have been developed with a focus on providing OD-related feedback to managers interested in making systemic interventions in organization.

After identification of the attributes that are likely to be possessed by healthy organizations, a few more references were sifted through to get a consensus on the attributes. Likert's System 4 management theory (1961, 1967) is also built on similar assumptions substantiating to the framework of the typological classification of healthy and sick organizations. Furthermore, the theoretical concept of organizational health by Clark (1961) and Blake and Mouton (1968, 1971) has also provided a strong theoretical base to standardize our instrument.

9.7.4 Preliminary Pool of Items

Initially, a pool of 157 items was prepared. This preliminary form was checked for its pertinence to the construct defined. A necessary modification in the wording of statements conforming to the conceptual definition of organizational health was also made. The preliminary form of the index was then presented to a group of experts for establishing content validity of the index. The first screening of the items seeking consensus on the items eliminated 19 items as considered irrelevant. All 138 items in the first form of the index had references to one or the other aspects of the organizational/management processes of bank branches as per the framework of the typology chosen. The dimensions under which these items were grouped were tentatively given a semantic label on the basis of the contents of the items central to that dimension. Thus, these dimensions referred to a priori intuitively selected criteria of organizational health; their presence or absence is more likely to be perceived by organizational members. The following is a list of the dimensions initially used in defining organizational health index:

1. Communication efficacy
2. Adaptiveness

3. Competitiveness
4. Leadership
5. Innovativeness
6. Human resource management
7. Conflict management
8. Task effectiveness
9. Structure
10. Involvement

9.7.5 Nature of the Measurement Scale

Unlike a dichotomous scale, organizational health was measured on a continuous 5-point Likert scale. This measurement scale was selected in view of its apparent utility in survey researches where flexibility in response style is highly demanded. Two category responses do put the respondents under extra pressure generated by suspicion and fear about the survey itself. However, it would be a viable scheme if a dichotomous scale (yes/no type) is also used on a different sample and the response patterns between the two are analyzed for checking the discriminative power of the scaling method to be preferred.

9.7.6 First Tryout

The first tryout of the index was done in four organizational units of a large commercial bank. The item pool so obtained revealed discrimination of items between two contrasting groups. It further paved the way for enhancing rigorous examination of items for final inclusion in the index. This attempt also helped in clarifying and correcting the items; ambiguities were thus removed from contents of the items. Those items which showed a little difference or no difference among criterion work groups, as shown by the chi-square test of significance, were removed from the index, resulting in total number of items being 99 from 138.

9.7.7 Second Tryout

After the first tryout, a new form of 99 items was prepared and sent to four bank branches working under three administrative circles. The details of branches are shown in Table 9.1.

The final pool of responses was obtained from 100 employees to compute the estimates of item validities. These item validities are the objective estimates that indicate the extent of discrimination between the responses of individuals on a

Table 9.1 Selection of bank branches in the second tryout

Name of the bank branch	Composition of branches			
	Employee strength	Age of the bank	Location of the bank	Respondents
1. Akola	128	95	Urban	40
2. Thiruvarur	53	13	Semi-urban	15
3. Vizianagaram	70	29	Semi-urban	15
4. Ootacamund	54	107	Urban	30

particular item. According to original ideas, we intended to compute item validities on certain identified branches of high and low organizational health. Since this could not be materialized due to non-availability of the data from such contrasting branches, we used the data from four branches where data were collected first.

9.7.8 Final Selection of Items

As we had an a priori categorization of items into different dimensions, item validities were, therefore, computed for each dimension separately. The most rigorous method of item to total correlations for obtaining item validities was point biserial correlation. Since there was a total of 99 items, 99 point biserial coefficients were computed.

For selecting the items from the item pool that systematically discriminated across 99 items, we ranked the coefficients from high to low. Those items which showed high magnitude of item-dimension association were ranked first, and those which showed less discrimination were ranked last. In this way, most discriminating items were preferred over the least discriminating items.

The item validities so obtained yielded a range of item-dimension correlation from −.07 to +.72. All the items showed positive significant correlation with the dimension scores except one item which showed negative correlation of −.07. The number of items which were eliminated on the basis of statistical evidence was 19, and the total number of items that were retained in the final test was 80.

9.7.9 Reliability of Organizational Health Index

The reliability of organizational health index was estimated separately for each subscale. Subscale reliability coefficient was summed up to obtain an average reliability coefficient for the whole index.

The kind of reliability coefficient computed for the index was an internal consistency estimate of the scores known as Cronbach's Alpha coefficient. The overall reliability coefficient of .96 order was obtained straight from item analysis statistics done separately on the mean scores of the branches.

9.7.10 Validity

As an instrument constructed to discriminate healthy and sick characteristics of organization, the index requires an objective statistically verifiable estimate. A questionnaire is said to be a valid measure only when it is capable of discriminating between healthy and sick bank branches. This objective estimate can be obtained by computing a validity coefficient which, in essence, would indicate the amount of association between actual scores assigned by the organizational members and the criterion scores received by a bank branch independently assigned to the branch by a group of knowledgeable experts, who knew the sick and healthy conditions of the bank branch due to their frequent transaction with and basic understanding of the bank's internal structure a processes observed by them as business units.

9.7.11 Selection of Raters

In order to obtain independent ratings on a group of branches, the Personnel Department of Hyderabad Local Head Office was initially contacted to facilitate in obtaining ratings on a set of bank branches. With the help of the personnel department, 20 branches were identified, forming a dichotomous group of 10 healthy and 10 sick bank branches or "business units" in each category.

Before approaching the regional manager under whose jurisdiction these branches were functioning, it was desirable to mix up the provisionally identified set of branches with another set of 20 branches selected at random. This procedure was followed to offset the tendency of raters to judge bank branches as we identified them initially.

The controlling authorities of this randomized sample of 40 branches were then identified and separated to form three groups of 13 branches each. Elimination of a few more branches was made later on when we could not get satisfactory ratings on them and also when the branches were not qualified to be included as per the assumption that organizational health can be measured only when branches' strength of employees should be not less than 25.

The concerned regional managers were then requested to give ratings on the branches we have listed out or suggest three knowledgeable experts who met the following criteria to rate the branches:

- Raters should have sufficient experience of at least 6 months with the branches in question.
- Based on the regional managers' experience, a rater should be one who is considered to be a good observer and a competent judge.

The officers who were suggested as competent raters for the present task were administrative officers, staff officers, area superintendents, and officer-in-charge. In the case of two branches (Vijayawada and Secunderabad) not falling under any of the three administrative districts, ratings from the deputy secretary (operations) and administrative officer were obtained.

9.7.12 Rating Scale for Validation

Global ratings were obtained on a rating form especially constructed for the purpose. In order to obtain fairly accurate ratings on the branches, the concept of organizational health as we defined it was provided to the raters. The rating scale consisted of a 9-point scale ranging from "not at all healthy (1)" to "completely healthy (9)." A complete description of the anchored rating scale together with a semantic description of each anchor is presented in Box 9.2.

Box 9.2: Showing 9-Point Rating Scale Used for Validation Study for OH

1	2	3	4	5	6	7	8	9
Not at all heal-thy	Much below aver-age	Somewhat average	A little below average	Average	A little above aver-age	Somewhat above average	Much above aver-age	Complet-ely healthy

Before obtaining ratings on the global rating form, rapport was established with the raters individually as well as in groups. Independent judgments to assign authentic ratings to the branches were encouraged. Technical steps of the study were explained to the raters so as to elicit open and frank responses. The raters were also asked to read the following description which depicted the characteristics of healthy organizations, and suitable ratings then may be assigned in terms of the description given below:

> A healthy organization is one that has a strong sense of own identity and mission, yet has the capacity to adapt readily to change. A healthy organization is most likely to search out and use the most effective methods for conducting its business. Healthy organization as a whole appears to be independent and growing. Everyone in the organization is really responsible for the behaviour towards an associate, a supervisor or an employee in a grown up way. Healthy organization is flexible and reflects team spirit, collaboration and sensible rivalry. A few more attributes noticeable in healthy organizations are strong and consistent flow of energy towards widely shared objectives, problem solving attitude, amicable human relations, willingness on the part of the members to learn from their jobs, high degree of trust and sense of freedom and mutual responsibility.

9.7.13 Inter-rater Reliability

Single ratings may not be a proper estimate of a branch, whether it is organizational health or organizational sickness being measured. It was, therefore, essential to verify the extent to which raters independently agreed with other's ratings given to the branches, being healthy or sick. Inter-rater reliability simply ascertained the degree of consistency among sets of judgments. In this connection, inter-rater reliability was estimated by computing Kendall's coefficient of concordance (W) for a set of ratings exceeded by two. In case, we had only two ratings, Spearman's *rho* was computed for checking the consistency between two ratings.

The analysis of ratings of agreement by 6 raters on 13 branches of Region I was found to be $W = .586$, chi-square = 42.192, and $p < .001$. The agreement of ratings on Region II was found to be rho = .80 and $p < .01$. Branches falling under Region III received homogeneous ratings with concordance coefficient value being .5074, chi-square = 15.222, df = 10, and $p < .13$.

9.7.14 Validity Coefficient

After having estimated the reliability of obtained ratings of the branches, a validity coefficient was computed by finding out the significant differences between the scores of employees working in healthy and sick organizations. Table 9.2 summarizes the validity results on each factor score of the organizational health index. It needs to be mentioned here that factor scores represent the composite scores obtained for each factor after the factor results are firmed up and accepted for further analysis. The subsequent analysis of checking validity coefficient for each factor is based on eight factorially defined dimensions of the study.

Table 9.2 Reliability coefficient (internal consistency estimates) of the organizational health index

Subscales of the organizational health index	Reliability coefficient
1. Involvement	.62
2. Structure	.72
3. Leadership	.68
4. Human resource management	.75
5. Adaptiveness	.66
6. Task effectiveness	.63
7. Conflict management	.69
8. Open communication	.78
9. Innovativeness	.59
10. Competitiveness	.61
Average alpha coefficient	.72

t-ratios suggested that the factor score of healthy and sick branches discriminated well in respect of adaptiveness, problem centeredness, conflict management, innovativeness, and initiation and outgoingness at the .05 or lower level of the confidence. Other factor scores such as considerate leadership and involvement dimensions discriminated the branches at a little higher level of significance ($p < .10$). The t-ratios for organizational excellence were very low, thereby indicating negligible discriminative power of bank branches or business unit of a large bank demonstrated on this dimension.

In addition, a series of phi coefficients were also computed between branch scorings high and low as classified by the ratings of independent judges. In this analysis, overall, 7 branches were considered since the data from employees of these branches were available. The data on ratings were dichotomous, but the scores were not. Therefore, it was considered necessary to dichotomize the OH scores, so as to calculate the degree of relationship between OH scores and rating scores obtained by the bank branches. The mean factor scores on each of the 8 OH dimensions were split on the median, and phi coefficients were computed for healthy and sick branches as rated by the independent raters (Table 9.3).

All in all, six validity coefficients were computed of which 5 were computed between single branch scores classified by the criterion rating scores, and one was computed between two healthy and two sick branches. Findings of these validity coefficients are shown in Table 9.4. The validity coefficients ranged from .27 to .88 with median value at .67. The validity coefficient for the combined sets of branches as seen in Table 9.4 was found to be .47. On the basis of these statistical results, we can say that validity coefficient of the index is promising.

Table 9.3 t-ratios between high and low OH branch employee scores dichotomized by OH ratings

Organizational health dimensions	High on OH branch ($N = 15$)		Low on OH branch ($N = 19$)		t-ratio
	Mean	SD	Mean	SD	
1. Adaptiveness	99.533	18.181	87.105	14.510	2.159*
2. Organizational excellence	73.800	11.882	71.842	12.465	0.466
3. Considerate leadership	14.600	4.421	12.211	3.853	1.650
4. Problem centeredness	21.267	3.712	17.737	2.207	3.268**
5. Conflict management	22.267	2.840	19.105	3.695	2.820**
6. Innovativeness	21.600	6.686	16.684	8.562	2.020*
7. Involvement	26.333	6.195	23.105	4.108	1.740
8. Initiation and outgoingness	11.000	2.619	8.579	1.924	2.550*

Note: Average ratings received by high on OH branch = 5.33; average ratings received by low on OH branches = 4.00

*Significant at .05 level; **significant at .01 level

Table 9.4 Validity coefficients (phi coefficients) of OH index computed between factor scores of branches classified by criterion ratings

High on OH branch	Average rating received	Low on OH branch	Average rating received	Phi coefficient
1. Tirupati	6.66	1. Adoni	4.00	0.67*
2. Vizianagaram	6.50	2. Adoni	4.00	.27
3. Tanuku	6.00	3. Adoni	4.00	.38
4. Nellore	5.50	4. Adoni	4.00	.78**
5. Maharanipeta	5.33	5. Adoni	4.00	.88**
6. Maharanipeta and Nellore combined	5.41	6. Adoni and Nandyal	4.16	.47*

Note: *Significant at .05 level; **significant at .01 level

9.8 Case Example # 2: Designing Productivity and Organizational Effectiveness Questionnaires

There is a range of productivity-related activities generally performed by the organizations. The subsystems of the bank or the bank branches are not an exception to the rule. Moreover, certain conceptual problems would arise if a single criterion of productivity is chosen. The criteria as found in business literature are not generally applicable to the banking subsystems. Therefore, the specificity of variables is an important step in measuring productivity and effectiveness of the bank branches. Thus, the assumptions to be considered for designing such questions are:

- Productivity and effectiveness of the bank branches should be measured through more than a single variable.
- Effectiveness and productivity variables should be specific to the organization for which these measures are being used.

In view of the above considerations, a group of participants fully well versed and knowledgeable in banking and managerial practices at the bank's staff college was requested to write up the criteria of productivity as they understood. The participants who were undergoing training and also had varied and rich managerial experiences were the *focus group*, and they were initially given a concept session for acquainting them with an essay writing task on measuring bank productivity. They were given full freedom to write up as many criteria of productivity as they could think of. It was, however, insisted upon that the ideas shall belong to their organization as experienced by them. It would be duly appreciated if they have understood the nature and function of such variables, which in turn would serve the basis to benefit the organization.

The written up criteria of productivity in the form of numbered items or an essay containing descriptive items of productivity were analyzed with a view to classifying them into a few areas of business operations. The objective was to eliminate the irrelevant and duplicate items. From an initial large pool of items, 167 tentative items were retained in the productivity index.

Another analysis was essential to retain them as objective indicators of productivity. Hence, an attempt was made to construct a 7-point scale ranging from "indispensable item must be included (7)" to "irrelevant item must be excluded (1)." Provision was also made for the raters to add some more items and at the same time weigh them if they want to retain them as objective criterion of productivity.

9.8.1 Sample of Raters

This analysis was done using a sample of supervising staff working at the local head office of the bank and also a sample of branch managers who were undergoing a training program at the staff college of the same bank. Certain criteria for the selection of supervising staff were observed. Only those supervising officers who had sometime back worked as branch managers were considered as raters for the productivity index. An overall sample of 20 officers rated the productivity index developed in the form of a questionnaire.

9.8.2 Final Tryout

The final tryout was conducted in two steps. In the first step, objective estimates in the form of means and standard deviations were computed for each item, and then items were provisionally selected for their inclusion. In the second step, the selected items were presented to a small group of faculty members individually to have a discussion on each item so as to establish their relevance and the measuring capability of the productivity index of the bank branches.

The objective estimates computed in terms of mean scores obtained by each item were used for item selection purpose. Only those items which have received 5 or more scores were finally included as a potentially useful item that can measure at an acceptable level productivity of the bank branches. The items with less than 5 mean scores were rejected. As a result of objective ratings, 6 fresh items were included in the productivity index, and 2 items scoring less than 5 were eliminated thereby making a total of 18 items.

9.9 Case Example 3: Designing Organizational Effectiveness Index (Questionnaire)

As outlined above, a similar procedure as followed for the development of the productivity index was repeated in constructing the effectiveness index. However, a few exceptions were kept in mind. The multiple criteria of productivity were followed for measuring organizational effectiveness of the bank branches. After obtaining the criteria from the *focus group* of the study, a pool of ratings on the criteria of effectiveness was obtained from the supervising staff. For this purpose, no specific criteria were observed in selecting the supervising staff except those who have enough experience as managers.

The selection of effectiveness items primarily contained both of performance and effectiveness variables, and these were finalized on the basis of mean value rating estimates of items. Those items with less than 5 scores were rejected, whereas items with more than 5 scores were retained. All in all, 38 items were retained in the effectiveness index after having a discussion individually on each item with the faculty members of the bank's staff college.

References

Blake RR, Mouton JS (1968) The managerial grid. Gulf, Houston
Blake RR, Mouton JS (1971) Corporate excellence. Gulf, Houston
Chattopadhyay S (1972) Organizational environment inventory. In Sarupria D, Madhavan S, Rao TV (eds) (1996). Measuring organizational climate. Academy of HRD, Ahmedabad
Christie R, Geis FL (1970) Studies in Machiavellianism. Academic, New York
Clark V (1961) A healthy organization. In: Bennis WG, Benne KD, Chin R (eds) The planning of change. Holt Rinehart and Winston Inc., New York
Fordyce JK, Weil R (1971) Managing with people: a manager's handbook of organization development methods. Addison and Wesley, Mass
Halpin AW, Crofts DB (1963) The organizational climate of schools. University of Chicago Press, Chicago
Jung CG (1971) Psychological types. Princeton University Press, Princeton
Likert R (1961) New patterns of management. McGraw-Hill, New York
Likert R (1967) The human organization: its management and value. McGraw-Hill, New York
Mintzberg H (1973) The nature of managerial work. Harper and Row, New York
Pareek U (2002) Training instruments in HRD and OD, 2nd edn. Tata-McGraw-Hill, New Delhi
Reddin WJ (1989) Organizational health survey. Fact sheet. Organizational Tests, Frederickton
Sarupria D, Madhavan S, Rao TV (eds) (1996) Measuring organizational climate. Academy of HRD, Ahmedabad
Stern GG (1968) People in context. Wiley, New York
Taguiri R (1966) Comments on organizational climate. Paper presented at conference on organizational climate, Foundation for Research on Human Behaviour, Michigan University, Ann Arbor

Chapter 10
Ethics in Research with Special Reference to Social Sciences

L.M. Bhole

10.1 Introduction

Formal research activity has widened and deepened enormously in the modern times. The types of research have multiplied, and very many new trends in research have emerged over the years (see Sect. 10.2 below). Students, faculty, committees, commissions and various organisations undertake research whose results may be used for the good or ill of the individuals and society. In other words, research at all levels and at all stages involves ethical considerations, i.e. the questions of right and wrong, value judgements, good or bad and so on. There is no doubt that ethical issues are involved in all research; the research in human subjects, medicines, etc. has a definite ethical dimension.

The research often involves elaborate deception, and the subjects in research are deceived in many ways to a limited or large extent. There exists a vast diversity or array of unethical acts which are committed by the researchers at various stages of research. There exist potential conflicts between ethical and professional values. The glaring example of how the subjects are deceived in research has come to light very recently in respect of Bhopal gas leak tragedy which occurred in India in the early 1980s. It was reported in the national press in June 2010 that hundreds of gas victims (patients) were subjected to same drug trials without their knowledge at the Bhopal Memorial Hospital and Research Centre (BMHRC) during 2004–2008. It was also further reported that the similar tests or trials were also conducted in other reputed hospitals in India. The several victims were not aware that they were being subjected to trials. All of them were made to sign consent forms without being clearly informed about the tests or that they could prove fatal.

L.M. Bhole (✉)
Former Professor of Economics, Indian Institute of Technology Bombay, Mumbai, India
e-mail: bholelm@gmail.com

D.S. Hegde (ed.), *Essays on Research Methodology*,
DOI 10.1007/978-81-322-2214-9_10

However, the researchers are often not aware of the existence of ethical considerations involved in their own research, and their perception of and approach to research quite often tend to be purely technical and devoid of ethics. All too often, researchers do not fully appreciate the complexities of ethical issues and dilemmas. It is in this context that the objective of this paper is to make the researchers at all levels, of all types and at all stages aware of the fact that the research should not be and it cannot be ethics-free. It tries to convey that values and ethics are a necessary part of a systematic and valid research that values cannot be eliminated from research and that values, ethics and research are linked with each other. The paper seeks to raise the ethical sensibility of all those who assume the role of researchers. It tries to clarify the range of ethical problems that might be encountered by the researchers in the process of research, and it tries to suggest some approaches for resolving those problems. The paper also seeks to make the researchers better equipped to anticipate ethical problems before they occur so that they can avoid them entirely or they become skilful in coping with them.

Some of the specific questions this paper tries to reflect upon are as follows: What is research ethics? What are the types of research, and can any type of research be ethics-free? What is the need for and importance of ethics in research? What are the ethical problems, issues, dilemmas usually faced by the researchers? What are the likely causes of unethical behaviour in research? How far research ethics can be promoted by issuing ethical guidelines by certain bodies or organisations? What are the typical ways in which researchers compromise with ethical failure?

10.2 Types and Trends in Research

Research or research activities refer to a systematic, scientific, critical investigation into or a study of a subject in order to establish old facts or discover new facts and reach new conclusions. It is an endeavour or a process directed towards innovations and improvement of understanding, skills and knowledge.

The taxonomy of research points towards theoretical research, basic research, pure research, applied research, prevention research, primary data research, field research, sponsored research, consultancy research, project research, in-house research, etc. Pure research is also known as basic research. The social scientists may direct their research activity from pure to applied orientation. Pure science remains unchallenged by practical, concrete, social problems and issues, while applied research is theoretical in nature.

The motivation behind research may be to earn academic degrees, or to earn money and power, or to publish books and articles or papers, or to contribute to human peace, happiness and welfare or simply the 'animal spirit'. It is obvious that research is undertaken in all disciplines, subjects and branches of knowledge. The nature of ethical problems or issues in research may differ in different types of research mentioned above. From the point of view of research ethics, it is useful to be aware of certain important evolving trends in research in various branches of knowledge, including the social sciences. Some of such trends are mentioned below:

- Increasing doctoral research (research leading to Ph.D. degree)
- The growing culture of 'publish or perish' in the academia
- Increasing number and types of institutions and organisations which sponsor and fund research
- Increasing funding of research by the states or governments
- Increasing international funding of research
- Increasing and huge amounts money becoming available to the researchers
- Increasing globalisation of research
- Increasing availability of research aids, tools and technology such as computational facilities, duplicating machines, computers, etc.
- Increasing clinical and corporate settings
- Increasing interdisciplinary and multidisciplinary research
- Increasing amount of social inquiry of all kinds
- Increasing dependence of universities on sponsorships and linking of government grants and salary raises to research performance
- Emergence and growth of new methodological patterns of working in social sciences
- Increasing emphasis on the cross-cultural and participant action research
- Increasing amount of attention is being now paid to questions of professional ethics
- Ethical and political questions are being faced now in systematic and institutionalised manners to an increasing extent
- More and more professional organisations are now issuing ethical codes to which their members are expected to conform
- Increasing corruption, scientific misconduct and impropriety in research activities
- Increasing public and institutional demands for individual accountability in research
- Increasing prospects and reality of legal action for misconduct in research

10.3 What Is Research Ethics?

Ethics, as per the Oxford Dictionary, means the science of morals in human conduct or moral principles or rules of conduct. Morals, in turn, are said to be concerned with the accepted rules, codes, norms and standards about goodness or badness, rightness or wrongness acceptability or unacceptability of general human character or human behaviour or human conduct or human duties. Research ethics, therefore, would mean the observance or practising of moral principles while doing research by any researcher. Certain ethical principles in research for example, are honesty, objectivity, carefulness, openness, respect for intellectual property, confidentiality, responsible publications, responsible mentoring, respect for colleagues, social responsibility, non-discrimination, animal care and human subject protection. Ethics and legal rules or laws are not the same; the action may be legal but unethical (Resnik 2011).

10.4 The Need for and Importance of Research in Ethics

It has been experienced often that research activity is afflicted by undesirable, wrong and corrupt practices of various kinds. This ethical problem in the world of research may not be on large scale, but there is no doubt that it very much exists in a sufficient degree to make us quite uneasy. There are many situations where ethical dilemmas are encountered by us. For example, there is falsification, fabrication and plagiarism in research.

There are various stages in all research: the decision to do research, choice of topic or definition of research problem, determining the aim and design of research project, collection of data and research material, choice of methodology and techniques, interpretation of data and research findings, etc. The ethical considerations are relevant in all these stages of research. For example, economics researchers often use statistical or econometric techniques even though the prerequisites for using those techniques (such as minimum number of observations required) are not met. They also often use techniques mechanically without seriously ascertaining the relevance of certain technique for their research. One often observes that there is a herd mentality in using econometric or statistical techniques among the researchers. The easy availability of computing facilities and statistical packages has aggravated the situation in this regard. There is also a high degree of complacency and sense of superiority in the minds of researchers who can use advanced, complicated and sophisticated econometric tools.

We, therefore, have to be bothered about the moral or ethical side or aspects of research. Research ethics is about proper conduct related to the processes and consequences of research. It helps to promote the aims of research; it promotes the values which are essential for collaborative research work; and it helps to ensure that the researchers are held accountable to the public. Research ethics also helps us to ensure that our scientific endeavours are compatible with our values and goals. The ethical norms in research also help to build public support for research. Research ethics can promote a variety of important moral and social values such as social responsibility, human rights and animal welfare. On the other hand, ethical lapses in research can harm human and animal subjects (Resnik, p. 2).

This need, as well as the importance of ethics in research, bears further elaboration. Research ethics has traditionally focussed its attention mostly on issues in biomedical research. The application of research ethics to evaluate biomedical research has been quite well developed by now, and it has influenced much of the existing statutes and guidelines for the ethical conduct of research. However, in humanities and social sciences, new and emerging methods of conducting research such as autoethnography and participatory action research are raising important but quite different ethical issues and obligations for researchers in humanities and social sciences.

Thus, research ethics can be said to help protect individuals, communities and environment and to offer the potential to increase the sum of the good in the world. If we do not practise ethics in research, we leave or put those who are attempting social change as a prey to the hucksters who are willing to put forth undocumented claims based on inadequate evidence. Ethical approach to research can help to promote the climate of trust in which the researchers can continue their socially useful labour. Ethical practices and ethical concerns help to promote integrity of research. If we can assure ourselves and others that we are conducting research ethically, we can be more confident that the results of the works we study are accurate and original.

Another reason why we have to care for research ethics is the increasing demand for individual accountability in research. Schools, universities, funding agencies, employers and professional societies seek to protect themselves from unethical actions in the field of research. The unethical practice in research can lead to community withdrawal of support for research, which, in turn, can reduce the capacity of institutions and individuals to continue research on groups and communities. The unethical research practices can end government research funding, travels to conferences, years of work and professional reputation.

The ethically poor practices affect not only individual and professional reputation but also the veracity and reliability of individual and collective works. It is vital that students, colleagues and others see us setting good examples by behaving ethically. The participation in and the observation of unethical conduct in research have an adverse effect on ethical beliefs of the students. The unethical researchers appear to model unethical behaviour for their colleagues. The moral observance in research is necessary for self-preservation. As a part of their claims to professional status for their members, professional bodies adopt processes and procedures for self-regulation of the moral conduct of their members. In return, the members of those organisations lay claim to professional status and receive special associated rights.

In short, there are, inter alia, three objectives of research ethics:

(1) To protect participants in research; (2) to ensure that research is conducted in a way that serves the interests of individuals, groups and society; and (3) to examine specific research activities and projects for their ethical soundness (Israel and Hay 2006, pp. 1–7).

10.5 Is Ethics Relevant in All Subjects?

Can any type of research or research in any field of learning be ethics-free? There are different viewpoints on this question, and the stand in this regard has been changing over the period of time. The two widely known approaches in this regard are positivism and normativism. The believers in the normative approach argue that the (social) scientists deal with phenomena that involves interpreting and endowing with values and meanings. The researchers deal with human and other beings, societies and social relations which affect and which are affected by values. The process of gathering 'facts' is not value-neutral; the researcher plays a significant role in constructing facts; and observations are theory-laden reflecting the interests of particular vested interests. The strive towards objectivism fails to see the historical influences upon our consciousness. The separation of means from ends is not sustainable. The 'facts' are not collected; they are produced reflecting and perpetuating unequal power relations which already exist. To follow the positivists such as the sociologist Max Weber and the economist Milton Friedman is to condemn researchers simply to a technical science of efficiency, unable to challenge morally the individual and society.

The positivists, on the other hand, argue that social sciences should strive to make social inquiry value-free. Despite their goal being to understand the subjective meanings, the social sciences can be objective. The social scientists provide a cost–benefit analysis of different means, but they refrain from making statements about the desirability of goals of ends. After committing to a particular area of research, the social scientists can pursue their investigation in an objective manner. The basic researchers particularly tend to view themselves as 'value-free technicians' who discover truth but are passive, in respect of the societal use of their findings. The assumption underlying such a position of scientific non-responsibility is that although research findings can be used for the good or bad ends, the knowledge is ethically neutral. They believe in 'value-free' tradition, and they claim that their work is objective and morally neutral since their goal is disinterested and an impersonal pursuit of scientific knowledge for its own sake.

Among these two positivists and normative schools of thought, the normative school appears to be more tenable and convincing. There are a number of arguments against the claim to value-free research. First, research, even pure research, cannot be value-free because it is immoral not to use the knowledge we obtain from research from reducing real-life social problems. Second, in real life, there have been many examples of abuse in the application of 'pure knowledge', viz., discovery of atom and research in genetics. Third, the basic research often entails the use of unethical procedures to obtain knowledge. The (pure) scientist's right to know often tends to conflict with the obligation to do no harm.

10.6 Research Ethics in Social Sciences

The foregoing discussion on the relevance of research ethics in all subjects can be strengthened further by briefly noting the distinctive features of social sciences and by comparing the extent and nature of ethical issues involved in research in social sciences on the one hand and natural sciences on the other. This discussion draws heavily on Barnes.

When compared with the natural sciences, the social sciences as a systematic and professional body of knowledge are of pretty recent origin. It is said that it is only in the twentieth century that the recognition has been granted to the existence of specific corpus of accumulated knowledge in social sciences, cultivated and added to by a specialist group of professional scientists. Further, social sciences differ significantly from natural sciences (and also from humanities) in respect of the relation between the phenomena the social scientist studies and the whole society. There are many problems and questions which arise in social sciences but not in natural sciences and even in humanities. It is because social sciences are essentially an activity in which human beings study themselves that complex ethical questions have to be faced as an abiding concomitant of the activity.

In this context, is the description of natural sciences as 'hard sciences' and social sciences as 'soft sciences' valid? The answer depends on what criteria are used to define hardness and softness of various disciplines. For example, if the kind of data used is the criterion, while the natural sciences have to be called 'hard sciences', the social sciences have to be called 'soft sciences' indeed. On the contrary, if the nature of problem is the criterion used, while the social sciences become 'hard', the natural sciences become 'soft'. This is so because the intellectual task of the natural scientist is greatly simplified because his or her data are hard and reliable and because the separation between the natural scientist and the natural phenomena he or her studies is clear-cut. On the other hand, the social scientist has to deal with data which, quite often, are unreliable and fuźzy, and his or her relation with the phenomena he or her studies is easily two-sided. From this perspective, the social science research is indeed a difficult, hard undertaking, and ethical problems constitute a major component of its intrinsic difficulty.

It has already been said previously that the ethical questions exist in all disciplines, whether social sciences or natural sciences or humanities. Even then, another distinctive feature of social sciences is that while the ethical questions are intrinsic, ubiquitous and unavoidable in social sciences, they are extrinsic and contingent in natural sciences. For example, there are ethical questions connected with atom bombs, germ warfare, environment destruction and genetic engineering, but they are not concerned with say, cruelty to atoms. The ethical questions in natural sciences are concerned with the effect of say, nuclear reactions on fellow human beings, yet human beings as such do not enter into the theory of say, physics at all. As opposed to this, fellow human beings are the essential ingredients of any social scientists' stock-in-trade. Hence, in social sciences, ethical consequences of professional activity are always present.

It is believed by many that the extent of concern for ethics in social science research has varied in roughly three different periods of evolution of social sciences:

(1) The social sciences emerged in a recognisable form in the middle of the nineteenth century, (2) the way they were practised in the 1930s or between two world wars when capitalism and imperialism still enjoyed widespread confidence and (3) the way they are practised currently after the second world war. In the first period, little attention was paid to ethical questions in social science research. There was an autocratic attitude towards the definition of the interests of the people whose lives were being investigated. Such attitude was reinforced by positivistic faith that the true facts of economic problem such as, poverty, unemployment, etc.

existed in some absolute and objective sense, and they were waiting to be discovered by unbiased investigators. This picture began to change during the interwar period (1920–1940) when the social scientist began to feel and appreciate that the natural science paradigm was not appropriate for social science in this context. The third period witnessed the strengthening of the trends and approaches initiated in the second period.

10.7 Some Aspects of Ethical Problems in Research

Given the importance of research ethics, many professional bodies, state agencies, universities, etc. have arrived at a kind of consensus on ethical principles, taxonomy of research conduct and characteristics of ethical problems. We list them below without elaborating on them. For details and full discussion, the reader may refer to (Resnik, pp. 2–6; Israel and Hay 2006, pp. 112–128; Kimmel 1988, pp. 30–41):

1. Ethical principles, codes and rules:
   - Honesty
   - Objectivity
   - Integrity
   - Carefulness
   - Openness
   - Respect for intellectual property
   - Confidentiality
   - Responsible publication
   - Responsible mentoring
   - Respect for colleague
   - Non-discrimination
   - Competence
   - Legality
   - Animal care
   - Human subjects' protection
2. Types of unethical conduct in research:
   - Fabrication or invention of data or cases
   - Falsification or wilful distortion of data
   - Plagiarism or copying of ideas, etc. without attribution
   - Silence about missing data
   - Conducting research without informed consent
   - Gifting authorship
   - Publishing the same paper in two different journals
   - Using an inappropriate statistical technique in order to enhance the significance of the research
   - Overworking, neglecting and exploiting research students

- Making derogatory comments and personal attacks while reviewing the author's submission
- Wasting animals in research
- Sabotaging someone's research work

3. Characteristics of ethical problems in research:

- Research problem can give rise to multiple problems about proper research conduct.
- Sensitivity to ethical issues is necessary but not sufficient for solving ethical problems in research.
- Ethical problems are the result of conflicting values.
- An adequate understanding of ethical problems often requires a broad perspective based on consequences of research.
- Ethical problems involve both personal and professional elements.
- Ethical problems can pertain to science as a body of knowledge and to research in it.
- Judgments about proper conduct lie on a continuum ranging from the clearly unethical to the clearly ethical.

4. Causes of research misconduct:

What are the possible causes of misconduct in research? It has been pointed out in this regard that while most of the researchers are highly ethical, there are some who are basically morally corrupt, economically desperate and psychologically disturbed, and the world of research becomes ethically afflicted on account of the nature and behaviour of such people. The research misconduct may also occur because of the 'stressful' or 'imperfect environment', i.e. various institutional pressures, incentives and constraints encourage or induce some people to commit misconduct. The peer pressures; the pressure to publish and obtain grants, contracts, consultancy and sponsored projects; career ambitions; the pursuit of fame and name; the pursuit of profit; the desire to maximise patents to one's credit; the poor supervision of students and trainees; and the poor oversight of researchers result in the emergence and entrenchment of unethical behaviour in research.

To put it differently, research misconduct may result from environmental and individual causes, i.e. when people who are morally weak, ignorant or insensitive are placed in a stressful environment, they easily commit misconduct in research. The deviations from research norms may also occur because the researchers simply don't know or have never thought seriously about the ethical norms in research. The lack of ethics in research sometimes may be due to the facts that certain practices which are in vogue (although basically improper) are regarded by the fraternity as normal and traditional. The failure to reflect critically on the mistaken or problematic traditions results in the continuation of research misconduct. For example, it is regarded that there is nothing wrong in naming the research supervisor as an author on every paper that comes from his or her students even if he or her doesn't make any or significant contribution to the paper. Similarly, the practice of drug companies to employ ghostwriters to write papers 'authored' by their physicians' employees is perceived to be ethically unproblematic because it is asked as to what is wrong about this practice, and it is pointed that it is just the way it is generally done (see Resnik, pp. 8–9).

10.8 The Role of Ethical Codes or Rules or Guidelines in Promoting Research Ethics

Since research ethics is of primary importance in research activity, what are the approaches to promote research ethics? The two approaches for this purpose are (a) external and (b) internal. The external approach emphasises the issuing of ethical codes by the external 'authorities'. The internal approach, on the other hand, requires the acceptance that research ethics is a value in itself, and it puts onus on every researcher to behave ethically without fear and favour while doing research. We show below that while there are certain limitations of the first approach, the second approach is the only ultimate guarantee to infuse ethics in research.

With the passage of time, certain professional organisations have issued ethical codes to which their members have to conform and adhere. Similarly, research sponsors have developed norms, codes, rules, regulations and guidelines which specify in details the ethical constraints which must be accepted by the researchers they sponsor. About 59 such codes have been developed and issued in the West during the period of 1945–2006. The most of these codes have been developed in the area of bioethics, but they have been extended across the research spectrum including social sciences. Nuremberg code (1947), Declaration of Helsinki (1964), Belmont report (1979) and Council for International Organization of Medical Sciences (1982) are some of the examples of such codes (for details see Israel and Hay 2006, pp. 23–29).

The survey of these codes in various countries such as the USA, the UK, Canada, Australia, New Zealand, South Africa and Scandinavia reveals that there have been diverse regulatory experiences in these countries. Many early regulatory initiatives were responsive to crises, but more recently, ethical regulation has emerged as a part of broader social trends towards individual and organisational accountability. Ethical review strategies based on biomedical experiences are being applied to social science research. This is achieved either through national legislation or through actions of funding agencies. One may come across two ways in which ethical codes have been issued and used, namely, 'top-down' and 'bottom-up' approaches in the former; the national strategies which are set out legislatively or by major government bodies and research organisations are common. In the latter, professional organisations and individual institutions drive multiplicity of codes. In the future, it is quite likely that international benchmarks for ethical research conduct may be established. One can expect that in the coming years, supranational approaches to ethical regulation of research may be developed.

Although ethical codes are useful and effective to some extent, certain limitations and problems associated with them cannot be ignored. The wide range of certain ethical questions cannot be resolved easily and satisfactorily by reference to these codes. It is difficult to draw up a set of research ethics norms which are commonly applicable to all situations and countries because of the diversity of the ethical position held by people and a great variety of social and cultural contexts in which the research is carried out.

Some of the problems associated with the ethical codes which have multiplied over the years are particularly relevant to the research in social sciences. As said earlier, social scientists face many difficulties in conducting research ethically. These difficulties have been the result of methodology chosen, the actions of participants and colleagues and so on. However, some of the problems have often arisen due to regulatory environment or procedures prescribed by research committees, funding agencies and the government.

One comes across a strong view that the research ethics regulators have given ethics a bad name. Ethical codes and regulatory mechanisms have been established and multiplied disproportionately. In the beginning, such codes had little to do with research in social sciences, but soon, there was net-widening, and what was mostly true in the field of biomedical research came to be applied to all research involving human beings. Funding agencies began requiring every institution which received money from them to abide by regulations. In turn, the institutions concerned about their funds established review structures whose decisions cut to the heart of social sciences research.

It may be noted that much of the above has happened with the minimal consultation with the social scientists and with little recognition that the social sciences research is not the same as biomedical research. As a result, the regulation of research ethics in many countries is now underpinned by an unsettling combination of biomedical research and institutional risk minimization models. An adversarial culture has emerged between regulators and researchers. There has been an imposition of bio-ethnically derived models of research ethics governance on social scientists. Given these problems, social scientists need to develop their skills in evaluations and determining ethical conduct and engage collectively and constructively with local and national regulatory bodies (Israel and Hay 2006, pp. 129–144).

All this goes to suggest that the internal approach to promote research ethics, particularly in social sciences, assumes great importance and relevance. The ethical conduct is not the same as regulatory compliance, and there are practical and philosophical reasons for all the researchers to take ethics seriously. The researchers ought to be committed to the virtues of trust and integrity. In the last analysis, the researchers must remain responsible as individuals for acting with integrity.

This need to remind researchers about the importance of honesty, integrity, trust and ethics as values in themselves, now and not sometime in the future, arise because sometimes, one finds that even the highly renowned social scientists regard expediency, plenty and money to be far more important and necessary than the ethics, and researchers prefer to listen and follow them.

One of the best examples of this is the following viewpoint of J.M. Keynes, the famous and influential economist. Once, while reflecting on the 'economic possibilities for our grandchildren', he or her concluded that the day might not be all that far off when everybody would be rich. We shall then, he or her said 'once more value ends above means and prefer the good to the useful'. 'But beware', he or her continued, 'The time for all this is not yet. For at least another hundred years, we must pretend to ourselves and to everyone that fair is foul and foul is fair for foul; is useful and fair is not. Avarice and usury and precaution must be our gods for a little longer still' (see Schumacher 1977, pp. 19–20). Such a 'religious' belief or faith that ethical considerations are not only irrelevant but also an actual hindrance can never promote research ethics even if hundreds of ethical codes or guidelines are issued.

10.9 Summary and Conclusions

The formal research activity has grown enormously over the years in modern times. There are many types of research, and they have witnessed quite a few new trends. Although quite often the researchers are not aware of and sensitive to the ethical side of their research, it cannot be gainsaid that research does have an ethical side. The research ethics refers to the observance of certain moral principles while doing research. There are many considerations as to why ethical approach is needed and important in undertaking research. This is true in the case of all subjects of study or fields of inquiry. Of course, there are certain distinctive features of social sciences as compared to natural sciences, and, therefore, ethical issues involved in social sciences research may be somewhat different from such issues in natural sciences. The various aspects of research ethics are ethical codes, types of unethical conduct, characteristics of ethical problems and the causes of research misconduct. There are two main approaches to promote research ethics: one, issuing ethical codes or guidelines and two, the acceptance of the need and importance of ethics by each individual researcher at his or her own volition. The ultimate guarantee to ensure ethical behaviour in research is this belief or faith that ethics is a value in itself and it must be practised by every researcher voluntarily without any external intervention or guidelines.

References

Barnes JA (1977) Ethics of inquiry In social sciences. Oxford University Press, Delhi

Brown N et al (2004) Social science research ethics in developing countries and contexts. ESRC research ethics framework, discussion paper 3, (V-2), April 2004, ESRC Research Ethics Framework Project Science and Technology Studies Unit (SATSU), Department of Sociology University of York and School of Social Studies and Law, Oxford Brookes University

Israel M, Hay I (2006) Research ethics for social scientists. Sage, London

Kimmel AJ (1988) Ethics and values in applied social sciences. Sage, New Delhi

Myrdal G (1970) The challenge of world poverty. Penguin, Allen Lane
Nazareth R Ethical principles. http://books.google.co.in
Resnik DB (2011) What is ethics in research & why is it important? http://www.niehs.nih.gov/research/resources/bioethics/whatis/
Schumacher EF (1977) Small Is beautiful. Radha Krishna, New Delhi

Appendix: Writing a Doctoral Dissertation

Dinesh S. Hegde and Lakshmikanth Hari

1. Thesis Writing

Thesis writing is one of the crucial and the final phases of a doctoral program. Producing a thesis either in soft or hard copy form is mandatory for the research degree and in a way it is the outcome of research which is communicated to the outside world and other researchers. Besides meeting the requirements of the degree, it reports the findings, draws inferences and implications thereon, and highlights the contributions of the research and their usefulness to the stakeholders. Also, the research process is as important as the research itself in that researcher is expected to demonstrate subject knowledge in the relevant area and familiarity with the methodology adopted, tools and techniques. Further, the limitations encountered in the research and leads/inspirations to other researchers by way of scope for future research are to be brought out. Based on these considerations, a doctoral candidate's research work is evaluated.

This chapter is aimed at providing some broad guidelines to doctoral candidates as to how to prepare, organize and structure the dissertation writing on completion of research work. Needless to say, the findings and inferences need to be integrated and connected to the other scholarly works previously undertaken.

D.S. Hegde (✉)
Former Professor of Economics and Dean (Academic), National Institute of Industrial Engineering, Mumbai, India

Present Affiliation: Visiting Faculty, IIM Raipur, India
e-mail: dshegde108@gmail.com

L. Hari
Assistant Professor & Chairperson, Centre for Sustainable Development, K J Somaiya Institute of Management Studies & Research, Mumbai, India
e-mail: kanthhl@gmail.com

D.S. Hegde (ed.), *Essays on Research Methodology*,
DOI 10.1007/978-81-322-2214-9

Cover Page *Certificate* *Abstract/summary* *Acknowledgement* *Table of Contents* *List of Figures* *List of Tables* *List of Abbreviations*	*Prefatory section*
1. Introduction 2. … 3. … 4. … 5. Conclusion	Main section (chapter scheme)
References *Appendix* *Publications*	*References and Appendix section*

Fig. A.1 Sections of the thesis

2. Structure of the Thesis

In general, a thesis can be divided into three sections as (1) Prefatory, (2) Main (chapter scheme) and (3) References and appendix. A typical thesis structure is as shown in Fig. A.1.

2.1 Prefatory Section

Prefatory section precedes the main chapters of the thesis. It includes cover page, certificate, abstract/summary, acknowledgement, table of contents, list of figures, list of tables and also a list of abbreviations. The sequence and format of these differ from institute to institute and one may follow the prescribed format in this section.

2.2 Main Section (Chapter Scheme)

As the name indicates, the main section constitutes crucial parts of the thesis. It comprises introduction, literature review, methodology, data sources including study design, analysis, discussion and conclusion. Unlike the prefatory part, this section largely depends on the candidate who has the freedom to organize the things in his/her own way in consultation with supervisor/s. However, there are certain rules to follow which will be elaborated in detail subsequently (i.e. Sect. 3).

2.3 References and Appendix Section

Reference and appendix part follows the main section of thesis. It contains references, appendix, list of publications, questionnaire and other supporting material. Similar to the prefatory section, the format and sequence depends on institute and one may follow the same pattern.

3. Organizing the Chapters (Main Section)

Compiling the years of research work into a single piece is a challenging task and one needs to pay due care and attention in doing so. All the chapters in the thesis should be connected to each other and there should not be any disjoint or break in the continuity and flow. In other words, each chapter should stand on its own and together there should be well integrated. For achieving this, chapters need to be carefully organized and connected.

Example 1
There are many ways to organize the chapters depending on the field of research. Let us begin with one simple example as shown in Fig. A.2.

As shown in the example, the main section of thesis contains seven chapters. The number of chapters may increase or decrease depending on the type research work and on the number aspects dealt with. Introduction and Conclusion are usually the common chapters in various types of structures of the thesis. Introduction being the starting chapter of the main section and conclusion the last. Following are the description of each of the chapters.

Introduction: This chapter should provide two things. First is introducing the topic (title) and the second introducing the thesis. Introduction chapter usually should have either following subsections or cover the following topics.

Prefatory section

1. Introduction
2. Literature Review
3. Objectivesand Methodology
4. Chapter 1
5. Chapter 2
6. Chapter 3

Data collection, analysis and discussion (Chapters 1–3)

7. Conclusion

References and Appendix

Fig. A.2 Thesis Structure (Example 1)

(a) Backdrop: introducing the topic, providing the background of the topic
(b) Need for the study: justification for choosing the topic
(c) Objectives of the study
(d) Scope of the study
(e) Chapter scheme

Literature Review: As the name indicates, this chapter should contain the review of literature as up to date as possible. The objective of literature review is to critically discuss the existing literature, how the various works relate to one another, organize them into sections following a suitable taxonomy/classification and finally identify the research/knowledge gaps. The basis of taxonomy can be periodization, spatial dimension reflecting different regions/countries, conceptual, model based, aspects based or broadly theoretical and empirical studies or phenomenological and positivist studies.

Apart from objectives, methodology and findings from various works/papers, a review must contain how the study under review connects to previous and subsequent studies and how they relate to one another. If one study is an extension of or improvement over previous one/s it should be clearly brought out. Similarly, studies dealing with same or related aspects are to be discussed together and points of concurrence/departure along with reasons/possible explanations should be pointed out. Towards the end of the critical review, there should be "summary" section giving an overview of the literature review followed by research gaps or issues raised. A few such research gaps thus arrived invariably leads to the research questions and objectives of the proposed study/thesis.

Objectives and Methodology: This chapter is very important as it describes the "what" and "how" aspects of the research being undertaken. It should contain objectives of the research and problem formulation followed by the methodology or approach to inquiry (positivist or phenomenological), research design, models adopted and delineating the tools and techniques employed. This is then followed by description of the data sources which maybe primary or secondary.

Chapter 1, 2, 3 … (Data collection, analysis and discussion): The chapters between "Objectives and Methodology" chapter and "Conclusion" chapter, there should be chapters containing main body of the work, say 3–4 in numbers. They broadly cover data collection, data analysis and discussion and can be named based on aspects covered by the research. For example, if topic of research is a study on urban transportation, the main chapters could be trends in urban transportation growth, modelling and forecasting the growth and scenarios for policy analysis. Whatever be the names, the chapters should include data description, modelling, analysis, validation, discussion, etc. In each of these chapters, major contributions of the study should stand out and how they are an improvement over the previous research, thus maintaining the link with the literature chapter throughout the main chapters.

Conclusion: The last chapter of the thesis viz. the concluding chapter should contain a summary of findings, implications for stakeholders such as industry, policy, research, etc., limitations of the study and scope for future work. Apart from culling the results and discussion from each of the main chapters, the summary section should highlight the salient features of the thesis including major contributions. This is then followed by limitations of the present study and scope for future work.

Thesis as one: Though every chapter in the thesis stands on its own, together they all should be connected and cohesive and appear as one complete piece of work. There should be continuity and flow from the first to the last chapter. As discussed earlier, the introductory chapter anticipates what is likely to follow. The literature review chapter identifies research gaps and also in a way anticipates gaps which are to be taken up for inquiry/investigation. The chapter on methodology describes the overall approach/ methodology, research design, tools and techniques and data sources. The subsequent chapters constituting the main body of research work focuses on some major aspects dealt with during the course of the study.

In addition to the above, the dissertation should reflect a broad knowledge of the subject, critical thinking, attempt to make the analysis rich by seeking possible alternative explanations, intelligently connecting to similar or related previous works. Further, the writing should be couched in a research language and suitably using riders in appropriate places. Finally, it should reflect ability to undertake research investigation independently with the use of suitable tools and techniques.

Prefatory section

1. Introduction
2. Chapter Describing about area/ field of study
3. Literature Review
4. Objectives, Hypotheses, Methodology & Data sources

5. Questionnaire Design/ Tool Design/ Tool Modifications
6. Data Analysis
7. Results and Discussion

Data collection, analysis and discussion

8. Conclusion

References and Appendix

Fig. A.3 Thesis Structure (Example 2)

Prefatory section

1. Introduction

2. Chapter 1
3. Chapter 2
4. Chapter 3

Literature review, Data collection, Analysis and Discussion

5. Conclusion

References and Appendix

Fig. A.4 Thesis structure (Example 3)

Example 2
Another way of organizing the chapters would be as shown in Fig. A.3.

Example 3
One can also organize the chapters as shown in Fig. A.4. The major difference in this structure compared to the previous ones is the absence of specific chapters on

Table A.1 Some licensed and open source software for data analysis

Licensed software	Open source software
MS Office	Open Office
MS Word	Latex
SPSS, Stata, Eviews, SAS	PSPP, OpenStat, R
MATLAB	Scilab

literature review, objectives and methodology. In this structure also, introduction and conclusion chapters serve the same purpose as that of previous ones. Each of the middle chapters (i.e. chapters between 'introduction' and 'conclusion') contains literature review, gaps, objectives, methodology, results and discussion. These middle chapters are generally three in number. All these put together and added with introductory and concluding chapters go to form a thesis.

4. Writing and Data Analysis Tools

While writing the thesis, certain format-related precautions need to be taken. The usually followed font is Times New Roman with font size 12. The font and size for headings may differ. The line spacing is generally 1.5. But again, these formatting standards differ from institute to institute and one should make note of it and adopt them early.

The other formatting issues are – table of contents, tables, figures, page numbers, numbers for tables, figures and equations. All these things can be taken care of with Microsoft Word automatically with minimum manual interface. But for this purpose, customization of word document settings need to be done. The alternative for Microsoft Word is Latex. In Latex, all the formatting conditions can be taken care of easily and it is highly recommended for thesis with a large number of mathematical equations.

The other tools which come handy while writing thesis are reference managers. These reference managers are useful for automatically formatting the references in required style and also adding the reference in the reference list whenever an article is cited in the text. There are many reference manager[1] softwares available in the market. To name a few: Endnote (against payment), Biblioscape (against payment), Mendeley (free) and Zotero (free add-on to Mozilla browser). One should try and adopt them at the early stages and start organizing the references right from the beginning it self (Table A.1).

Data Analysis
Use of data analysis software depends on the area of research. Statistical Package for Social Sciences (SPSS) is generally the most preferred data analysis software in social & management sciences. When it comes to economics or econometric analysis, the preferred software are Stata, Eviews, SAS, R, etc. When the data analysis

[1]http://en.wikipedia.org/wiki/Comparison_of_reference_management_software

requires elaborate technical analysis such as neural networks, genetic algorithm and support vector mechanism (SVM), the preferred software is MATLAB. Only a few software are mentioned here. There are others used by researchers in various fields depending on the specific requirements.

Some Useful Readings

Davis GB, Parket CA (1997) Writing the doctoral dissertation: a systematic approach. Barron's Educational Series, Woodbury, New York, USA

Dunleavy P (2003) Authoring a Ph.D.: how to plan, draft, write and finish a doctoral thesis or dissertation. Palgrave Macmillan, Houndmills, New York, USA

Glathorn A, Joyner R (2005) Writing the winning thesis or dissertation: a step-by-step guide. Corwin Press, Thousand Oaks, California, USA

Gosling P, Noordam B (2006) Mastering your Ph.D.: survival and success in the doctoral years and beyond. Springer, Heidelberg, Germany

How not to write a PhD thesis. http://www.timeshighereducation.co.uk/news/how-not-to-write-a-phd-thesis/410208.article

How to write a PhD thesis. http://www.phys.unsw.edu.au/~jw/thesis.html

Lunenburg FC, Irby BJ (2008) Writing a successful thesis or dissertation. Corwin Press, Thousand Oaks, California, USA

Murray R (2011) How to write a thesis. Open University Press, Maidenhead, England

Oliver P (2004) Writing your thesis. Vistaar Publications, New Delhi, India

MIX
Papier aus verantwortungsvollen Quellen
Paper from responsible sources
FSC® C105338

If you have any concerns about our products,
you can contact us on
ProductSafety@springernature.com

In case Publisher is established outside the EU,
the EU authorized representative is:
Springer Nature Customer Service Center GmbH
Europaplatz 3, 69115 Heidelberg, Germany

Printed by Libri Plureos GmbH
in Hamburg, Germany